THE

HISTORY

OF

FRANCE.

BY

EYRE EVANS CROWE.

VOL. II.

NEW YORK:
HARPER & BROTHERS, PUBLISHERS,
FRANKLIN SQUARE.
1869.

CONTENTS.

THE

HISTORY OF FRANCE.

CHAPTER I.

1610—1624.

LOUIS THE THIRTEENTH'S REIGN TO THE ASCENDENCY OF CARDINAL RICHELIEU.

THE noble character of Henry IV., his early distresses, his valor, and final triumph, render his life a drama, the interest of which hurries on the historian, forbids him to pause for reflection or remark, and rigidly confines his task to that of simple narrative. If the fate and progress of political society be overlooked by us in this rushing throng of personages and events, we but imitate the age itself, which unfortunately lost sight of any principles save those of bigotry and self-interest. Never did a nation throw away such advantages, as France at this period. The royal authority was in the dust, yet the shadow of an attempt was not made to establish civil rights. A great portion of the kingdom had embraced reform, and yet no means could be devised for securing even tolerance to this body, except the verbal promise of a despot on the one hand, and organized revolt on the other.

It is not always just, however, to condemn a country for its loss of liberty. Representative freedom, that great political result of modern times, was as little the effect of human providence, as the great physical discoveries that have contributed with it to change the face of civilization. Had not England preserved the boon more by a devoted attachment to old institutions than by any legislative skill, it is to be feared that not even all our modern ingenuity could have invented a durable constitution. If the French, then, are to be blamed, it is more for fickleness than servility; and even this censure will be rendered lighter by considering the causes that led to the different fate of liberty in the two countries.

Many of these have been already pointed out. The aristocracy on either side of the channel differed essentially in character. The noblesse of England, crushed by the imperious spirit of the Conqueror, were subjects, and sympathized with the mass; in France, the same class were either princes, or the followers of princes. Thus, whilst the former raised the standing bulwark of law around their privileges, including, for greater security, those of the people, the French aristocracy, aiming at nothing short of independence at one time, at ll times more eager to share than to limit the royal authority held a contempt for aught like constitutional maxim or law and, full of recklessness and presumption, sought no other guarantees for their existence than intrigue or the sword.

The blending of classes was another fortunate circumstance for England. Nobility, considered in France to extend to the whole blood, was here confined, with the most beneficial injustice, to the eldest son. The younger branches fell into the ranks of the lower aristocracy, or lesser landholders, who again found themselves assorted with the chiefs of the burgess class in the lower house of parliament. Thus was solved, and apparently by chance, one of the greatest difficulties of social organization; a difficulty which convulsed the republics of Greece and Rome, and proved the great stumbling-block to upset the latter. France, less fortunate, adopted the classic division of patrician and plebeian; a line equally dangerous to draw as to efface.

The consequence of this was the absolute extinction of what is called the middle orders. In the present day we can scarcely conceive the non-existence of this immense and predominant class, composed, as it is, not only of small commercial and landed proprietors, but of the professional men of all ranks. In France, however, every owner of land was then a noble, if not in wealth, at least in privileges and spirit. The professions held apart; the church, the legists, each forming an aristocracy of its own. Commerce rarely afforded the means of amassing large fortunes. Paris was no sea-port, like London: its citizens could not arrive at the same degree of wealth, enlightenment, or influence. Moreover, the great cities of France had never succeeded in obtaining any thing like chartered rights. Nor is this mere speculation. We have manifest proofs of the absence of a middle class. In the elections for the *tiers-état*, or commons, we find those chosen to epresent the people to be universally either lawyers or financiers; the only two issues, indeed, for the plebeian to rise to eminence. Hence it was, that in the past times of trouble, when the great towns stood forth in behalf of liberty, butchers and men of vile trades were its leading supporters; and their ferocity marred the cause, more than their zeal aided it. Hence, when the rational doctrines of the Reformation were preached, the citizen of London listened and adopted: he of Paris, on the contrary, held fast to Catholicism, and sacrificed at once his civil and religious liberty on the altars of orthodoxy.

All this, however, is much more true of the north than of the south of France. This latter region had, in the early ages of the monarchy, started before its neighbor in the race of civilization. It was far superior to the north in industry, commerce, wealth, in letters and refinement, in the development of municipal freedom, and in religious tenets drawn from uncorrupted tradition and a rational knowledge of the Scriptures. The conquest of Provence and Languedoc by the bigoted followers of De Montfort covered this bright prospect with a cloud of ignorance and oppression. But still the region was not all spoiled of its advantages. There are several proofs of this. Montaigne is one, who owed much of his free spirit to his residence at Bourdeaux, a commercial town of the south. The schools of law, and the study of the pandects, so strengthening to reason and restorative of common sense, were far more active and famous in the south than in the north. De Thou, who wished to hear Cujas lecture, was obliged to betake himself to Valence, in Dauphiny, for that purpose. To these causes was in great part owing the adoption of reform by the cities of the south. Nismes, Montauban, Thoulouse, and La Rochelle, were its fortresses. The majority of the population southward of the Loire were Huguenots. Their churches were registered, and found to number 760, at the time of the edict of Nantes.

The reformers had established a perfect representative system. On the conversion of the king to Catholicism, in 1594, they had held an assembly of deputies, by which a council general, or executive committee, was appointed to represent and manage their interests, now that the prince had deserted them. The reformed provinces were declared to be ten in number: each was to appoint a member of the council, which was to consist of four gentlemen, four commoners, and two clerics. Provincial or inferior councils were at the same time formed, to take care of the fortresses of surety, to see that they had Protestant governors, and that the troops were regularly paid: they even agreed to stop the produce of the *taille* for this latter purpose, if necessary. Moreover, the reformers levied an annual revenue of 450,000 crowns. Here was a federal assembly, as complete as could be desired. By its influence and exertions the edict of Nantes was procured, which Henry was too much in the power of the Catholics to have granted, without the plea of necessity pressing him from the opposite side. By this edict all their privileges were guarantied to the reformers. Its spirit is evident from one important article. This is—The king appoints the governors of the fortresses of surety, but the *colloque*, or assembly of reform, must approve the appointment, ere it be valid.

Despite the veneration of the Protestants for the edict of Nantes, and their just indignation at its total and final repeal, it must nevertheless be allowed, that such a system of organized anarchy, as that which it established, could not endure. A representative assembly, with a religion adverse to that of the sovereign and the capital, possessed of fortresses, of funds, with a militia trained to war, and taught the doctrine of resistance, formed an *imperium in imperio*, or one empire within another, as the Catholics justly termed it, as incompatible with any regular government as with monarchy. Even Henry IV. perceived this. The annual assemblies of the Huguenots kept the flame of treason alive. The pretext for holding them was, to watch over the interests of the new religion, to offer advice, and make remonstrances thereon to the sovereign. Henry bade them, in lieu of assembling and debating continually, to appoint two or three of their body to reside at court, and act as deputies or ambassadors from the Protestant body. The Huguenots grasped at the offer of having ambassadors; a trap in which their power fell a sacrifice to their vanity. Their deputies were appointed for three years. The king afterwards obtained, that six should be chosen, of which he would select two; by which means those tribunes near his person were less turbulent and odious.

Such materials of opposition to the sovereign power, without any prospect or possibility of their assuming a legal, a fixed, or constitutional shape, formed a state of things sufficiently dangerous and insecure. The independence and frowardness of the nobility, always supplying leaders and instigators to the malcontent religionists, rendered it still more dangerous. It has been seen that the noblesse, humbled under Louis XI., recovered its influence under Charles VIII. and Louis XII. Francis favored the order, whilst he wisely kept down its chiefs. But these—the Guises for example, and the Montmorencies—rose up during the civil wars. Henry IV. whose ideas and policy in this respect were those of Francis, wished also to favor the order at the expense of its chiefs. But his position compelled him, instead of humbling the latter, to make compromises with them, and to distribute the remaining force of the monarchy, towns, appanages, and provinces, amongst an aristocracy already too powerful. Their attempt to consolidate this power, and to re-establish the old feudal system, has been mentioned; but Henry, if he could not humble them, at least prevented them from out-topping the crown, and the execution of Biron was a menace and an example, which answered its intentions, and kept the ambitious caste of nobles for the time in quiet.

Of this aristocracy, by far the greater part drew additional strength from their orthodoxy, their attachment to Rome, and the consequent support of Spain whilst others professed the Huguenot doctrines, and aspired to lead this formidable party. When the house of Bourbon, in the person of Henry, became converted to Catholicism, the young prince of Condé was at the same time taken and educated in the now orthodox creed of the court. The first rank amongst the reformers thus fell to La Tour d'Auvergne, vicomte de Turenne, and by his marriage duc de Bouillon. He was powerful by possessing the independent sovereignty and fortress of Sedan. The noble house of Rohan professed the same creed, as well as Sully, D'Aubigné, De Mornay, and other distinguished families. It is singular to remark, that in little more than half a century's time, all these had abjured the Protestant belief; so great was either the fickleness of the nation, the influence of the court, or the natural distaste of the nobly born to the democratic spirit of Calvinism.

The last dispositions of Henry, on his intended departure to head his army, had appointed his queen, Mary of Medicis, regent: this was strongly in her favor as dowager; and she now found little difficulty in assuming the same authority. The duke of Epernon, her partisan, summoned the parliament, and procured their acquiescence, not, however, without having made some show of menace. This seemed unnecessary: of the princes of the blood, three in number, who could alone have pretended to the regency, Condé was absent in the Netherlands, his brother of Conti was imbecile, whilst their uncle, the count of Soissons, also absent, was at enmity with every influential personage.

It was to Sully that Henry's death came as the greatest blow. The duke had ridden from the arsenal, and was coming to the rencontre of the court, when he heard the fatal tidings: Sully was panic-struck; he saw in the murder a Catholic plot, and dreaded a renewal of the massacres of St. Bartholomew's eve; he accordingly turned back, and shut himself up with his followers in the Bastile, which he hastily provisioned by carrying off all the bread from the bakers' shops around. By the morrow, however, his suspicions had subsided, and he appeared at the court of the regent.

Mary of Medicis was of a weak character; she was simple

womanhood, unenforced by either firmness or sagacity. She had come to France a stranger; and wanting both charms and wit, she had never acquired any influence either with her husband, or amongst the followers of his court. Mary, therefore, shrunk back into her private circle, and made confidants and counsellors of two domestics of her country, Galigai, a female attendant, and Concini, the husband of this woman These upstart personages, full of all the meanness and narrowness of their calling, had frequently fanned the pett jealousies of the queen against Henry; and now it was to be feared their influence would be perniciously felt. Mary, however, was as yet too conscious of her weakness and inability. She had a vague idea of the justice of the late king's policy in keeping down the noblesse, that now pressed around her, and terrified her with their pretensions and their quarrels. She therefore had recourse to those best fitted to guide her—the ministers of the late monarch, Villeroi the secretary, Sillery the chancellor, the president Jeannin, and Sully, superintendent of finances: these, except Sully, had none of the pretensions and haughty bearing of the noblesse; and Mary felt not deprived of her will and authority in being guided by them.

The warlike measures of the late king first fell under the consideration of the government. Henry had provided two puissant armies; one destined to invade Italy, the other to conquer Flanders. It is singular that the design of the great Henry was the identical one that is still the darling project of French warriors,—to annex Savoy to France, and make the Rhine the boundary of the kingdom by the conquest of Flanders. Henry intended to recompense the duke of Savoy by the territories of Milan. To humble the house of Austria, and confine that family to its German dominions, made part of the project. But even the enterprising Henry slumbered over designs so vast, and paused to undertake them, till the chance flight of the prince and princess of Condé, and their protection by the vice-regal court of Flanders, induced him to draw the sword. This latter motive of course ceased to be one with the queen-regent, to whose narrow mind and timid spirit the profound and daring views of the monarch's policy were equally incomprehensible. The army intended for Italy was accordingly dismissed; the more speedily, as its Huguenot commander, Lesdiguières, was thus deprived of power. The force in Champagne was still kept on foot for the sake of dignity and defence.

Foreign enemies were not the great objects of dread to Mary of Medicis. It was against the princes of the blood, the rivals of her power, that she felt need of fortifying herself. The absence of the count of Soissons from Paris had been owing to a fit of discontent, occasioned by observing the *fleur-de-lis* embroidered on the gown of the duchess of Vendôme at the ceremony of the queen's coronation. The duke being but an illegitimate son of the king, the purer blood of Soissons was indignant. On learning Henry's fate, the count hurried to the capital, too late to contest the regency, but not too late to utter formidable discontent at the queen's ascendency. The government of Normandy, and a pension of 50,000 crowns, appeased for the time the resentment of the count of Soissons. The prince of Condé next came to play the same part: he entered Paris at the head of 1500 armed gentlemen. The present of a magnificent hotel, the county of Clermont, and 200,000 livres pension, were the price of his submission. The nobles, it may well be imagined, did not leave such examples unimitated; and the regent soon found it as troublesome to be pressed by such powerful claimants, as to be menaced by their hostile rivalry.

As long, however, as the rigid Sully held the finances under his care, there was a check to spoliation, as well as a generous voice in the council to support the sage, the firm, and yet conciliating measures of the late monarch. He was at first retained, indeed, for the sake of the stern negative which he was wont to put on the demands of the greedy courtiers, as well as from fear or respect of his influence with the Huguenots. But his economical temper became soon a disagreeable restraint upon the queen herself; and the duc de Bouillon, an indefatigable votary of intrigue, offering to effect more than even Sully in conciliating and quieting the Huguenots, this old and upright minister of the great Henry was dismissed. Despite his probity, his able administration, and the esteem of Henry, a cloud would rest on the character of Sully, but for the honest and simple exculpation contained in his own memoirs. His austere and rude manners made him many enemies. Most of his contemporaries unite in accusing him; and, strange to say, the only family beyond his own, whose friendship and good-will he preserved in his retreat, was that of Guise.

The disgrace of Sully left the treasure of the late king completely at the regent's disposal, who dissipated it by bribing prince and noble to remain quiet. The favor of Eleanor Galigai and her husband Concini, now mareschal d'Ancre, became more apparent. The avarice of these foreigners knew no bounds: not content with the purchase of a marquisate, and the dignity of marshal, Concini contrived to get some of the principal fortresses of the kingdom in his possession; Peronne amongst others, and the citadel of Amiens. Epernon, on his side, secured Metz; whilst the count of Soissons and the prince of Condé, despite their pensions and their submission, by turns thwarted the court, and threw it into disorder by their private quarrels. Although the mareschal d'Ancre and his wife were the chief favorites of the queen regent, Villeroi was nevertheless the counsellor whose views, in matters of serious policy, she principally adopted. Villeroi, say the memoirs attributed to Richelieu, bred in the civil wars, had imbibed their virulence, which he repressed during the life of Henry. Instead of now recommending that monarch's conciliating policy, which Sully upheld, Villeroi said that that there were but two parties in the state, Catholic and Protestant, and that the government must necessarily embrace one or the other. He leaned to the Catholic side, and supported the project of strengthening it by marrying the young king to a daughter of Spain, rather than to a princess of Lorraine or Savoy, as had been the advice of Henry. The prince, however, urged by the duke of Bouillon, opposed the ministry in this, for no reason, apparently, except the sake of making opposition. And for the time, Louis XIII. being as yet but nine years of age, the project was allowed to slumber.

The assembly of the Protestant representatives took place at Saumur. The duc de Bouillon was called on to make good his promises of allaying any hostility that might lurk therein towards the court: the government of Poitou and a pension were to be his reward. But De Bouillon had over-estimated his influence. Sully, and his son-in-law the duc de Rohan, countermined and defeated his intrigues. The assembly showed itself refractory, and, instead of rendering the Protestant body well disposed towards the regent, it had a very contrary effect; betrayed suspicions, drew up remonstrances, and displayed a lively resentment at the disgrace of Sully. Bouillon accordingly went unrewarded; and he became again hostile to the court, against which he united, and exasperated the princes.

All the largesses of Mary of Medicis had not secured the attachment of a single magnate; and she had now left herself without the support of any one influential personage amongst the Huguenots. She had exhausted the treasure; the provinces were all bestowed; the fortresses in powerful and independent hands. Nothing preserved to her the shadow of authority, but the division and mutual enmity of princes and nobles. Standing alone, and uncompromised by the rapacity and folly of her favorite, Mary might have succeeded in balancing and thus quieting the contending parties of the state. But the madness of the mareschal d'Ancre, who, nov making the most intolerant demands for himself, then, irritated by refusal, leaguing with the princes, supporting demands of theirs equally insufferable, finally quarrelling with them, and adding the odium of his own conduct to the un popularity of the queen, rendered useless all the pruden efforts of the regent and the minister Villeroi. The latter again brought forward the project of an alliance betwixt the young king and a Spanish princess, by which he hoped to prop the tottering authority of the regent. The princes saw through his design: a union was effected amongst the whole body of nobles; jealousy of the queen and of her favorites was its bond; and the pique of the powerful dames of the court, on finding themselves excluded from the queen's private parties and amusements, was one of the principal causes of the revolt which ensued.

In the spring of 1614, the chief noblesse, with the princes at their head, retired from court, each to his government and province. They levied troops, and made a show of war. Villeroi proposed to march instantly upon them; but the chancellor and the favorites seconded the queen's wish to temporize and negotiate. She accordingly sought an accommodation. The demands of Condé were the assembly of the states-general, and the postponement of the Spanish match. These stipulations, made by the princes merely to give a popular color to their revolt, were acceded to by the regent; but large sums were, at the same time, paid to the several malcontents. Condé had 450,000 livres, and the château of Amboise. The treaty was concluded at St. Menehould, and was not a month old ere Condé showed himself again refractory, having, perhaps, spent his bribe. He quitted the court. The regent and the young king took a journey to Poitou, in order to counteract rebellion. The reunion of all parties in the states, which were summoned in October, gave some respite to hostilities and intrigue.

The states-general, assembled at Paris in 1614, demand especial attention, not only as the last of these national assemblies previous to the Revolution (at the commencement of which it was continually referred to as affording precedent), but as a scene in which the political feelings and views of the age were completely developed. We have an ample account of the sittings and discussions of the commons or third order, written by Florimond Rapine, a member, one of the king's advocates. From this we learn, that the majority of the lower chamber were lawyers, and a considerable portion nobles, almost all the king's lieutenant-generals being elected by their several governments. The most important consideration in the eyes of all was evidently the respective dignity of persons and classes. The first two months were consumed in disputes of precedence, in ceremonials, in mutual compliments between the orders at first, and afterwards in mutual abuse. Miron, provost of the merchants of the city of Paris, was elected president. The address of the commons to the king was spoken by this magistrate on his knees; the deputies were clothed in simple black, whilst priests and nobles shone in gold, and an attempt of the president to wear his city robes of red and blue in a procession was looked upon as a monstrous piece of ambition.

The grievance most odious to the nation was, the enormity of pensions granted to the princes and chief officers. Against these the commons and the clergy joined in lifting up their voice. The next demand was to abolish the venality of the judicature, and the right of the *paulette*, a kind of annual fine, paid by the officers of parliament, in consideration of which their offices were considered hereditary.* This demand the chamber of the commons could not in decency oppose; but being principally lawyers and provincial governors, it was their interest to preserve the *paulette*, and they therefore slurred over the question, and laid greater stress on the necessity of abating the *taille*, which pressed upon the people. Thus, the nobles insisting on abolishing the hereditary right to the offices held by the legists, the legists or commons retaliated by demanding the retrenchment of pensions; and a struggle ensued between them. Savaron, an orator of eloquence in the *tiers*, exclaimed against the mercenary spiri of the noblesse, which, he said, had forsaken the pursuit ot honor for the worship of the goddess Pecune, and bartered even its fidelity for a price. The nobles were indignant at this, and demanded an apology. De Mesme, another member of the *tiers*, was deputed to explain, and he made matters infinitely worse. "France," said he, "had three children.—The clergy, if not the eldest born, had at least, like Jacob, gotten the heritage and the blessing, and therefore were to be considered the eldest. Next came the noblesse, the second son: fiefs, counties, and commands, were its share. The youngest born was the commons, whose portion was the offices of the judicature. But," concluded the orator, "let not the

* The amount of pensions was calculated at six millions of livres. The *paulette* produced 1,500,000 livres annually. This last was an arrangement made by Henry IV. in the days of his distress.

noblesse presume too much over the *tiers* ; since it often happens, that the cadets of a great family restore to it that honor and illustration, which has been thrown away by the elder brethren."

The difference of interest between the states rendered their meeting productive of no effect. The regent would willingly have reduced the pensions of the great, and destroyed the *paulette*, or hereditary right of the legists to their offices; but she feared to outrage the princes by the first, whilst uncertain of the support of the commons. Nothing accordingly was decided on. The *cahiers* or remonstrances of the states were presented, were smilingly received, and slept in the king's hands. The assembly was dissolved. The queen took her own inactivity and inability for prudence. It proved the contrary. The party of the princes leagued with that of the legists, the union being effected by the exertions and intrigues of the duc de Bouillon. As the assembly of the states had proved an empty ceremony, all its advice and remonstrance being disregarded, the legists of the parliament were urged to put themselves forward as the popular representatives, and finish the work that the states had vainly attempted. The chambers of parliament accordingly assembled, and began by summoning the great peers to join them, and form a court of peers for taking into consideration the affairs of the kingdom. This bold act was the inspiration of de Bouillon. The court was terrified, and with good cause; but the parliament itself was almost equally intimidated by its own boldness, and showed but hesitation when the queen put forth her authority. Nevertheless, the peers being forbidden to join the parliament,—an injunction that Condé had the weakness to obey,—the legists prepared their remonstrances; amongst which were not only all the demands of the states, but also a claim, that no act of the king should have force unless freely registered by the parliament, and that the parliament should have the right of summoning a court of peers and great officers, when occasion required. These remonstrances they insisted on reading in public before the young king, who showed a favorable and benign countenance, whilst that of the regent was convulsed with anger. But this bold attempt to put a check on the royal authority utterly failed: an edict of the king reproved the audacity of the parliament; and the latter, who had been urged on more by the intrigues of the princes than by any conscientious or firm love of liberty and the public good, yielded pusillanimously, when affairs began to assume the appearance of an open rupture. Condé acted pusillanimously also, in not declaring himself, and taking his place in the parlian.ent, ,o which his secret promises of support could not impart sufficient confidence. It ended by the court obtaining the upper hand, and in the consequent revolt of Condé; the queen resolving, at the same time, to fulfil the project of the double marriage with Spain.

Mary of Medicis, with the young king, set out for Bour deaux, to meet his future spouse. It was a military enterprise rather than a nuptial procession, the court marching at the head of an army, whilst it was pursued by Condé with an equal force. Both sides avoided an action. The king arrived at Bourdeaux, dispatched his sister Elizabeth, who was to espouse the infant of Spain, to the Pyrenees, and received in return Anne of Austria, a young and not unlovely princess of fifteen. The marriage was celebrated at Bourdeaux in November, 1615. Louis XIII. was now of age (the kings of France enjoy this privilege at fourteen), the possession of a wife gave him the consciousness of manhood; and he began accordingly to feel and to express a will of his own, that disquieted and constrained the queen-mother, no longer regent. He had already chosen a favorite, De Luynes, who of course excited his sovereign against the domineering queen, and her favorites, the marquis and marquise d'Ancre. Feeling her influence undermined, and humoring the impatience of the young monarch and his queen, who longed to visit Paris, she concluded a new accommodation with Condé, greatly to the advantage of that prince. He was allowed to participate in the government, and to sign the decrees of the council. The queen objected to granting this power, but she was overruled by Villeroi, who observed, that this would put the prince always in the king's power, by bringing him to the Louvre.—"There is no danger," said he, "in trusting th● pen to a hand, the arm of which you hold." The duc de Longueville superseded the mareschal d'Ancre in the government of Picardy. The Huguenots, who had armed for Condé, had also their recompense. The court and royal authority was, in fact, at the feet of this young chief of the noblesse.

The queen-dowager saw the condition to which her weakness had reduced her. The mareschal d'Ancre was her only friend, and, from the general odium borne to him, he proved more a weight than a support. Another counsellor indeed she had, a man attached both to her and d'Ancre, and who was well capacitated to counsel her in this extremity. This was Richelieu, bishop of Luçon, who had somewhat distinguished himself in the states-general of 1614. Mary was not aware of the merit of this personage; yet it may have been by his bold counsel, that she ventured a stroke of policy, of boldness unusual to her, in arresting Condé in the Louvre, and sending him to the Bastile. The noblesse, his partisans, instantly fled to raise their followers. The Parisian mob collected, and showed its humor by pillaging the hotel of the mareschal d'Ancre; there, however, its fury subsided. The queen was victorious, and the fugitive partisans of Condé were reduced to impotent exclamations of vengeance and rage. Their cause, however, was not lost. The young king had joined his mother in the project of getting rid of Condé; but in delivering himself from one master, Louis was mortified to find that he had given himself another. The mareschal d'Ancre now ruled uncontrolled at court and in council; and the pride of Louis was even more hurt by the ascendency of the upstart Concini than by that of Condé. De Luynes, his favorite, and the young nobles who composed his court, flattered the monarch's pride, and fanned his resentment. Mary of Medicis deemed this knot of striplings to be occupied in pleasure, whilst they meditated a plot. The arrest of Condé was a precedent and an example. Accordingly, as the mareschal d'Ancre was proceeding to the council-chamber in the Louvre, Vitri, captain of the guard, stopped him by the king's order, and demanded his sword. D'Ancre moved his hand to his weapon, whether to draw or to surrender it never could be ascertained, for he received at the moment several pistol-shots, and instantly expired. Louis immediately came forth, and declared himself to have ordered the deed, whilst the court hastened to abandon the queen-mother, and to throw itself at the feet of the monarch, who had thus manifested his authority. The body of the murdered Concini was seized and torn in pieces by the populace. His wife, Galigai, marchioness of Ancre, was torn from her affectionate mistress, and sent to prison.

The position of the queen-mother was mortifying and distressing. She had been deceived by the boy-king; stripped of her power; of her dearest friends one had perished, the life of the other was menaced; whilst of the band of courtiers, who so lately hung upon her smile, Richelieu alone evinced a determination to adhere to the fortunes of his mistress. Mary of Medicis besought an interview with her son. This favor wa long denied. De Luynes feared a mother's influence over a being so young and so weak as Louis. Mary was allowed to retire to Blois, whither Richelieu accompanied her. She saw her son at the moment of her departure. Louis was cold, and his mother in tears. She ventured to utter a word of intercession for her follower, Galigai, marchioness d'Ancre. The king's silence showed that the poor victim was not destined to be spared The unfortunate widow of Concini was brought to trial, and accused of a long list of crimes. Sorcery formed the climax of these. "By what process of the black art," they asked her, "did you acquire such influence over your royal mistress?" "Simply by that power which a strong mind ever has over a weak one," was the triumphant and well-known reply of Galigai. But her judges, alive only to the pernicious results of favoritism, were deaf to reason as to mercy, and condemned the marchioness d'Ancre to be beheaded and burnt as a sorceress; a verdict that was soon after carried into effect in the Place de Grêve.

This act of cruelty and vengeance did not deter a new favorite from springing up. The wealth as well as the influence of Concini fell to the share of De Luynes, who was, however, neither a foreigner, nor so rash and avaricious as his predecessor. Louis XIII., from his very first moment of grasping power, showed the same incapacity of wielding it that ever distinguished him. The love of the chase was the only active quality the young monarch seemed to have inherited from his father Henry. De Luynes became hence sole master of the state. He found two parties aspiring to influence; that of the prince of Condé, and that of the queen-mother. One was in prison, and the other exiled; so that De Luynes found no difficulty in flattering and giving hopes alternately to both, whilst he permitted neither the liberation of the prince nor the return of Mary of Medicis. The body of the noblesse, who had flown to arms upon Condé's arrest, and who had returned on learning Concini's fall, thought it a more serious step to rebel against the king than against his mother and her favorite. The young court, too, had charms; and the prince of Condé was now but ill supported by that aristocratic band that had shared his envy and hatred towards the family of Ancre.

Mary of Medicis bore her disgrace with impatience. For some time she lulled herself with the hope that Luynes was incere in his promises of allowing her return. She expected n vain; and at length resolved to work her deliverance by eaguing with the prince of Condé and her former enemies. These intrigues coming to light, Richelieu, who was considered to be the source of them, was ordered to quit Blois, where the queen resided, and retire to his bishopric. But Mary had already profited by the advice of this able counsellor. She kept up an active correspondence with the duke of Epernon, who was master of Metz, and through him with such of the nobility as were envious of Luynes. Having by these means formed a party, Mary escaped by night from the château of Blois: was met by Epernon at the head of an armed body of gentlemen; and, retreating south, soon found herself at the head of a party strong enough to defy her enemies. There cannot be a stronger example of the overgrown power of the nobles, and of the manner in which they absorbed the whole force of the crown, than the authority wielded by Epernon at this time against his sovereign. The duke had no less than five governments, viz. the provinces of Saintonge, Auxerrois, the Limousin, the Bourbonnois, and the three bishoprics. Add to these Metz, the bulwark of the kingdom adjoining Lorraine, and Loches, the strongest fortress of Touraine, which he held, together with the command of all the French infantry, as colonel-general; and it can be no longer a wonder that the defection of such a grandee should have immediately reduced Louis and his favorite to treat with the queen-mother.

Richelieu was recalled from his diocese, and employed to effect an accommodation, which took place. Mary of Medicis was the principal gainer: she obtained the government of Anjou, and the towns of Angers, Chinon, and Pont-de-Cé, as fortresses of surety. The king promised to restore Mary of Medicis to his confidence, and to her place at court. But this was postponed for the time. An interview took place betwixt Louis and his mother. A light remark on one side, answered by a cold compliment on the other, is all that is recorded of the meeting. "How your majesty has grown!" exclaimed Mary. "Grown for your service, madame," was the young monarch's reply. The queen-mother remained at Angers, whilst the court returned to Paris. Epernon received a written pardon for his rebellion, but otherwise derived no advantage from it; a circumstance that caused him to be taxed with folly by his contemporaries. Disinterestedness was inconceivable to the age. As to Epernon, his grandeur, wealth, and commands, could scarcely have supported an increase.

The first step of Luynes, in order to counteract the revived party of the queen-mother, was to liberate Condé from Vincennes. But his long captivity had secluded this prince from his ancient followers; and Richelieu, who saw the object of Luynes, was able to succeed in not only drawing over the whole body of the noblesse to the queen-mother, but even in exciting the Huguenots to stir in her favor. These measures of Richelieu, who was at the same time amusing Luynes by feigned friendship and communications, became ripe in 1620, when, upon a fresh refusal to admit Mary of Medicis to court, all the great nobles, who had most of them formerly conspired against her, now espoused her cause, and quitted the court. Almost all France was in array against Louis and De Luynes.

Epernon armed his five governments and his many towns. Mary herself was in Anjou. The duc de Longueville held Normandy, the duc de Vendôme Britany, the count of Soissons Perche and Maine, the mareschal of Bois-dauphin had Poitou. De Retz, La Tremouille, Mayenne, Rouen, and Nemours, held the southern provinces betwixt them, except Languedoc, where Montmorency remained neuter. The Huguenots were also against the court, as was the duc de Rohan, their principal leader, and Rochelle, their chief town. Thi was owing to a decree issued by Luynes, that the church lands of Bearn, where Henry IV. had established Protestantism, should be restored to the Catholic priesthood. Thus Richelieu enlisted under the banners of his mistress these two great malcontent and independent powers in the monarchy, the aristocracy and the reformers, which it was afterwards the great aim and achievement of his policy to crush. In thus wielding them successfully against the monarch, Richelieu became acquainted with their danger, their strength, and their secret springs.

Condé, however, inspired De Luynes this time with additional vigor. The prince himself was excited to avenge his long confinement upon the queen-mother, who had caused it; and the king, therefore, was induced to march with an army, headed by Condé, to reduce the rebels. He was successful in Normandy; the insurgents retired everywhere before the royal army, which turned southward, and drove the queen from even Angers, her principal fortress. Luynes, contented with these advantages, showed himself willing to treat, as did Richelieu, who was somewhat disgusted by the want of alacrity and resolution evinced by the noblesse, his partisans. Condé, however, pushed on the war; and although a treaty was on the eve of being concluded, he attacked the forces of Mary's adherents, and put them to the rout at Pont-de-Cé. This success, instead of breaking off negotiations, accelerated them; for Luynes became instantly jealous of Condé, and feared his predominance, if the queen-mother should be completely crushed. A treaty was therefore concluded on similar terms to the preceding one, with the important addition, that the king should become really reconciled to his mother, and that she should reside at court. Many doubts and accusations exist against the good faith of Richelieu in these transactions. The loss of Angers, and the defeat of Pont-de-Cé, were said to be arranged and allowed by him; and it is more than probable that, in disgust with the noblesse, who were at once domineering to their friends and feeble towards their enemies, Richelieu had conceived the project of reconciling Louis and the queen-mother, as well as their respective favorites, De Luynes and himself; thus uniting the scattered elements of the government, and enabling it to set its turbulent enemies at defiance. Richelieu, by this plan, hoped to secure to himself a place in the council, where he felt confident he would soon rule such weak spirits as Louis, the queen-mother, and De Luynes. But the latter had the sagacity to dread Richelieu's superiority. Although the bishop sedulously sought the favorite's friendship, and although an alliance took place betwixt their families, nevertheless Luynes persevered in his jealousy; prevented, by his intrigues, the cardinal's hat stipulated for Richelieu in the late treaty, and kept the doors of the council-chamber inexorably closed against him.

Although Luynes had risen to power as a mere favorite, he still held it with a firmer hand than Concini; nor was he without the views or the sagacity of a statesman. Even previous to his having at court so able a prompter as Richelieu, he had anticipated the future policy of that minister in endeavoring to crush the Huguenots. Luynes was determined upon restoring to the Catholic priesthood the church lands of Bearn, which had been in the hands of the Protestants since the days of Jeanne d'Albret. Louis was equally bent on rescuing from heresy the native province of his family. After the treaty of Pont-de-Cé, the king marched into Bearn, and reduced not only the church lands to his will, but the little province itself, the privileges of. which he annulled. The Huguenots were of course indignant and alarmed. This was not the only infraction of the agreements made with them. Favas, their deputy at court, declared that the government intended to reduce them altogether. They accordingly summoned a general assembly of reform at Rochelle, despite the prohibition of the king; and their consistory published a bold decree, dividing the Protestant regions of France into circles, after the manner of Germany, uniting again these circles in a general government, and establishing the rules by which this government was to raise troops and taxes, to levy war, and exercise independent jurisdiction. The scheme was a direct imitation of the United Provinces of Holland. It manifested fully the republican ideas and leanings of the Huguenots, and roused the court, and above all Richelieu, to crush them.

An army was raised by Luynes. The command was given to Lesdiguières, a veteran soldier, a Huguenot, indeed, but one who showed no disinclination to recant. He was debauched, unprincipled, and mean enough to recommend Luynes as fit to wield the constable's sword; a choice that the monarch himself, despite his blind affection, was ashamed to make. Although the noble Huguenots were displeased with the froward conduct and republican principles of their party, nevertheless, the duke of Rohan took the command of their army in the south, whilst his brother, the comte de Soubise, was placed at the head of that in Poitou. The royal army passed the Loire, and soon drove the Huguenots before it. St Jean d'Angely, the principal fortress belonging to Rohan, wa besieged and taken, with Soubise in it. The Huguenot chiefs Bouillon, La Tremouille, Chatillon, submitted. Rochelle itself trembled. The duc de Rohan alone, who seemed to have inherited the constancy and stubborn virtues of his father-in-law Sully, remained firm against all the offers of Luynes, and determined not to despair of the cause; but for him, indeed, reform would have been crushed at once in France. Owing to the imprudent conduct of the Rochelle assembly, and to their inopportune manifestation of rebellious designs and republican principles, at a time when they could expect no aid from abroad, nor from the Catholic noblesse, the northern provinces of reform were in fact reduced, except Rochelle, in the neighborhood of which the royal troops were busied in erecting a strong fort. The royal army had marched into the south, entered Montpellier, and besieged Montauban, the conquest of which would have decided the war. It was defended by the marquis de la Force, a veteran Huguenot who had escaped the massacre of St. Bartholomew's eve, whilst Rohan hovered in the vicinity. The resistance of Montauban proved successful. The royalists lost nearly half their force beneath its walls. Young Mayenne perished amongst others. Not the least illustrious victim was De Luynes, who died, not indeed in arms, but of a fever caused by the chagrin of defeat.

This check saved the Huguenots for the time, although it was counterbalanced by the ascendency of Guise in Poitou. The treaty was concluded in the following year at Montpellier, by which it was stipulated that affairs should be replaced as they were before the war, new conquests restored, and new fortifications demolished. One point the king gained; this was, that the Huguenots should no more have a lay assembly. A synod of ecclesiastics was alone allowed them; thus obviating the revival of that republican assembly at Rochelle, which had roused all the suspicions and energy of king and court. The duc de Rohan lost his government of Poitou, but was given Nismes in recompense for St. Jean d'Angely. Lesdiguières, who had by this time recanted and returned to the Catholic faith, was rewarded with the staff of constable. Louis, returning to his capital, was welcomed as a hero. The two queens rivalled each other in the brilliancy of their fêtes.

But neither applause nor pleasure could prevent the king from relapsing into that state of apathy which was natural to him. Louis XIII. was as completely the *roi fainéant* as were the last of the race of Clovis and Charlemagne. But times were altered; the tree of royalty had taken root, and stood as erect, when withered and sapless, as when in spring and leaf.

CHAPTER II.

LOUIS THE THIRTEENTH'S REIGN DURING THE ADMINISTRATION OF CARDINAL RICHELIEU.

1624—1643.

Armand du Plessis de Richelieu was born in 1585. Intended for the army, he was diverted from a military life by the piety of his brother, who abandoned his bishopric of Luçon and became a monk. Richelieu stepped into his place. The pope, however, objected to a bishop of one-and-twenty; and the young prelate was obliged to journey to Rome, where his talents and address soon overcame the scruples of the head of the church. In 1610 the bishop visited Paris, and began to court popularity by preaching; a mode of eloquence and influence that emulation of the Huguenot divines had excited amongst the Catholics. It was reform that thus produced a Massillon and a Bossuet. Richelieu, chosen member of the clergy in the states-general of 1614, became orator of that body, and spoke its address to the king, in which may be remarked a complaint, that there was then not a single ecclesiastic in the council. He intervened with success in the squabbles betwixt the different orders, became known to the queen-mother, and was by her appointed grand almoner, a post which he sold to satisfy his debts. Thus Richelieu, like Cæsar, began his public career with a course of interested extravagance. Paying court to the mareschal d'Ancre, and attached to Mary of Medicis, the gradual rise of his influence has been seen.

The state maxim of that day, the usual policy of weak minds, was to trim a middle course, to hold a balance betwixt contending parties, and allow none, if possible, to be predominant. Such had been the rule of conduct of Mary of Medicis, by which she perpetuated all the evils of the state, disunion, rebellion, and aristocratic independence. In this continued game of intrigue, this play of petty motives and petty forces, every head and every thought was absorbed. There was neither leisure nor elevation to afford views of foreign policy or public good. Selfish interests could be the only aim, and these were so numerous, so universal, and so complicated, that it required the capacious mind of genius to grasp, in conjunction with them, a patriotic or a public feeling. Such, however was the mind of Richelieu: he at once towered over the heads of those dwarf statesmen of the court, and saw at a glance the evils that preyed upon France, and neutralized her power. To remove these, and elevate her to her rank amongst nations, was his instant conception. Henry IV. had effected this: he had raised the country to its just pre-eminence, and made it respected. But this he did merely by his personal character and ascendency: he had not done it permanently: he left all the materials of dissension and insurrection in force. These were principally two, the independent noblesse, and the Huguenots. To overthrow and crush these, to tread them beneath the feet of the monarch, became Richelieu's first object; and towards this he marched through every difficulty, and shrunk from neither peril nor blood. He threw aside the trimming, the balancing policy that had hitherto prevailed, and adopted in its stead that bold, decided, straightforward line of conduct, which suits a mind conscious of superiority and confident of force.

Louis XIII. had been inspired by De Luynes with an aver sion for Richelieu. It was with great difficulty that Mary of Medicis obtained for him in 1622 the cardinal's hat stipulated in a former treaty; but all her efforts in procuring him admission to the council were resisted. The marquis de la Vieuville was favorite for the moment, and he strengthened the king's prejudices against the cardinal. Mary was persevering; and at length Louis yielded. He permitted Richelieu to take his seat at the council-table, but on the express condition that he was to be without office, and that he should not consider himself a minister. The cardinal expressed himself perfectly contented with this arrangement: he took his seat; and the inefficacy of all the precautions taken against him soon appeared. They had bound the arms of a giant, who broke his bonds the instant that it pleased him to be free. From the first moment that Richelieu spoke, his genius dominated; and the monarch himself, as well as La Vieuville, cowered beneath an ascendency that they found it vain to dispute.

To secure this ascendency over the monarch, Richelieu scorned to make use of the same means which sufficed Vieuville and De Luynes. Instead of flattering Louis, and directing him in the way of pleasure, the cardinal at first strove to awaken the young king to a sense of the country's debasement, to its true interests, and its possible glory. He pointed out the turbulent disobedience of the great, the sedition of the Huguenot assemblies, the weakness of ministers, and the disorder of the finances; the consequent poverty and misery of he kingdom, as well as the decay of its influence and dignity n its relations with foreign potentates. He pointed to the nouse of Austria, daily increasing its strength and extending its territories, at that very moment triumphant from the conquest of the Palatinate, and threatening to crush those Protestant states of Germany which had defied the might of Charles V. Louis listened, and was excited, not indeed to take vigorous counsels himself, but to confide in a minister who had shown himself able to conceive and execute them.

The chief object then coveted by the house of Austria was the possession of the Valteline, a strip of Alpine territory which might serve to connect the dominions of that family in Germany and in Italy. It had been in subjection to the Grisons, a Protestant race; and Spain seized this pretext to conquer it in the name of the pope. France had opposed this with the usual feebleness of her diplomacy. The first act of Richelieu was to cut short the negotiation, to defy both the pope and Spain, and to send an army under the mareschal d'Estrées into the Valteline, which expelled the Spaniards, and restored the region to its ancient masters.

Richelieu dared to show the same bold front to the Huguenots at the same time. Determined on completely reducing them, his first endeavor was to drive them from Poitou and Rochelle, where they could at all times receive succors from England, and to circumscribe their influence to the provinces of the south-east. It was with this view that the governments of Nismes and Uzes were given to the duc de Rohan, in exchange for those of St. Jean d'Angely and Poitou. By the last treaty all new fortifications were to be demolished; but Richelieu, on the contrary, kept Fort Louis, lately erected in the vicinity of Rochelle, in good order. He refused to evacuate Montpellier also; and the Huguenots were thus provoked to rebel. The cardinal at the same time deprived them of the aid of the English monarch, with whom he was negotiating the marriage of Henrietta of France, sister of Louis. Rohan, and a great number of the Protestants, thought it on this account imprudent to recommence war; but his impetuous brother, Soubise, made an attack on the port of Blavet; seized some ships that were fitting out there; and, sailing thence, made a descent upon the Isle of Rhé. He was defeated; the Huguenots being neither decided nor prepared for a general insurrection. The consequence of the rash attempt of Soubise was, that in the accommodation that ensued the royalists kept Fort Louis, merely promising not to annoy from it the inhabitants or shipping of Rochelle.

Richelieu here postponed his design of completely reducing the Huguenots. The conquest of Rochelle could alone do this effectually, and that required a large naval force, as well as such preparations of every kind as would insure success. Besides, for the present, the cardinal was aware that he would soon have to encounter a court intrigue, a triumph over which was more requisite to establish his power, than even the subjugation of Rochelle. The marriage of the princess Henrietta with Charles of England, which had been desired by Richelieu, as securing the previous neutrality of the latter country in a war against the Huguenots, had proved a source of difference rather than of alliance. The gallant Buckingham, who had come to demand and escort back the princess, had excited the jealousy of the cardinal. He had shown at the French court the sample of such a minister as the age esteemed; gay, liberal, handsome, looking as well as wielding command. He had admired the young queen, and had boldly expressed his admiration. His friend, lord Holland, had paid court to the duchess de Chevreuse, the companion of the queen, and the most lovely woman of the time. Richelieu admired madame de Chevreuse, nay, by some is said to have pretended to the queen herself. Whatever was the truth, Richelieu and Buckingham conceived for each other a mutual hatred, which afterwards produced a rupture betwixt their respective sovereigns. And a strong pique at the same time arose betwixt the cardinal and the queen.

Another personage at court, now grown into importance, was Gaston duke of Orleans, brother of the king. Louis was extremely jealous of him. A tutor, under whom the young duke improved and began to give promise of good conduct and manly virtue, was superseded by a mere courtier, calculated to give lessons in vice and dissipation. Ornano, who succeeded this man, found the prince absorbed in pleasure and debased. He endeavored to rouse Gaston, by explaining to him his rank, his hopes; and he did succeed in awakening his ambition. The young duke of Orleans demanded to enter the council. Richelieu, then in the commencement of his influence, replied by banishing Ornano for a time. Gaston relapsed into dissipation, and seemed little inclined to give umbrage or uneasiness to the government.

The worst part of feudal tyranny was, that it interfered

with tne private affections of all men. Richelieu, wielding the power of Louis XIII., was not content with commanding the loyal submission of the first prince of the blood. He thought proper to impose a wife upon him, nay, to choose one. The lady selected was mademoiselle de Montpensier, rich, lovely, allied to the crown, and heiress of the house of Guise. There could be no objection to such a bride, excep the compulsion that gave her. Gaston rebelled. The projected marriage convulsed the entire court, and well-nigh the kingdom also.

Richelieu's object was to provide an heir to the crown, which Louis seemed not destined long to wear. Anne of Austria, the little queen, as she was called, to distinguish her from the queen-mother, was on the other hand averse to Gaston's marriage; and she joined the friends of the latter in endeavoring to thwart the cardinal's plan. Ornano had resumed his influence and station in the prince's household; and he it was who chiefly urged Gaston to resist. Ornano was arrested. This increased the rage of the duke of Orleans; and at length a plot was entered into and approved by him, to get rid of the domineering Richelieu in the same manner that d'Ancre had been removed. The cardinal then inhabited a country-house at Fleury. Gaston's servants were to betake themselves thither, under pretence that their master was about to honor Richelieu on that day with his company to dinner, and the murder was to have taken place. Richelieu received warning. The count de Chalais, who was to have been the chief perpetrator, ventured to sound a friend, who expressed at once a lively abhorrence of the attempt, and threatened to denounce it. Chalais became alarmed, and resolving to anticipate the informer, went himself to the cardinal, and made a disclosure. Gaston was astonished, in consequence, by the appearance of the cardinal in his apartment, on the morning appointed for the deed. "I am sorry," said Richelieu, smiling, "your highness did not give me warning of your intention to make use of my residence. I should have been prepared. As it is, I abandon it to your service." Having so said, Richelieu handed his shirt to Gaston (one of the ceremonials of etiquette observed at a prince's levee) and then retired.

The cardinal, not content with thus confounding his enemies, was resolved to punish them, and intimidate others by their example. By probing Chalais and his family, it was discovered that the nobles, upon whose aid Gaston reckoned, were the duc de Vendôme and his brother the grand prior, illegitimate sons of Henry IV. The former was governor of

Britany. Richelieu, dissembling his suspicions, enticed them to repair to the court at Blois, where both were instantly arrested. The imprisonment of all his friends, and the danger of some, would have roused to serious resistance a prince of more energy than Gaston. The young duke was not wanting in indignation; but Richelieu had prepossessed the monarch's mind, and had taught Louis to believe that his royal life had been aimed at as well as his minister's; that the young queen, Anne of Austria, was privy to the plot; and that she was to have married the duke of Orleans on his accession to the throne, These accusations hardened and enraged the mind of Louis XIII. Gaston, in the power of the court, was forced to espouse mademoiselle de Montpensier; the count de Chalais perished on the scaffold; the queen was publicly reproached by her husband with having sought a second marriage, to which she indignantly replied, "That there was not so much to be gained by the change." Her friend, madame de Chevreuse, was banished from court. Thus Richelieu, triumphant over his foes, amongst whom the queen and the king's brother were numbered, showed how fatal it was to provoke his enmity, how fruitless to resist his power.

No sooner had this storm blown over, than another assailed the cardinal, from England. The dismissal of some ecclesiastics attached to queen Henrietta had caused Bassompierre to be sent to London. Buckingham proposed to proceed himself to Paris, and conduct negotiations for an alliance: the duke was moved by a desire to re-behold the queen, Anne of Austria, the object of his admiration. By humoring the gallant whim of the British minister, Richelieu might have secured the friendship of England, most valuable whilst Rochelle remained in the power of the Huguenots; but the cardinal, himself enamored of the queen, at least detesting Buckingham and his pretensions, peremptorily forbade the proposed visit of the latter to Paris. "I will see the queen in his despite!" exclaimed the duke. The first pretext for reaking with France, and of thwarting its proud minister was hence seized by Buckingham. Soubise was then in London, smarting from his recent defeat, and from the thought that his rash expedition against Blavet and the Isle of Rhé had enfeebled the Protestant power. The Catholics and royalists had taken that opportunity to fortify themselves in the isle, which blockaded and menaced Rochelle. Soubise urged Buckingham to break with France, to openly uphold the Huguenots, and to commence the war by driving their enemies from the Isle of Rhé. The headlong Buckingham flung himself and the country into the scheme, and fitted out an expedition, of which he took the command himself. Neither Soubise nor the duke had tarried for the necessary preliminary of consulting the Huguenots. The inhabitants of Rochelle were in doubt and suspense on beholding the English fleet, and by neither opposing nor supporting it, they affected to observe a kind of neutrality. Buckingham landed in the isle of Rhé: inept as rash, he allowed the commander of its only fortress time to strengthen himself; he undertook the siege, which lingered unsuccessfully and ingloriously. The royal army approached Rochelle; the king himself and Richelieu were in its ranks. The neutrality and forbearance affected by the town were disregarded by the cardinal, who ordered it to be instantly invested; whilst a reinforcement dispatched to the Isle of Rhé kept Buckingham in check, and converted the besiegers into the besieged. It was then that the Rochellois exhausted their store of provisions, of which they were soon to stand in need, by supplying the English. Their efforts served no purpose: Buckingham evacuated the island, and sailed for England.

Richelieu then turned all his efforts to reduce the Huguenot strong-hold. For this purpose he imagined to throw a mole across the harbor, so as to shut out all succor. This gigantic attempt he commenced on the last day of November, thus braving all the elements. A winter's storm scattered in one night the mass of his labors; the only thought of Richelieu was to recommence. He had taken the idea from a similar attempt of Alexander to shut up the harbor of Tyre; but here was the ebbing and flowing ocean to contend with, in lieu of the still waters of the Mediterranean. Richelieu, with the volume of Quintus Curtius in his hand, directed the works, overruled the objections of the engineers, and the jealousies of commanders. The latter dreaded the ascendency of Richelieu, should he prove victorious. "We shall be mad enough to take Rochelle," said mareschal Bassompierre. In despite of all these obstacles, the mole was terminated; the English fleet, which arrived in spring with succors, came merely to recognize the impossibility of penetrating into the harbor, and then retired. The besieged, already wasted by famine, watched with despair the retiring sails of their allies: still they refused to surrender. England surely, said they, will not abandon us, will not forsake the cause of reform; which, if Rochelle be subdued, must inevitably perish in France. The feelings of the English nation were indeed with the brave Rochellois. Buckingham was about to lead a powerful expedition to their aid, when he fell by the hand of Felton; the expedition sailed, nevertheless, came in sight of the beleagured town; and that was all. Attempts to break through the mole were found impracticable; and, after a fruitless cannonade, Rochelle was abandoned to its fate; a melancholy example how insecure and treacherous is foreign aid. Had Rochelle been left to itself, been unexcited by Buckingham, she would not have commenced war until prepared for it, or until the encroachments of Richelieu had roused the Huguenots to arm and take the field, as they had done under Henry IV. They, however, relied upon the strength of Rochelle, Rochelle relied upon the English and Reform, that in France had fought so many battles, and survived so many defeats, fell almost ignominiously before the arm of a churchman.

Richelieu, however, was not a bigot: he showed himself clement towards Rochelle: there was no vengeance taken no victims sacrificed. The town lost its independence, which was, indeed, incompatible with the idea of sovereignty: but its worship and its religious opinions were left free; "the only avowed and open toleration," says Hume, "which at that time was granted in any European kingdom." Rochelle surrendered on the 28th of November, 1628. In a few days after, the sea broke through the mole and opened the harbor; an event that, to superstitious minds, proved the great good fortune of the minister, and the favor shown by Providence to his cause and his designs.

No sooner had the French monarchy thus got the better of its domestic enemies, than an opportunity was presented for measuring its power with Spain and the house of Austria, its great European rival. The duke of Nevers, having married the daughter and heiress of the duke of Mantua, succeeded to his dominions: Spain opposed the establishment of a French prince in Italy, and disputed the succession. Olivarez, the Spanish minister, had recourse to arms: the duke of Nevers shut himself up in Casal, and sent to claim the aid of Louis XIII. Great debates ensued in council, whether the duke should be supported or abandoned, and Richelieu was foremost of those who insisted on a bold and warlike policy.

He was opposed by the queen-mother, and for selfish reasons, which we must explain. The wife of Gaston, duke of Orleans, had expired, in giving birth to a daughter, who was afterwards the celebrated mademoiselle de Montpensier. Mary of Medicis, anxious to see heirs to the throne descended from her, and despairing of offspring from the king, turned her exertions to re-marry Gaston: she fixed upon a Florentine princess, one of her own blood; but the widower prince had already given his preference to Mary of Gonzaga, daughter of the duke of Nevers: hence the hatred of the queen-mother to the duke of Nevers and his cause. Richelieu, in his lofty and patriotic views, despised the petty motives of Mary of Medicis; and, though he endeavored to soothe her anger, urged the king to war. Mary was indignant that th minister whom she had raised should prove disobedient, an she vowed vengeance: hence arose the feud betwixt Riche lieu and the queen-mother. The cardinal's advice prevailed The army was ordered to march into Italy to the relief oı Casal: Gaston was at first appointed to the command; but Louis, in a fit of jealousy against his brother, crossed the Alps as his own general, delivered the duke of Nevers and Mantua from the siege of the Spaniard, and compelled his recognition by that power.

Thus was Richelieu's triumph complete. The army, on its return from Italy, completed the defeat of those Huguenots who still remained in arms, and utterly annihilated them as an independent party. Peace was at the same time concluded with them and with England. But nothing could soothe the resentment of the queen-mother. Unable as yet to strike Richelieu, she wreaked her vengeance upon Mary of Gonzaga, daughter of the duke of Nevers, whom the duke of Orleans persisted in seeking to espouse. She caused the unfortunate princess to be seized, and immured in the Bastile: an order from the king released her, a fresh mortification which Mary attributed to Richelieu. Shut up in her palace of the Luxembourg, this queen brooded over the ingratitude, the wrongs, she experienced from the cardinal. A weak, selfish woman, she could not comprehend how great public motives could come into competition with private interests and obligations. The chief confidant of her hate was Marillac, chancellor and finance minister, and his brother, who was marshal of France. They took Richelieu for an ordinary minister; and hoped, by the usual means of court intrigue, to remove and supersede him. On the king's return to Paris, Mary made trial of her influence. She commenced hostilities with the cardinal by a step certainly neither unjust nor arrogant. Richelieu held the office of superintendent of her household: she sought to displace him; but Richelieu, who had no moderation in his despotic ideas, determined to keep the place, and, by the king's express interference, did so; thus reserving the command of the domestic servants of his enemy, and that enemy a queen:—one instance, which shows that feudal despotism can be even more tyrannical and absurd than its oriental rival.

The late pacification of the quarrel in the north of Italy, proved but momentary. No sooner was the royal army withdrawn, than the duke of Savoy displayed his old hatred to France. A Spanish force under Spinola invaded the duchy of Mantua, and again laid siege to Casal. The resolution of Richelieu was instantaneous to march another army to the Alps. The cardinal had been just declared prime minister; he now assumed the title of generalissimo (a word by the by of his own special invention), and at the head of 40,000 men, armed with superb cuirass and sword, a page bearing by his side a plumed casque, the prelate-warrior advanced to humble the pride of Austria. Louis followed in his minister's suite, as did the queen-mother, who now determined to keep near her son, and to make use of every opportunity to undermine the great usurper of authority. At first the war proved successful: Pignerol was taken; the duc de Montmorency defeated the enemy in action; but to succor Mantua required concentrated force, as well as the undistracted attentions of the minister and leader. The king fell dangerously ill at Lyons: Richelieu had reason to tremble for his personal safety. The monarch, on his bed of sickness, showed a generous solicitude for the safety of his minister. "Should I expire," said Louis to Montmorency, "do you promise me to protect the cardinal of Richelieu to a place of safety." Montmorency promised. Louis, however, recovered; but it was too late to prosecute the war with vigor. Marillac, who had commanded during the illness and the occupation of Richelieu, had held back, owing, it was said, to the traitorous wishes of the queen-mother. Mantua, the duke's capital, was taken by storm and pillaged; and Casal was surrendered, after a long defence, by the brave Thoyras. The powerful diversion, caused by the arms of Gustavus Adolphus in Germany, alone saved France and Richelieu at this time from the disgrace of a dishonorable peace, including the loss of Mantua to the duke their ally. The pope interfered, and negotiated a treaty: his envoy on the occasion was Giulio Mazarini, a name afterwards famous. He showed himself most active, and at one time personally interfered betwixt the French and Spaniards, who, on account of a doubtful interpretation of a certain article of the treaty, were about to proceed to fresh hostilities. After all the ill success of the campaign, Mantua and Montserrat were ceded by the emperor to the duke of Nevers.

The termination of war was the commencement of new perils for Richelieu. He foresaw the fresh efforts of his enemies, and on the return of the court to Paris, he used all the resources of his address to avert and conciliate the resentment of the queen-mother. She dissembled, and did not forgive. Leagued with the Marillacs, and favored by many of the nobility, Mary labored to overturn the minister, who defended himself with firmness and adroitness. Louis XIII. was of a feeble mind, still more enfeebled by a weak temperament and languid constitution. Resolution was a state above his powers; it was to him an unnatural tension, menacing at each instant a relapse. Despite of this, he was clear-sighted. He loved France, was alive to its glory and prosperity, and saw that it required the strong hand of Richelieu to govern and to guide. He did not love the minister, indeed; and it was thus the more to his credit that he upheld him from a sense of his talents and utility. When Mary poured into his ear complaints against the cardinal's insolence, against his tyranny and domineering ambition, Louis allowed that she was right. He acquiesced; and the queen-mother argued from this passive assent, that the king shared her aversion and her views against the minister. She would hurry home to her palace of the Luxembourg after such interviews, and confidently assure her followers that her ascendency was complete, that the fall of Richelieu was near. By that hour, however, Richelieu was closeted with the monarch, was unfolding to him his high and masterly views of policy, was exposing the selfish manœuvres of Mary of Medicis; and had at length gained in his turn such complete ascendency, that the feeble Louis would not only assent, but kindle up for the moment with warmth and friendship towards his minister, and then, in confidence, betray the very secrets of his mother's converse with him. Richelieu thus drew from a certain source the hopes, the plans, and the names of his enemies.

This is the story of the famous *Day of Dupes*, the 11th of November, 1630. In an interview with his mother, Louis, assenting to the justice of all her complaints against the cardinal, had proposed that his niece first, and then Richelieu himself, should come publicly and ask pardon of Mary at the Luxembourg. The king intended this as a measure of conciliation. The queen accepted it for the sake of seeing her enemy humbled. Accordingly, on the appointed day, Madame de Combalet, the cardinal's niece, entered, and flung herself at the feet of Mary, imploring her forgiveness. The latter, instead of preserving the disdain that suited her purpose, or of assuming the air of forgiveness that the king desired, was unable to contain her temper, and burst forth in invectives against the suppliant lady. Madame de Combalet retreated terrified and in tears. The cardinal himself succeeded, equally suppliant, and was received by the same volley of coarse vituperation. Louis XIII. scrupulous in his ideas of dignity and delicacy, shocked at the conduct of his mother, took the part of his minister, and reproved her; but at the same time bade Richelieu, in the same tone of anger, to retire. The court remained uncertain as to the issue of this scene. Richelieu felt himself, or affected to feel himself, disgraced. He made preparations for leaving the kingdom whilst Mary of Medicis at the Luxembourg gave full scope to her exultations, and was surrounded by crowds of courtiers who welcomed her return to influence. Louis in the mean time had retired to Versailles,* wearied and sick of these squabbles. He held to his mother by filial affection, to the cardinal by a sense of the absolute necessity of his services. Still he was in doubt; when a word of one of his attendants, St. Simon, in behalf of the minister, turned the scale in favor of the latter. Richelieu's brother, the cardinal Lavalette, was summoned to the royal presence. Richelieu himself was commanded to repair thither, when Louis assured him of his support against every enemy. The news of the cardinal's being with the king at Versailles, fell like a thunderbolt on the Luxembourg. Exultation ceased. The crowd of courtiers slunk away, and hurried with servile speed to reiterate their assurances of devotion to Richelieu. Mary remained mortified. She and her friends were the dupes. Marillac the chancellor was arrested. His brother, the mareschal, suffered at the head of his army the same disgrace. The duke of Orleans was obliged to humble himself before the cardinal; and even the young queen, Anne of Austria, was punished by the exile of several of her companions.

The popular feeling was nevertheless against Richelieu and in favor of Mary of Medicis, whose munificence and fête-loving habits had won the good-will of the Parisians. This had no small weight in detaining the king at St. Germain, where he held his court, and where the two queens appeared, although Louis scarcely spoke to them. Mary bore disgrace and contempt with impatience; but she could now find no one hardy enough to brave the cardinal and espouse her quarrel, except Gaston, her second son, the rash and weak duke of Orleans. The prince imagined a singular mode of

* It was Louis XIII. who commenced the château of Versailles. He had not the magnificent taste of Francis I. or of Henry IV. in building, and left nothing of this kind behind, except what Bassompierre describes as "the miserable château of Versailles, of which a simple gentleman could scarcely be proud."

vengeance. Accompanied by a body of young and armed companions, he entered the cardinal's palace, came rudely into his presence, and apostrophized him in a rough and menacing speech. After this bootless outrage, Gaston retired, left the capital, and proceeded to levy troops in the provinces. Louis, on learning this sally of his brother, whom he peculiarly disliked, took up the cause of his minister more warmly; and attributing, not unjustly, the turbulence of Gaston to their mother, he openly reproached her, and warned her to become reconciled to Richelieu. Mary would not abandon her hate; and monarch and minister were obliged to proceed to extremities. It required much address to bring the king to this point, and Richelieu was only enabled to reconcile Louis to use harsh measures towards his parent by means of the confessors whom he himself had provided for his master. These smoothed away the difficulties presented by the king's conscience, or rather by his filial habits; and the queen-mother was arrested at Compiegne. After this decisive step, some months passed in vain attempts at accommodation: but the ultimate result was the flight of Gaston and of Mary of Medicis out of the kingdom. The latter retired to Brussels. Thus Richelieu came triumphant from the second struggle. Bassompierre was sent to the Bastile, the duke of Guise was deprived of his office of admiral, and went on a pilgrimage to Rome. Even the proud and veteran Epernon was obliged to crave for pardon. The parliament objected to an ordinance of the king, declaring the partisans of Gaston guilty of high treason. They rightly argued, that such a condemnation could not be issued without trial, or by other than a judge. But even from this just position they were compelled to recede. They were summoned to the Louvre; their edict of objection cancelled in the presence of Louis and his minister, and the obnoxious ordinance registered in its stead. Richelieu showed a still more culpable contempt for the forms of justice, in the trial of the mareschal de Marillac. He was brought before a commission, which sat in the cardinal's country-house at Ruel, accused of a long list of crimes, of all save his true fault of conspiring with Mary of Medicis. Being convicted, he was beheaded in the Place de Grève.

Marillac was the second victim sacrificed to the supremacy of the minister. The desire of vengeance and of blood grows, like other criminal tastes, upon those who indulge and gratify it; and Richelieu stained deeply his high reputation. Hitherto the nobility bore the tyrannic ascendency of the cardinal with jealousy and impatience. They saw plainly that his designs were directed against their power and independence. Still, from want of union, and from the absence of a spirit amongst them capable of coping with their great enemy, they held back in trembling, though indignant submission, looked on while their chains were preparing, and even aided to forge them. Thus they had helped to put down the Huguenots, ever the main stay of rebellion. They then, when too late, sought to intrigue with Mary of Medicis against the cardinal. The trial of Marillac, not by his peers but by a mock commission, and the execution of that marshal on no grounds save enmity to the minister, filled all the noblesse with fresh indignation and alarm. And one who, from birth and position, might well take the lead of the high-born of France in this its cause, declared himself unhesitatingly on this occasion.

The duke de Montmorency was governor of Provence. He had distinguished himself in the Italian war; had never been foremost to complain or to intrigue; but, like his family, had been remarked for moderate and independent principles; tolerant though orthodox in religion; a loyal subject, though no fawning courtier. In the king's extreme illness, he had given his word to protect the minister, and Richelieu had other causes of gratitude. But Montmorency was now indignant at the insult offered to his rank in the person of Marillac. He felt it equally a shame that the king's brother, the son of Henri Quatre, should be driven into exile by the enmity of an upstart minister. Gaston had fled to Lorraine, and there passed his time in the wooing and espousal of the duke's daughter. Richelieu advanced to Lorraine, and Gaston was obliged to fly. He applied to Montmorency for protection and support, and the duke was both imprudent and generous enough to grant it. This could be done with arms alone. The dukes of Orleans and Montmorency therefore raised a little army, cantoned themselves in Languedoc, and resolved to fight the royal forces, which under Schomberg advanced against them. It appears that the population of the south looked with disfavor on the enterprise of the dukes, either in dread of Richelieu's power and vengeance, or in dislike of the aristocratic cause. The issue of the rebellion was decided in a skirmish at Castlenaudari, where Montmorency, at the head of 500 followers, charged the royalists, and was unhorsed and taken prisoner, owing to his imprudent valor. The news of his capture dispersed his army, and left Gaston no resource but to join his mother at Brussels.

It was now in the power of Richelieu to give an example of his moderation. In pardoning Montmorency, he would have gained many hearts nor would his power have been less formidable. Gaston even promised to submit, if his generous protector was spared: but Richelieu was inexorable; he knew what would be his own fate if overthrown. He recollected the fall of Ancre, of every favorite and minister, whom the nobles had overthrown; and private reasons of vindictiveness concurred with the wish of making a striking example and by the death of Montmorency giving the same salutary warning to his order as the execution of Biron had proved in the last reign. Richelieu had the power of communicating his own firmness to the king. Louis resisted the supplications of all the nobles of his court, of the princess of Condé, Montmorency's sister, and even the clamors of the mob, who cried under the windows of the Louvre for mercy. The mareschal de Chatillon begged the king to show himself to the people, and to grant to their prayers the life of the first noble of the land. "Should I obey the suggestions of the rabble, I should not act as a king," replied Louis, displaying that extreme of monarchic arrogance which his posterity so deeply cherished and so dearly expiated. The kingdom's safety might have been an excuse for cruelty,—the pride of the monarch none.

Montmorency owned his crime, and promised to redeem the disloyalty of a moment by devoting his after-life to the king; but he made no mean submissions. In passing to the place of execution, he regarded the statue of Henry IV. with emotion. He was the godson of that monarch, who knew how to unite clemency with firmness. But shaking off thoughts of the past, he pointed onward to the scaffold, which he said was the surest road to heaven. In him perished the last of the lineal descendants of the great constable, the most illustrious of which were still said to be only the younger branch of that noble family.

Whilst Richelieu was thus reducing the party of the noblesse, and the princes of the blood, of old so formidable to the crown, his negotiations excited fresh enemies to the house of Austria. The imprudent bigotry of the emperor Ferdinand, in attempting to restore to the Catholics the church property appropriated at the Reformation by the Protestants, roused the whole body of the latter in a league against him. Richelieu supported the Protestants, as Francis I. had done before, and at length found out and raised a potent leader and auxiliary for them in the celebrated Gustavus Adolphus, king of Sweden. Whilst Louis XIII. was on the borders of Lorraine, in pur suit of his fugitive brother, Gustavus was quartered not far from the Rhine, after his victory of Leipsic. Richelieu invited the Swedish monarch to an interview with himself. Gustavus, however, was too proud to meet any personage less than a monarch; and the cardinal feared lest the presence of a warlike and renowned prince might excite the jealousy of Louis, or disturb his own ascendency. Gustavus continued to humble the party of Austria, until the hero of Sweden, a few weeks after the death of Montmorency, fell in the arms of victory at Lutzen. Richelieu still upheld his alliance with Sweden and the Protestant powers; and thus keeping the force of Austria employed, he was enabled to effeot his next ambitious project, which was the occupation of Lorraine.

That province was in its origin feudatory to the empire, and was totally independent of France, except that from vicinity and interest its dukes were far more French than German. The Guises had drawn these ties closer. And now that the duke of Lorraine had harbored the duke of Orleans, and, against the king's consent, had given him his daugnter Margaret in marriage, the latter had reason or pretext for anger. Richelieu, as usual, caused an army, with the king at its head, to march to Lorraine. The duke was alarmed, and sought to parry the attack by offering to espouse madame de Combalet, niece of the cardinal; but Richelieu refused to sacrifice the interests of the state to the aggrandizement of his family. Perhaps he saw in the offer a trap laid for him. Lorraine was invaded; and Nancy, its capital, besieged. The duchess of Orleans contrived to escape from it to Brussels; but Nancy fell into the power of the king. In vain did the duke negotiate, and make submissions; equally in vain did he resign his duchy in favor of his brother. The capital and fortresses were held in firm possession by Richelieu.

Here fell another noble, or rather an independent prince, from having espoused the quarrel of the duke of Orleans. Whilst the queen-mother gave signs of increased exasperation, by suborning an attempt to carry off the cardinal's niece, Gaston began to be weary of exile. His favorite, Puylaurens, who had chief influence with him, was still more anxious; and Richelieu offered great advantages to the latter, if he would induce the prince to submit. Gaston at length did so, quitted Brussels abruptly, and repaired to Paris, where he was graciously and splendidly received. Puylaurens received the hand of the cardinal's niece, and was created duc d'Aiguil lon for his services. But Richelieu was a dangerous friend, except to an all-devoted servant. He sought to break Gaston's marriage; and Gaston was obstinate in resisting. The cardinal laid the blame on the new duke d'Aiguillon, and without further pretext arrested and shut him up in the Bastile, where he soon after perished. Gaston was, as usual, enraged; and, as usual, allowed his rage to evaporate in vain menaces, and in vainer enterprises.

Richelieu, victorious over every enemy, had now reached the height of power.. No longer occupied with climbing, or distracted by the task of keeping his supereminent position, he had leisure to look around and before him. The career which he had run, his private fortune and public achievements, had been such as might content the most soaring ambition; but the cardinal's avarice of fame was insatiable. In every direction, in every path, he sought it. The navy of France was re-created by him; commerce and industry reawoke at his call; and, except the noblesse, whose pride and power he blasted, all other classes seem to have started to fresh life beneath his sway. With all this care, this ubiquity of purpose and exertion, the minister was not the mere slave of office. He had the leisure and the power to shake off the calculations and dark thoughts of policy, and, adopting the recreations of the time, to act the gallant and the courtier. Thus greedy of the petty but flattering distinctions of private life, as well as of the greater honors of the statesman, Richelieu could not be blind to future fame. He had, in fact, the general characteristic of genius,—he was endowed with the instinct of immortality: and he sought it, where indeed it was not yet found, in his country's literature. This was yet to be called into existence; and Richelieu has all the honor of that act. He collected the talent and taste of the capital into a privileged society for fixing and polishing the French language. Thus the French Academy took birth in the year 1635. In the realm of criticism, the cardinal sought to be as despotic as in that of state policy. He compelled his new doctors to censure the Cid of Corneille: but taste he found to be more stubborn than politics; and the minister who over came princes could not crush the fame of a poet.

These formed Richelieu's minor cares, the play and relaxation of his power. Sterner projects filled his mind. The nobles checked, the Huguenot power destroyed, it remained to abase still lower the house of Austria, and to extend the territories of France at its expense. To make the Rhine the limit of the empire was the darling aim of Richelieu, as of Henry IV. Gustavus Adolphus and the Protestant princes of Germany had hitherto been instruments in Richelieu's hand to effect or further this; but, since the death of the king of Sweden, the emperor had recovered his superiority, had defeated the Swedes, and reduced his enemies. It behoved France no longer to confine her efforts to negotiation; but to draw the sword, if she wished to preserve her ascendency or to prosecute her political schemes. She demanded certain advantages for thus declaring herself; and neither Sweden nor the malcontent Germans were backward in paying the price. Oxenstiern, the Swedish chancellor, ceded the fortress of Philipsburg to France. The league of Protestants put the entire of Alsace and its important fortresses under her protection. Lorraine was already occupied; and now Richelieu pushed northwards, and garrisoned Treves, forming, at the same time, a defensive alliance with Holland. Spain, informed of this treaty, sent an expedition to surprise the town of Treves: and war was in consequence declared by France against the emperor and the king of Spain, in the commencement of 1635. A herald was sent to Brussels to announce it; the last time that this species of feudal etiquette was observed.

Richelieu, the destroyer of the Huguenots, was thus leagued with the Protestant powers of Europe against its Catholic princes; a clear proof that his principles were politic, not bigoted. This war, which lasted thirteen years against the emperor, and twenty-five against Spain, produced little glory to the minister, at least from its victories, and has brought as little interest to history. It is marked by as much want of spirit as of talent. Yet the thirty years' war in Germany, then drawing to its close, was marked with both. But religious differences had given ferocity to this war, which was carried on in the heart of Germany, and which put daily at stake the fate of kingdoms, capitals, and creeds. On the contrary, the war which we enter on was merely an extended line of frontier skirmishes, idle sieges, and fitful expeditions, in which Richelieu had the advantage, not from military but ministerial superiority. His vigorous administration enabled France to bear the expense and weight of the war, whilst the house of Austria, from the bad husbandry of more immense resources, became exhausted, and towards the close of it was in a tottering state. As to the lack of able generals, it may be observed, that great military talents must necessarily be wanting at the commencement of a war, and that it requires half a score of years' campaigning for the age and the nation to form its military system anew,—the old never sufficing,—and to find for that system a head and an arm capable of directing it. Turenne was a young officer at this epoch. It was not till the following reign that he and Condé were able to assert the superiority of French generalship.

France entered on the campaign with four armies, one in the Low Countries, one on the Rhine, the others in Italy and the Valteline. The first exploit was one of promise and éclat. The mareschal de Brezé was marching to join the Dutch through the country of Liege. Prince Thomas of Savoy, at the head of the Spanish, sought to prevent the junction. He was defeated by Brezé at Avein, and lost all his cannon and colors. Tirlemont was given up to the pillage of the victors. Louvain was besieged, and Brussels threatened. The unfortunate Mary of Medicis was obliged to fly from the latter town, with the duchess of Orleans, pursued by the good fortune of her enemy Richelieu. Chance, however, may give a victory talents can alone make the most of it. The French were obliged to retire behind the Meuse. They and the Dutch, most ill-assorted allies, laid the blame of the tardiness upon each other.

In the following year the Imperialists had all the advantage. They penetrated into Picardy, passed the Somme, and took Corbie. Paris was in alarm, and her citizens began to retire southward. It was a critical moment for Richelieu. His ascendency over the king consisted solely in the monarch's opinion of his sagacity and good fortune as minister. This opinion was greatly shaken; yet Richelieu kept a good countenance, and did all that the emergency required. He made the king show himself to the people; he dispatched reinforcements to the count of Soissons, who commanded in Picardy. The Spanish knew as little as the French how to push an advantage. Instead of advancing upon the capital, they passed the time in pillaging, and were soon obliged to retreat. The court advanced to Amiens, whilst the army besieged and endeavored to retake Corbie.

Here Richelieu's good fortune saved him from new peril. The count of Soissons, son of that prince of the blood whose turbulence made him conspicuous in the first year of the regency of Mary of Medicis, had stepped from the obscurity in which he had been kept, on the unexpected invasion of his government by the enemy. He had valiantly resisted; but the cardinal, who dreaded the renown of a prince of the blood, avoided placing any large force at his disposal, and at length brought the king himself to command, and eclipse Soissons. The count vowed vengeance; he leagued with Gaston, ever ready to commence a plot; and they agreed to assassinate the cardinal at Amiens. Two gentlemen, named St. Ibal and Montresor, were charged with the execution, but were to wait for the signal to be given by the duke of Orleans. An opportunity offered. Richelieu was alone at the foot of his staircase, which he had descended to his carriage, and in the midst of the conspirators. The agents had their hands on pistols, eagerly watching the countenances both of the count of Soissons and the duke of Orleans for the signal. Neither had the courage to give it, and Richelieu walked on, for the moment unsuspicious of the danger that he had escaped. On reflection, the princes perceived that the danger lay in having meditated the deed, rather than in having executed it. They tried other means, leagued with the Spaniards, and endeavored to rouse the nobility to rebel. Epernon, to whom they chiefly applied, bade them, in answer, recollect the fate of Marillac and Montmorency. They did so, and fled from court; the count of Soissons to Sedan, and Gaston to Blois. But the latter was soon brought back by fair words.

In the midst of these intrigues, this warfare, these struggles betwixt nations and parties, Louis XIII. was perhaps the personage who felt the least interested. "He led," says madame de Motteville, "the most wretched and sad life; without court, or friends, or power; spending his time in catching birds, whilst his armies were taking towns." He was plaintive, melancholy, retiring; not wanting either in good sense, or in any other manly quality perhaps, but cursed with a diffidence that neutralized them all. Thus he despaired of ever finding a minister like Richelieu; and, in fear of offending the cardinal, whom he might have controlled as well as employed, he resigned all authority into his hands. Another idea of his, proceeding from the same diffidence, and a great cause of discontent and sadness with him, was, that he despaired to render himself agreeable to the fair sex. He was cursed with a bashfulness and a backwardness that he blushed to avow, and that he concealed under the color of apathy and suspicion. This kept Louis XIII. for a number of years a stranger to his young and not unlovely queen; as the same defect produced, in after years, a similar result with his descendant, Louis XVI. Anne of Austria, piqued by this coldness of her spouse, avenged herself by ridicule and sarcasm. The king's indifference or distance thus became hatred; and Richelieu, who had cause to dread the young queen, fanned the latter sentiment. Louis nevertheless felt attracted towards female society, and he paid a kind of distant and formal court to mademoiselle de Hautefort. This young lady as little understood his bashful and susceptible temper as did the queen, and Louis soon accused them both of leaguing together to mock him. The attentions of the king were then turned towards a new object, mademoiselle de la Fayette, with whom the novel of De Genlis has perhaps rendered the reader familiar. She, of tenderer feelings and more penetration, knew how to appreciate the timid affections of the monarch. She cherished and returned them; never, however, overstepping the bounds of modesty. Louis, whose reserve, or "wisdom," to use the words of madame de Motteville, "equalled that of the most modest dame," at length ventured to propose an apartment at Versailles to mademoiselle de la Fayette, who replied, after some hesitation, some intrigue, and certain interference, by retiring to a convent. The king wept, and was in despair; but his scruples would not permit him, like Louis XIV., to tear a beauty from the altar. He did not cease, however, to visit mademoiselle de la Fayette at her convent; and long conversations were wont to pass between them through the *grille* or iron railing of the parlor. The monarch felt the influence of this virtuous young woman; her counsels, to which her piety now gave weight and her secure position boldness, prompted him to mistrust Richelieu, whom she represented as supporting heresy against Catholicism, and to give peace to Europe.

Another voice, of equal weight with the king, was pouring the same sentiments into his ear. This was his confessor, the father Caussin, whom Richelieu had placed in that station, but who betrayed his confidence. To resist at once a mistress and a confessor was difficult, and the influence of the minister began to totter. One urgent counsel given to Louis by mademoiselle de la Fayette and Caussin was, that he should become reconciled to his queen; they showed, and even proved to him, that his suspicions against her were unjust. Richelieu, who observed the changed sentiments of the king towards Anne of Austria, was alarmed, and tried to prevent the reconciliation that he feared. Suspecting that the queen held a correspondence with Spain, he caused the police to visit and search her apartments at the Val de Grace. But his enemies were too adroit; no discovery was made, and the insult served but to display the unfounded rancor of the cardinal. After this the pious and generous voice of La Fayette had more influence; and, obedient to it, Louis XIII. became reconciled for the time to his queen. The happy and unexpected consequence was the birth of a prince (afterwards Louis XIV.) on the 5th of September following (1638). To this, however, the result was limited. Richelieu regained his ascendency over the king; the confessor was banished; La Fayette forgotten; and the queen, though no longer banished from the king's presence, had as little share as before of his influence or friendship.

The fresh hold which Richelieu here took of the monarch's confidence was owing, in a great measure, to the success of the war. In the beginning of the campaign two actions were fought at Rhinfeld; in the first of which the gallant duke of Rohan perished; in the second, the duke of Saxe Weimar defeated the imperialists, and took their two generals, one of whom, the famous John der Werth, was sent to Paris. The principal consequence of this victory was the conquest of Brisach, the chief fortress of Alsace. The name of the town reminds us not to pass over the celebrated father Joseph, a capuchin friar, the follower and confidant of Richelieu. We can scarcely imagine a statesman and an ambassador clothed in a monk's frock and sandals: yet such was father Joseph, a name more or less mingled in all the intrigues of the French court, and its negotiations with others. His influence was known, and he was dreaded by the court as a kind of evil spirit, in fact the demon of Richelieu. Although the latter never procured for his monkish friend the cardinal's hat which he demanded, still the people called father Joseph his "gray eminence," at once to distinguish him from and assimilate him to his "red eminence" the cardinal. They had been friends from youth; congenial spirits in ambition, depth, and talent: the monk, however, sacrificed his personal elevation to that of the cardinal. Richelieu was much indebted to him:—it was Joseph that roused and encouraged him, when stupefied and intimidated by the invasion of Picardy; and it was said that after his death Richelieu showed neither the same firmness nor sagacity. When father Joseph was on his death-bed, Richelieu stood by it: it was a scene such as a novelist might love to paint. The conversation of the two ecclesiastics was [illegible]l of this world; and the cardinal's last exhortation to the expiring monk was, "Courage, father Joseph, Brisach is ours!" a form of consolation characteristic of both.

A triumph without a victim was unintelligible to cardinal Richelieu; or, in other words, vengeance had become such a habit with him, that he could not live without an object to pursue and to crush. In this too he scorned ignoble game; and, one after another, the first nobles of the land fell sacrifices as well to his humor as to his policy. Bad success in an assault upon Fontarabia afforded a handle against the duc de la Valette, son of the famed and haughty Epernon. Richelieu brought the duke before a commission, despite the remonstrances of the parliament, who in vain expostulated, and represented to the cardinal from year to year their maxim, that the great should be judged only in a court of peers. Richelieu mocked at their legal scruples; tried La Valette after his own convenient fashion; and condemned him to an enormous fine and banishment. The entire family was included in his disgrace; and even the duke of Epernon himself, a grandee whose power had counterbalanced that of the great Henry, was compelled by the minister's mandate to surrender all his governments, and to retire alone to his château of Plassac. He was soon after conveyed to the castle of Loches, where he died at the advanced age of eighty-six.

Fortune smiled everywhere upon Richelieu. Alsace was now in the hands of the French. Arras surrendered to them in Flanders, and Turin in Italy: whilst the insurrections of Portugal and Catalonia against Spain paralyzed all the force of that kingdom. The intrigues of the cardinal fanned or excited all their troubles. Portugal is mainly indebted to him for her independence under the house of Braganza, now established. Catalonia, after a vain attempt at a republic, was brought to own Louis XIII. for sovereign; and the mareschal de Brezé was sent as viceroy to Barcelona. It was high time for the enemies of the cardinal to think of submitting. The duke of Lorraine took this step; ceded some of his dominions, and received the rest on the condition of forfeiting all right to them in the event of his ever proving unfaithful or hostile to France. The queen-mother, Mary of Medicis, herself thought it vain to struggle longer, and made overtures to return. But the cardinal would not admit her into France. He pointed out Florence as the place to which she should retreat. But the widow of Henry IV. shrunk from making her native city witness of her distresses and her fall. After having spent some time in England, she settled in Cologne; where she died a few months before the cardinal. It is impossible to regard without compassion the misfortunes of one who had held the sceptre, and who was the wife of a monarch and the mother of a line of kings. But her unfitness to reign, and, at the same time, her tenacity to grasp at sway, gave reason for the severity of Richelieu. In any other than him, the creature whom she had raised, it would have been justifiable. But *reasons of state* were set by him over every motive, virtue, honesty, and gratitude included.

The count of Soissons, on the failure of his scheme against the cardinal, had taken refuge with the duke of Bouillon in Sedan. All the enemies of the latter, especially the exiles, looked towards this prince of the blood as the rallying point, the support of their cause. Richelieu employed every art to pacify the count, remove his distrust, and entice him to court. All efforts proved vain; and Richelieu was even obliged to purchase the tranquillity of Soissons, and tolerate his independent posture. It was dangerous, however, to let such an example of disobedience subsist; and the cardinal at length sent an army, under the mareschal of Châtillon, to reduce Sedan, and take or humble the count of Soissons. Châtillon was both valorous and skilful; but nothing could compensate for the ill-humor and backwardness of the troops, who, with their officers, felt more inclined to a gallant prince of the blood than to the domineering cardinal. In an action that took place at Marsée, near Sedan, the royal troops showed neither alacrity nor determination; and Châtillon, despite his efforts, was completely put to the rout. No obstacle seemed now to prevent the count of Soissons from marching to Paris, when the almost miraculous good fortune of Richelieu saved him from ruin. As Soissons rode over the field of battle, he pushed up his visor with his pistol; it was accidentally discharged, and the victor perished. Report did not fail to say that he was assassinated, and, of course, by the order of Richelieu; but there is no evidence to support such a rumor. Louis, who, on receiving tidings of the defeat, was preparing, with equanimity, to sacrifice the obnoxious minister, was now struck with his unvarying good fortune; and, with a superstitious feeling, bowed still lower to the cardinal's will.

The court did not share the monarch's obsequiousness; and every fresh triumph of the tyrant, as they considered him, filled his enemies with fresh indignation, and inspired them with new devices for getting rid of him. Cinq-Mars, son of the mareschal d'Effiat, was, for the present, the favorite of Louis: he had been chosen by Richelieu for his agreeable person, his frankness and frivolity, to fill this station, where the minister deemed him little dangerous. The youth, indeed, showed himself at first little ambitious of such eminence. Though loaded with wealth, honors, and the title of Grand Equerry, he shared the solitary habits and mean amusements of the king with impatience. These were to quarrel and complain of inattentions, to hunt the badger and the thrush in the forest of St. Germain. After the king retired for the night, Cinq-Mars used to gallop to Paris, join the gay society of the capital, and be back to attend Louis, when he rose. Such a life robbed the favorite of the spirits and vivacity requisite to please. The monarch complained of his apathy, and reproached him with ingratitude in return for wealth and favor. "And what have I to do with wealth?" replied the petulant youth; "I am ready to give it up. As plain Cinq-Mars I shall be happier than as grand equerry. One day in the societies of the Marais* would afford me more pleasure than a month spent here."

A powerful cause soon came to remove this impatience of ennui, and to awake the ambition of the favorite. He became enamored of Mary of Gonzaga, that daughter of the duke of

* The Marais or Marsh was then the fashionable quarter of Paris. Though still containing the vast hôtels of the old extinct nobility, it is now the quarter of the obscure and humble citizen.

Nevers, the object of Gaston's love and the queen-mother's hatred. To obtain the hand of a princess, it was necessary to become more than a court favorite. He sought to become duke and peer: the minister refused. The youth dissembled, applied himself to please Louis, attempted to enter the council, and again the stern cardinal put back the pretender with a frown, which even the king dared not gainsay. Henceforth Cinq-Mars vowed vengeance against Richelieu; and in this he was strengthened by the friendship and counsels of De Thou, a son of the famous president, an enemy to the cardinal on account of his oppression of the magistracy, and attached to the fortunes of Anne of Austria, whose wrongs, owing to the calumnies of Richelieu, he compassionated. Through De Thou, Cinq-Mars became connected with the queen, and through her with all the malcontents of the kingdom; with Gaston, with the duke of Bouillon, with all the exiles, and the personal enemies of the minister. It was a formidable league, and became more formidable by the adhesion of the king himself; but a passive adhesion, however. The monarch complained of the tyranny of his minister; Cinq-Mars instantly proposed as a remedy to assassinate Richelieu: Louis showed no horror at the crime, nor any aversion to the act.

The cardinal, in the mean time, had his own views, and was plotting in the depths of his policy and ambition. The king's health was evidently on the decline; and Richelieu, though not without the warnings of disease, reckoned on surviving. Under a new reign, Anne of Austria being queen-mother, he must look for dread retribution. The cardinal, therefore, from views of personal safety as well as of ambition, was necessitatd to aim at the regency for himself, to the exclusion both of the queen Anne and the duke of Orleans. In the furtherance of this plan, Richelieu determined to lead an army to the conquest of Roussillon, and to drag the monarch along with him; thus separating the latter from his queen, who remained in Paris. The duc de Bouillon he sought at once to gain, and to entice from Sedan, by offering him the command of the army in Italy, which the duke accepted with mistrust, but in obedience to the private solicitations of the queen. Amongst the nobility, Richelieu's only dependence was on the prince of Condé, and his son the duc d'Enghien, who had married Clémence de Maillé, niece of the cardinal.

Such were the views of both parties, when the court set out for Roussillon. Cinq-Mars had gained on the spirit of the king; and Richelieu was in such comparative disgrace and distrust, that he kept aloof from the monarch, and when arrived near to the seat of war, he took his quarters at Tarascon, a fortified place, some leagues distant from Narbonne, where Louis had his court and camp. With common prudence the conspirators might have completed their project; but they unwisely sought to strengthen themselves by a treaty with Olivarez, the Spanish minister, whilst, at the same time, Cinq-Mars conducted himself with so little secrecy that the plot universally got wind, and at the same time with so little discretion as to give cause of disgust to the susceptible and feeble monarch. Richelieu, informed of the manœuvres of Cinq-Mars, had no means of defeating them until he procured a copy of the treaty entered into by them with Spain. He dispatched Chavigny, secretary of state, to lay it before the king, who was roused and irritated by what he looked on as gross treason. To have plotted with him against the life of the cardinal was no crime, but to have leagued with Spain, and without his privacy, was guilt. All his mistrust of Cinq-Mars gathered at the moment. Chavigny and Mazarin gained ground for the cardinal, and kept possession of the monarch's ear, till warrants were procured for the arrest of those implicated.

Thus did the good fortune of Richelieu triumph to the last. Cinq-Mars and De Thou were taken. The duc de Bouillon underwent a similar fate, though at the head of his army; so dreaded was the ascendency of the minister. Gaston, duke of Orleans, found himself equally in his enemies' power: and the first act of this weak prince was to make submissions, and to offer himself as informer against his friends. Richelieu was restored to full confidence. It was not he, however, who repaired to court. The monarch came to visit him at Tarascon; although so little able to bear the voyage, that a couch was instantly obliged to be prepared for him by the side of that of the cardinal. There, extended each on his bed, did these personages, both menaced by the slow but sure approach of death, discuss the punishment of the baffled conspirators. Louis showed no more pride nor heart than his brother: he betrayed all the plans of the grand equerry against Richelieu. The latter repaid the confidence by covertly reproaching Louis with conspiring his death. The wretched monarch wept, and murmured excuses. The tiger-like cruelty of Richelieu was preferable to this.

Cinq-Mars might well exclaim with Strafford, "Put not your trust in princes." The king and his brother deposed against him. Both, however, gave their evidence only in writing; Gaston stipulated that he was not to be confronted with the victim of his treachery. Richelieu, ascending the

Rhone in a boat to avoid the fatigues of land travelling, dragged the prisoners after him in another bark, thus glutting his vengeance with the near view of its unfortunate objects. They were judged by a commission; Cinq-Mars, of course, condemned. Against De Thou no crime could be proved, except that he knew of the Spanish treaty, without revealing it. This satisfied the judges; and the friends were both con demned. The execution of these youths was a touching scene: they embraced on the scaffold: Cinq-Mars died with the physical courage of light-hearted youth; De Thou with the constancy of a reflecting mind, trembling, yet full of hope.

Richelieu, in the mean time, had reached his palace in the capital. Roman despot was never more courted, nor more feared: but death was coming fast to close his triumphant career. A mortal malady wasted him; yet the cardinal abated nothing of his pride, nor of his vindictiveness. He exiled some of the king's personal and cherished officers; he insulted Anne of Austria; remained seated during a visit that she paid him, and threatened to separate her from her children. Even his guards no longer lowered their arms in the presence of the monarch. His demeanor to Louis was that of one potentate to another. In December of 1642, three months after the execution of Cinq-Mars, the malady of the cardina became inveterate, and every hope of life was denied him. He summoned the king to his dying bed, recapitulated the great and successful acts of his administration, and recommended Mazarin as the person to continue its spirit, and to be his successor. Louis promised obsequiousness. Richelieu then received the last consolations of religion, and went through these pious and touching ceremonies with an apparently firm and undisturbed conscience. The man of blood knew no remorse. His acts had all been, he asserted, for his country's good: and the same unbending pride and unshaken confidence, that had commanded the respect of men, seemed to accompany him into the presence of his Maker. He died like the hero of the Stoics, though clad in the trappings of a prince of the church. Most of those present were edified by his firmness; but one bishop, calling to mind the life, the arrogance, and the crimes of the minister, observed, that "the confidence of the dying Richelieu filled him with terror."

Louis XIII. survived his great minister but a few months: during that time he scarcely exercised the royal will, except upon one great occasion. Though supporting Mazarin and the policy of Richelieu, he tolerated rather than permitted the return of all the exiled nobles. Condé alone remained constant and respectful to the memory of the cardinal. But the party of Vendôme, united to the house of Austria, already usurped the authority that the speedy death of Louis seemed about to leave them. The monarch, however, made a struggle to thwart them. Mazarin, a foreigner and an upstart, could not pretend to the regency that Richelieu might have grasped but he prepared a plan for balancing parties and personages dividing power so between them as to neutralize their force and thus leave the existing ministry predominant as umpire. To effect this, Louis drew up a will, declaring Anne of Austria regent, and the duke of Orleans lieutenant-general; at the same time appointing a council, whose approbation was necessary to all acts of government, and which was to consist of the queen, of the duke of Orleans, the prince of Condé, Mazarin, and three other ministers. This vain attempt of despotism to prolong its power beyond the grave was rightly judged invalid by the queen, who persuaded the parliament to register it, rather than disturb the death-bed of her husband. He to the last remained suspicious of her faith, and deaf to her protestations. Louis expired at St. Germain on the 14th of May, 1643. His character, one of the feeblest of humanity, is sufficiently marked in the preceding pages: that he did not want sagacity, is proved by his choice of Richelieu, and his adherence to him; beyond this he possessed not another respectable quality. A more contemptible character was never raised to the eminence of a throne. Louis appears as a phantom, into which Richelieu had the power of breathing, from time to time, his own passions and feelings; and which, when released from the influence of these, relapsed into its own shadowy nature, and complained of the violence and the tyranny which compelled it to energy. Thus we see him acting now informer and spy for his minister, and placing himself in the judgment-seat to make the condemnation of a victim more sure; another page of history represents him pouring out his plaints against the cardinal to Cinq-Mars, declaring his disgust of life and of the crown. The memoirs of Brienne record a striking picture of his remorse. When at Ecouen, the old palace of the Montmorencys, he fancied that he perceived the spectre of the duke, who had been decapitated, coming to upbraid him: the affrighted monarch fled the château, and no more returned to it.*

Richelieu was the true monarch of the reign: it was he who stamped upon it the impress of his genius and despotic character. True, he did but adopt and follow up the plans of

* Chantilly and Ecouen were spoils of the Montmorencys, forfeited in this reign to the crown, and given by it to the branch of Condé.

the great Henry, in humbling the Huguenots, the noblesse, and the house of Austria; but the execution of three such enterprises in the short space of twenty years, and by a minister risen from obscurity, and obliged to act as often in despite of the monarch as with his countenance and aid, places Richelieu in the first rank of statesmen. His address, his firmness, his sagacity, were unequalled. He was naturally magnanimous, loving wealth and splendor more as the symbol of power than as the gratification of selfish vanity. The cruelty of his character is its great blemish; yet he was clement to the Huguenots, and shrunk early from the severe acts which he foresaw his plans for raising royalty would throw upon him. In the states-general for 1614, he proposed to do away with the punishment of death for political crimes, yet he soon came to be unsparing in its infliction; and the decapitation of each new victim increased in him the taste for blood, until his prelate's robe assumed the crimson dye of the murderer and the tyrant. On a superficial view, this minister's unvarying success is the most striking feature of his career; and yet all of this that his own sagacity might not produce, the extreme imprudence and feebleness of his enemies may account for.

The crime of having trodden out the last spark of his country's liberties, and of having converted its monarchic government into pure despotism, is that for which Richelieu is most generally condemned. But the state of anarchy which he removed was license, not liberty. The task of reconciling private independence with public peace, civil rights with the existence of justice,—and this without precedent or tradition, without that rooted stock on which freedom, in order to grow and bear fruit, must be grafted,—was a conception which, however familiar to our age, was utterly unknown, and impracticable to that of Richelieu. With the horrors of civil war fresh in the memory of all, the general desire was for tranquillity and peace, not liberty; to which, moreover, had it been contemplated, the first necessary step was that of humbling the aristocracy. It was impossible that constitutional freedom could ever grow out of the chaos of privileges, and anarchy, and organized rebellion, that the government had to contend with. In building up her social fabric, France had in fact gone wrong, destroyed the old foundations, and rebuilt on others without solidity or system. To introduce order or add solidity to so ill-constructed a fabric was impossible; Richelieu found it necessary to raze all at once to the ground, except the central donjon of despotism, which he left standing. Had Richelieu, with all his genius and sagacity, undertaken for liberty what he achieved for royalty, his age would have rejected or misunderstood him, as it did Bacon and Galileo. He might, indeed, as a man of letters, have consigned such a political dream to the volume of an Utopia, but from action or administration he would have been soon discarded as a dreamer. Liberty must come of the claim of the mass; of the general enlightenment, firmness, and probity. It is no great physical secret, which a single brain, finding, may announce and so establish: it is a moral truth, which, like a gem, hides its ray and its preciousness in obscurity, nor becomes refulgent, till all around it is beaming with light.

Had we space to enter into the minor details of Richelieu's administration, much might be found to abstract from his merit, much to add to it. His management of the finances was grasping and unwise. France paid dearly for her glory and ascendency. The 20,000,000 of revenue, that enabled Henry IV. to amass, were quadrupled and yet expended by Richelieu; the greater part being wasted ere it reached the treasury. Thus the proud monarchy which Richelieu founded, owed to him also the canker that was destined to destroy it,—the extravagance and mismanagement of its pecuniary resources. For the sake of a certain revenue, there were 40,000 employments in finance and law left in the hereditary possession of subjects; an anomaly in a despotism scarcely credible. But the minister could not venture to attack at once the noblesse of the sword and that of the robe. He destroyed the former, and contented himself with humbling the latter.

CHAP. III.

1643—1661.

LOUIS THE FOURTEENTH'S REIGN TO THE DEATH OF MAZARIN

A SHORT time before the death of the late king, his young son of five years old, the dauphin, was brought to his bedside. "What is your name?" asked the languid monarch: "Louis the Fourteenth," replied the boy, who had early learned the secret of his dignity. "Not yet, not yet," observed his sire. Anne of Austria showed similar haste in usurping power. Surrounded by the exiles whom she had recalled, supported by the duc de Vendôme, by his son the duc de Beaufort, a handsome youth, whose devotion to her was as gallant as politic, and by the duke of Orleans himself, the queen was enabled, immediately on the demise of the king, to assume not only the name but the authority of regent. The late monarch's will, appointing a council, in which the partisans of Richelieu, Mazarin, and the prince of Condé, were to con trol the government, was set aside without difficulty by the parliament. Condé felt that he was powerless, and Mazarin made preparations for retiring to Italy.

Guilio Mazarini first appears in history as envoy from the pope. He was an Italian ecclesiastic, of no illustrious birth, and had been a follower of the Barberini; his sagacity discovered the French court to be a sphere where there was more room for his talents than the papal afforded. He came to Paris, attached himself to secretary Chavigny, and rose to be the confidant of Richelieu, who even intrusted him with the management of foreign affairs on the death of the friar Joseph, procured him a cardinal's hat, and recommended him as his successor. The Venetian ambassador described him, at this time, as possessing "a well-formed and agreeable person; as polite, adroit, impassive, indefatigable, prudent, eloquent, plausible, persuasive, an apt dissembler;" in short, a perfect statesman of the Italian school. Yet, if he now remained at the head of affairs, it was owing more to good fortune, and to the complete dearth of rival talent, than to his own foresight. He had drawn up the late king's will, which had sought to limit the power of the queen-regent. Could Anne of Austria forgive this? She did so. Enemy as she was of Richelieu, and vilifier of his policy, no sooner did she find herself at the head of affairs, than she perceived this very policy to be the only one consistent with the welfare of the state and the security of its ruler. Brienne recommended Mazarin, who, on being applied to, promised the most scrupulous devotion to the queen.

The announcement of this reconciliation, of this return of Mazarin to power, was received with surprise and mortification by the returned exiles, the enemies of Richelieu, those who had deemed themselves possessed of the heart and confidence of the queen. They were for the most part young men, such as the duc de Beaufort, and a host of noble striplings, who were all, nevertheless, profound statesmen in their own esteem. With pretensions to govern, they found it necessary to alter or conceal their juvenile and frivolous habits; they affected to be grave and sententious, and some even thought it necessary to give time to study and reflection; a whim, the characteristic and beneficial consequences of which are seen in the Memoirs of De Retz, and the Maxims of the duc de la Rochefoucault: the latter was at this time one of the young friends of the queen. Despite the talents that some of these youths afterwards displayed, their present pretensions and demeanor were considered as absurd, and the party was ironically called *les Importans*, that of the Important. On the side opposed to them were drawn up cardinal Mazarin, the old partisans of Richelieu, and, amongst the noblesse, the prince of Condé and his gallant son, the duc d'Enghien.

The queen-regent, as became her position, affected neu rality, but supported her newly chosen minister. The *Im portans*, however, hoped to regain the ascendency throug the means of Anne of Austria's old favorite, madame de Chev reuse, who was now returning from her long exile. This lady had once been all-powerful with the queen: her misfor tunes, occasioned by that attachment, gave her, she thought, an increase of claim; she totally put out of consideration how far the policy of a regent might interfere with the affections of a queen, and her party pretensions were as high as her resentments. She was warmly and cordially welcomed back by Anne; Mazarin hastened to conciliate her will, and commenced by placing 50,000 crowns before her, asking, might he count her amongst his friends. Madame de Chevreuse required the dismissal of Chavigny, and the cardinal instantly consented to sacrifice the secretary: then came the great demands of the party, viz. that Sedan should be restored to the duc de Bouillon, the government of Britany to the duc de Vendôme, and that of Guienne to young Epernon; Havre, too, was required for the future duc de la Rochefoucault. These demands were no less than to re-constitute the power and independence of the grandees, that Richelieu had spent his life, and steeped his memory in blood, in order to reduce. Anne of Austria and Mazarin, now in the place of authority held by Richelieu, could not but see with his eyes: the adroit Mazarin, however, did not give to madame de Chevreuse the flat and peremptory denial that would have come from Richelieu's mouth; he looked complaisant and yielding, and drew on the negotiatrix of the *Importans* to fresh pretensions. One of these was to supersede the chancellor Seguier by Château neuf. Now Châteauneuf had presided at the commission which condemned the duc de Montmorency, and to favor him would be to outrage the princess of Condé, sister of that duke. Mazarin pretended to stand out on this point, hesitatingly, no oubt; madame de Chevreuse insisted; and the cardinal, etermined to break with a party whose pretensions were xorbitant, and which sought to replace the aristocracy on its old footing of superiority to government and ministry, affected to break with them rather than insult the family of Condé; thus securing powerful support, and averting the suspicions of the young noblesse from the political jealousy which he bore them.

A rupture was declared; and a lady's quarrel soon after occurred to precipitate hostilities, and give the minister a pretext for acting. The duchess de Longueville, of the family of Condé, and one of the beauties of the court, was maligned by madame de Montbazon, sister-in-law of madame de Chev reuse. The latter found a *billet-doux* in the handwriting of the former, and addressed, she asserted, to comte de Coligni. This piece of scandal or calumny convulsed the entire circle of influential personages. The duc d'Enghien challenged the duc de Beaufort; the duke of Guise and comte de Coligni fought in the Place Royal, madame de Longueville being spectatress of the discomfiture of her chevalier, who died of his wounds. The queen in vain endeavored to bring about an accommodation. The *Importans* were too deeply mortified, and nothing short of the disgrace of the cardinal would satisfy them. The queen peremptorily refusing this, the duc de Beaufort entered into a scheme for making away with the cardinal by violence. Circumstances occurred to baffle and interrupt the design. Epernon was sounded in the mean time by one of the conspirators, and he instantly betrayed it. The duc de Beaufort was consequently arrested on the following day. Mesdames de Montbazon and Chevreuse were both exiled, as well as the duke and duchess of Vendôme, the dukes of Guise and Mercœur, and other less illustrious nobles. Here is the exculpation of Richelieu, and the excuse of his severity. No sooner is Anne of Austria, his rival and enemy, in the place of power, than she is obliged to adopt his policy and his strong measures, notwithstanding that such acts did violence to her private feelings. She wept on ordering the arrest of Beaufort; but, like the late monarch, she was compelled to sacrifice her feelings to her own interest and that of the state.

Whilst Louis XIV.'s reign thus commenced at court by a struggle betwixt the aristocracy and the ministers of royalty, t was signalized on the frontier by a brilliant victory. One of the bad effects of stern despotism is to check the development of talent in those who serve, and to paralyze their efforts. Thus few feats of war were decisive under Richelieu, unless the siege of Rochelle, which he personally directed. Had the cardinal lived, the duc d'Enghien had never dared to give battle at Rocroi, against the advice of the mareschal de l'Hôpital, who superintended as it were the movements of the young general. The action took place but five days after the death of Louis XIII., whe. the future

Condé felt himself at liberty. The Spaniards, 25,000 strong, besieged Rocroi. The duke marched to its succor with an army somewhat less in numbers. De l'Hôpital commanded the left of the French, and Sirot, who boasted to have been the antagonist of three kings, Gustavus Adolphus being one, commanded the reserve. Albuquerque, an active general led the Spanish left wing; he had strengthened it by a pos of a thousand mounted musqueteers, concealed by a wood, an destined to distract and take in flank the attacking enemy The vigilance of Condé discovered the manœuvre. He ordered Gassion with the infantry of the right to disperse this force. The prince himself, after a delay well calculated, led on its cavalry against Albuquerque; and the infantry having cleared the wood of the musqueteers, appeared in flank to second him. Albuquerque's division was routed and driven off the field. De l'Hôpital in the mean time had been beaten on his side and put to flight. Sirot, however, supported him and rallied the fugitives, until the victorious Condé, turning and taking the victors of De l'Hôpital in flank and rear, decided the action. The Spanish reserve, commanded by the veteran count de Fuentes, themselves veteran bands, and the most redoubtable infantry in Europe, alone stood their ground, or prepared to make a lion's retreat from the French. Condé charged them. The Spaniards allowed him to advance within fifty paces, and then a battery of eighteen cannon, which their body concealed, opened upon the advancing column, and drove it back. Twice the prince rallied and led his cavaliers to the charge; he might have perished like Gaston de Foix at Ravenna, in rashly pressing a desperate enemy, when Sirot and the reserve arrived, surrounded the valiant phalanx of Spaniards, broke it after many efforts, punishing ungenerously its stubborn resistance by indiscriminate slaughter. At Rocroi was overthrown the military superiority of Spain. Its veteran infantry was destroyed, and so weakened by misgovernment were the resources and spirit of the country, that to renew this army, or rather to renew its ancient confidence, was foun impossible. The moral effect of the victory of Rocroi was its most important consequence. The capture of Thionville was all the advantage immediately drawn from it.

The four years which succeeded 1643 were years of tran quillity to the regent, triumph to Mazarin, and glory to France. The petulance of the noblesse was checked by the discomfi ture of the *importans*. Mazarin, instead of imitating Richelieu and reigning by terror alone, sought to captivate by giving scope to pleasure, and creating a general taste for light and social amusements. He encouraged fêtes and gallantry

He was prodigal of favors, of money, of every thing save authority. He bound the noblesse, and their still more froward dames and mistresses, in golden and in flowery chains; and those, who a year before were clamoring for independent governments, then limited their ambition to a duke's title. The sage La Rochefoucault himself has recorded in his Memoirs how he pleaded for this important distinction, in order, as he observes, that his wife might enjoy the privilege of a *tabouret* or stool at court.

The year 1644 is marked by the brilliant manœuvres of the duc d'Enghien and Turenne, who drove the imperialist general, Mercy, from his lines near Fribourg. The Austrian, however, had his revenge. In May, 1645, he surprised Turenne in his camp, and defeated him. D'Enghien was instantly ordered to the Rhine to repair this defeat. It was August ere he could bring Mercy to action, and not then without a risk that might have been fatal. The imperialists had taken a strong position near Nordlingen. They occupied two eminences and a valley that lay between, a village of some size being the centre. Here Mercy had fortified himself, and, seconded by the famous John der Werth, thought he might turn the hero of Rocroi. Strongly against the opinion of Turenne, the prince determined to attack. He himself led his troops against the village in the centre. It was valiantly defended; and the houses and wall offered so many means of neutralizing attack and rendering resistance stubborn, that the young general despaired of overcoming on this point. He therefore flew to his left, led them with impetuous valor up the fortified eminence, and took it after a desperate struggle. Its cannon, turned on the village in the centre, soon gave the victory on this point also to the French who attacked. To the right the imperialists, under John der Werth, had beaten the mareschal de Grammont, but this advantage did not now avail. Mercy himself was slain, and his army suffered a complete defeat. In this battle it was evident that the personal valor and exertions of the young d'Enghien decided the day. His generalship was heroism, Turenne's was science.

The paucity of result arising from these brilliant victories disgusted the French government with the war. Spain and Austria were both wasted by the prolonged struggle, and negotiations commenced for peace. Hostilities ceased in 1647 betwixt Spain and Holland, and a treaty followed betwixt these belligerents. France was thus exposed without an ally. Her domestic tranquillity began again to be disturbed, and the house of Austria entertained in 1648 sanguine hopes of preluding to peace and facilitating it by a victory. The duc d'Enghien, now prince of Conde by his father's death, afforded them the opportunity sought. The archduke Leopold commanded an army of 18,000 men. He had taken Lens in the month of August, and lay encamped beneath its walls. Condé advanced, meditating an attack, but retreated on observing the force of the position. Nordlingen and years had taught him prudence. As he retired he was followed by the Austrian general Beck, and a combat ensued betwixt him and the French rear, in which the advantage was alternate, each general supporting his men with reinforcements, till the two armies were drawn up in full presence. Condé as usual commenced and led the attack, was victorious wherever he personally appeared, and by his activity succeeded in routing an enemy whose order of battle was from the first confused.

This victory decided the superiority of France, and the peace of Westphalia was signed in October of the same year. By it the war with Austria was concluded. Its chief consequences beyond the Rhine went to establish the independence of the Protestant powers, and to give an existence to that country, which afterwards grew into the kingdom of Prussia. Protestantism may almost pardon Richelieu for reducing Rochelle, in exchange for having established its predominance in Germany. France made important acquisitions. The empire at length acknowledged her claim to Metz, Toul, and Verdun. Alsace was finally abandoned, by which the boundary of the Rhine was on that point secure. Lorraine was indeed to be nominally restored to its prince, but with retention of its fortresses, and on such conditions that the duke refused to take advantage of the stipulation. As to Spain, she refused to be included in the treaty, and war still continued with that branch of the house of Austria.

So low had the French aristocracy been brought by Richelieu, that after his death, Mazarin, a foreigner and an upstart, a mild and even timid minister, was able to triumph over them. Their petulance overcome, the course of his administration ran smooth, until it encountered the resistance of the magistracy. The rise of this body to independence in the state, by being allowed to purchase and bequeath their offices, has been stated. The wealthy families of the commons, secluded from the hope of being admitted amongst the territorial noblesse, directed their ambition to the offices of parliament, and therein formed an aristocracy of their own, that of the robe. The commons, or burgess class of France, cheated of their political rights by the cessation of the states-general, and of their civic rights by the abolition of municipal privileges, looked up to the eminent of their own body, whom their wealth had invested with the dignities of judicia office These were considered as the chiefs, the representatives of the commons. The force of the magistracy lay in this sympathy and support. The growth of this third or fourth estate did not escape the jealous eye of Richelieu. He found no difficulty in depressing it. Had he found more, had he lived longer, or had he the same sagacity in finance, which guided him in other branches of administration, it is probable that he would have abolished and replaced the parliaments; no easy task to complete, since not only were the prices of each place to be repaid, but the revenue arising from the yearly fines, which perpetuated them, was to be supplied from some other source.

Under Richelieu the parliaments had the wisdom to desist from their principal pretension, that of acting the part of a representative assembly, in examining and refusing to pass the pecuniary edicts of the crown. But the claim, though dormant, existed; and the despotic minister did all that his wars, his enemies, and his occupation would permit to undermine the power not only of the magistrates, but of all who held offices by right of purchase. He appointed intendants of justice, of finance, and of police, in the several provinces. State criminals he handed over to commissioners, not to the parliament; whilst in ceremonies of etiquette, an important matter in those days, the legists were made to feel their humble origin, by being compelled to walk, to kneel, to bare their head in the midst of courtiers seated and covered. But the supple Mazarin could not wield his predecessor's sceptre of iron; and when a few years allowed the parliament to recover breath and courage, a reaction took place, and the struggle recommenced betwixt the crown and that assembly; the latter putting forth all its dormant pretensions, and a great portion of the discontented nobility rallying round it.

And here may be stated that unpleasant part of the historian's task, in which the reader must participate, condemned to choose betwixt two parties, neither of which he can applaud; compelled to bestow his interest when but a small portion of approbation is due, and forced, by an immediate and as it were local sense of impartiality, to lean to the side which his general feelings abhor. It is thus that, in narrating Richelieu's conquest of the Huguenots and of the aristocracy, it is impossible not to sympathize in a degree with the despot, however his cruelty and crimes may from time to time excite a burst of indignation. But when the historian is convinced that the independence of Huguenot and aristocrat, had both lasted, would but have prolonged anarchy, without ever producing liberty, he resigns himself, not without tacit reluctance, to admiration of the minister's genius and success.

The want of these two qualities, at least of the first, shown by Mazarin in the quarrel which we are about to relate, leaves impartiality more free. The parliament revived its claim to refuse taxes. This claim, though spirited and salutary if employed merely to deter the avarice of government was certainly as much an usurpation as the unlimited prerogative of the crown. The parliament was selfish and wrong It assumed the rights of the states-general, the assembly of which it took care not to provoke. At the same time the despotic aims of the court were pregnant with ill. The reader will judge betwixt them by the light of modern experience, looking with favor probably on any check that could be established against the royal authority. But the intrinsic merits of either side at the time call from the historian but strict impartiality.

Finance was then, as now, and as ever, the great, the insuperable difficulty of government. Richelieu had shown little skill in its management. Mazarin, a foreigner, ignorant of the habits of the people whom he governed, and of all the complicated mechanism of society, so necessary to be kept in view by him who would draw fresh revenue from the public, was less likely to succeed; and even his subaltern, especially charged with this part of the administration, was an Italian also, though wearing the French title of D'Emery. These ministers had an instinctive dread of the parliament; and when the expenses of the war and the court rendered an extraordinary supply indispensable, Emery rummaged in the book of ordonnances to find some old law, long registered, which might sanction a new levy, without having recourse to the legists. He found one a century old, which forbade any new buildings in the *fauxbourgs* or suburbs of Paris, under pain of demolition. It had been forgotten, and hundreds of new mansions had since arisen within these forbidden precincts. Emery proposed to raise a fine upon every such house, thus infringing the maxim of despots, "to feed their capital and tax the provinces." The outcry was general; the parliament stepped out of its jurisdiction, and forbade the fiscal officers to enforce the levy. Hence arose quarrels, negotiations, and finally sedition. The fines on houses in the suburbs were withdrawn, and a loan of eighteen millions to be forced on the notables of Paris was proposed in its stead. The parliament was to have the power of distributing this loan, and by thus allowing them to take part in finance arrangements, Mazarin induced them to register the decree.

The whole force of the legists was here seen to consist in the support of the citizens. The decree, though registered, could not be executed. The parliament was divided into several chambers or courts, of which the several chiefs and members were wont to unite in the great hall, to register any edict of state, or to consult on important affairs. The grea hamber pretended to the exclusive right of convoking thi eneral assembly. It was composed of the elder and least violent of the body. They refused to summon the other chambers on the present occasion; and the younger members, of whom these were composed, became clamorous and indignant They assembled of their own accord. Mazarin lost presence of mind. Fear quenched his natural astuteness. The inferior chambers were bursting into hostility against the great. A schism was declaring itself, by which the minister might have profited. He precipitated matters, however; arrested the most turbulent chiefs of the inferior chambers; and thus afforded an opportunity for the elders of the great chamber to make common cause with their opponents, and redeem their having supported the minister by now demanding the liberation of their brethren. The consequence was, that Mazarin was obliged to yield, and to meditate another measure of authority. He brought the young king to parliament; and in a bed of justice caused him, sitting on his throne, to order the registry of nineteen fiscal edicts. The parliament dared not to murmur in the presence of royalty, though but infant, and the minister for this time triumphed.

In the following year Emery attempted to establish an *octroi* or tax on all articles of consumption entering Paris; but this he was obliged to abandon, and Mazarin in his distress recurred to the old ruinous routine of creating new offices and selling them. This he thought the scheme most acceptable to the parliament. But they were now acquainted with their strength, and with the timid character of the minister, who felt once more obliged to make use of the dignity of the king's presence. A bed of justice was accordingly held in February, 1648. The parliament registered in silence, but on the following day declared its assent to have been forced, and the registry invalid. The queen was enraged at this audacious act. She warmly expressed her indignation against the *canaille*, or rabble, who, to use the words of madame de Motteville, were infected with such a dangerous love of the public good. Confident of the royal rights, Anne of Austria sent to ask the parliament, "Did it believe itself to possess the right of limiting the king's authority?"—a dangerous question, at a time when the commons of England, bearing the same name of parliament, by which the French judicial body was designated, had proclaimed republican principles, and were that very moment warring upon their monarch. There is no doubt that some of the younger members of the French judicature entertained a wish at this moment to imitate their insular neighbors. This was but a latent and rarely entertained idea, and whatever slight root it had, was utterly destroyed by the catastrophe of king Charles's execution in the following year.

At present the parliament gravely deliberated on the queen's question, and the speeches of many of its members no doubt echoed the great principles of liberty. We find some of these maxims in De Retz. "There is none but God who can subsist alone,"* said that personage, whose volume of memoirs appears to be one of more value, and to testify more genius than all the boasted chefs-d'œuvre of the age immediately succeeding. "The firmest monarchies, the most despotic kings, can only be supported by men and by laws united. One of them without the other will never suffice." He afterwards proceeds to assert, that kingly authority had ever been limited in France. The aristocracy and the parliament he considers the proper check, but the word states-general never drops from his pen. He thus describes the conduct of the parliament:—"It grumbled on the subject of the edict, and no sooner was it heard to murmur, than the public started up. Half awake, we set about groping for the laws of the state. They were nowhere to be found. We were frightened; we clamored; we asked them of each other; and in the general agitation questions arose, exciting animosity here, dissatisfaction there. The people entered into the sanctuary, tore away the veil that ought for ever to cover all that can be said or thought upon the rights of subjects and the rights of kings, interests that can never agree but in silence. The hall of the judicial palace profaned these mysteries."

The question of the queen, and the debate upon it, instead of terrifying the magistrates, gave the younger fresh spirit to advance in opposition. These were moved by the free spirit of the times, and the wish to imitate the English parliament; the elder as well as the less speculative and tranqui members joining in the opposition from hatred to the cardinal, whose last edicts proposed a considerable reduction in their

* From De Retz, who could speak for order as well as liberty, though he so little practised the one or comprehended the other, is this other powerful maxim, analogous in its allusion,—*Dieu obéit toujours à ce qu'il a commandé une fois.*

salaries. This latter was a finesse on the part of Mazarin, to make it appear that the opposition of the magistrates proceeded from their private interests; another blunder of his over-astuteness. In fine, the younger and more violent members, the reformers as they might be called, succeeded in carrying their plan, which was a union of the chiefs of the magistracy, with deputies from the inferior members and, with the municipality of Paris, forming an assembly for the reformation of the state.

The queen lost all temper at this practical reply to a question that she deemed unanswerable. She accused Mazarin of weakness, because he sought to calm her. The assembly was forbidden. It met in despite of this, and the prohibition was recalled. At length, in July, it produced its plan of reformation. This recommended, in the first place, the removal of the intendants, whom Richelieu had appointed; the diminution of the taille;* the illegality of all taxes not consented to by the sovereign courts of law; and, finally, a kind of habeas corpus, by which every prisoner was to be interrogated within twenty-four hours after his arrest, and brought before his natural judges. No marvel that the court, in the words of De Retz, felt itself "touched in the apple of the eye" by these bold demands, which constituted no less than a free constitution. It cost Anne of Austria fresh tears, and new bursts of rage. The blood of Charles V. and Philip II. might well boil within her. Not in a position to deny, the minister determined to evade. In a bed of justice the young king was made to grant some immaterial part of the demands; but the principal articles were found to want the expression which gave them force. The presence of royalty did not now keep down the murmurs, and the boyhood of Louis XIV. unfortunately saw his dignity insulted and his authority denied. Bred up in these quarrels, his young ears drank in the continued complaints and imprecations of his mother against the parliament; and the circumstances increased that strong bias to despotism which was but natural to his station.

Nevertheless, the queen and Mazarin had no thought but of yielding, and of deferring the recovery of authority to a future period; when tidings of the victory gained by the

* The yearly taille, levied on the poorest classes only, amounted to 50 million of livres, equal to double the sum in our day. The present land-tax in France, paid by all, does not exceed that amount by more than one half. And now there are neither tithes nor feudal exactions. The weight of taxes on the French population under Mazarin may be thence imagined. The whole revenue amounted to 80 or 90 millions of livres, equal, if doubled, to the value of about 7,000,000*l*. sterling.

prince of Condé at Lens arrived, roused the drooping spirits of the court, and excited it to resistance. On the 26th of August the king went in state to hear *Te Deum* sung in honor of the victory.* The opportunity was taken of the military force attending this ceremony to arrest six of the chief magistrates. Broussel was the name of the principal. The news of his imprisonment created a tumult, which soon grew into a seditious mob, clamoring for the liberation of the prisoners. The mareschal de la Meilleraye with 200 guards tried to disperse them; he drove them back to the Pont Neuf, where his progress was impeded, and where he met De Retz, coadjutor of the archbishop of Paris, who had rushed out in his robes amongst the mob. After having harangued and momentarily tranquillized the populace, De Retz hurried with the mareschal to the Palais Royal, to represent the alarming state of the city to the queen. Anne of Austria, who knew the coadjutor's character, suspected him as one more likely to throw oil than water on the flame. "It is rebellion itself to imagine that the people can rebel," said she: "you would have me deliver Broussel; I will first strangle him with these hands." This resentment, seconded by the jeers of the court, had the ill effect of converting De Retz into a dangerous enemy. The mob, however, dispersed for that day; and it was not till the morrow that, on the meeting of the parliament, and in full cognizance of the matter, the more respectable citizens joined the populace in renewing the tumult. The queen had troops. Defence was necessary, and tradition pointed out the means. In a few hours the barricades of the league were renewed. The streets were every where broken up; and these intrenchments, guarded by an armed population, became, as the military men of that day avowed, impregnable to a force of whatsoever magnitude.

The presidents and chiefs of the parliament now proceeded to supplicate the queen to allay the tumult by rendering up the prisoners. At first unhearkened to, the people drove them back into the palace, and into the queen's presence; to whom a sister queen, the wife of the unfortunate Charles I., then present, observed, that the troubles in London were

* I cannot refrain from here remarking, how similar scenes are reproduced in French history. This has been noticed in relating the *barricade* of the league. The *barricades* of the *fronde* we now enter on, and they too had their points of resemblance with the last. It was the capture of Algiers that raised the confidence of Charles X. to resist. We saw him proceeding to the *Te Deum* amidst the silence of his people. And in a few days the barricades of 1830 had driven him from his capital. The reader will find that the *Fronde* had also its *garde bourgeoise* or national guard, its mobs its moderate royalists, astonished to find themselves revolutionary, &c. &c

never more passionate nor more alarming. The court was forced to yield. Broussel and Blancmenil were restored to liberty. The barricades were immediately levelled, and the people ceased their turbulence and clamor. "Never was disorder more orderly managed," says madame de Motteville; "the citizens who had taken up arms to prevent the ascendency of the rabble and to check pillage, were little more peaceable than the populace itself, and roared for the liberation of Broussel with equal violence." The court in yielding had but temporized, however; and it soon made its escape from the capital to St. Germain's. Such was the first insurrection of the *Fronde*. As it had been commenced by troops of urchins, who at that time amused themselves with slings, the wits of the court called the insurgents *frondeurs*, or slingers, insinuating that their force was trifling, and their aim merely mischief. The young lords and dames, who afterwards embraced the party, willingly adopted a name which so well characterized their petulance, and sportive rather than serious rebellion.

The hopes of the queen were now in the young prince of Condé. But that young hero, though opposed to the party of the *importans*, was not prepared to martyrize his popularity for Mazarin. He proposed his mediation. Mazarin accepted it, well knowing how soon the hot prince would lose patience at the formal and democratic pleadings of the parliamentary statesmen. De Retz, now the leading man of the popular party, made every effort to gain Condé, who replied, "My name is Louis de Bourbon: I will not shake the throne." Through his means negotiations were entered into with the court; the elders of the parliament, and Molé, the president, at their head, being anxious to avoid a civil war, whilst the violent party, bestowing on the pacific chiefs the nickname of *barbons*, pushed matters to extremities. They had revived an old law, passed after the fall of the mareschal d'Ancre, which prohibited the administration of the kingdom by foreigners, thus aiming at Mazarin. Still a second accommodation took place: a royal declaration, dated the 28th of October, accepted the principal articles of the plan of reformation, and the court once more took up its residence in the capital.

This proved but a hollow truce, entered into by both parties out of respect for Condé, whom both feared, and both hoped to gain. The popular party was suspicious; De Retz continued his intrigues; whilst the queen urged Condé to make preparations for defending the royal authority by force. It has been the fate of all attempts to establish liberty in France to be frustrated, not by the opposition of the aristocracy, but by their affecting to abet and to adopt its princ'ples. Having under this pretext obtained the lead, they have ever perverted the force of the cause to their own selfish or frivolous interests, thus proving equally fatal in their friendship as their enmity. The nobles and princes of the blood, taking the lead of the popular party, destroyed all its efforts for freedom under Charles VI. The struggle of the Huguenots for religiou liberty was perverted in the same way. To what end was al the blood of the French Protestants spilled, and their victories achieved? To the establishment of the house of Bourbon, and to the oppression and ruin of themselves. In the *Fronde*, the magistracy of Paris, supported by the citizens, endeavored to supply the want of a national assembly. They framed a constitution; forced it on the court without effusion of blood, and might have succeeded in upholding and perhaps amelior ating it, when the young noblesse interfered, drove the citizens to insurrection first, then to submission, and for the sake of their selfish quarrels, which all their light-heartedness and valor cannot redeem, they sacrificed the last hope that the French had of even a degree of liberty; they pierced the last plank that shut out the overwhelming ocean of despotism. We certainly, of the present day, can look but with a small degree of hope or approbation on a judicial body which grasps at legislative power. But had the noblesse known its true interests, and acted its natural part of mediator, the states-general might have superseded the parliament in its political functions; the moderation of the provincial deputies would have tempered the ardor of the capital, and the ever consecutive extremes of insurrection and pusillanimous submission might both have been avoided.

The old party of the *importans* now roused itself. The duc de Beaufort escaped from prison. The duc de Bouillon, smarting under the loss of Sedan, joined counsels with him; and both intrigued with the violent men in the parliament to form an insurrection against the court. The duchess of Longueville brought her charms to support the same cause: these decided De la Rochefoucault, her lover, to adopt it. She used all her influence to the same effect with her brother Condé in vain. In default of him, the prince of Conti, of the same family, was won over. No cause could subsist, in the opinion of these gentlemen, unless it could boast the name of a prince of the blood. The duchess of Chevreuse, though still in exile, corresponded with the party, and promised to it the accession of the princes of Lorraine. Madame de Montbazon was found united in the same cause with her rival, madame de Longueville. The mareschal d'Hocquincourt offered 's strong and important fortress which he commanded, in homage to the charms of the former. "Peronne," wrote he to her, "is at the disposal of the fairest of the fair." A crowd of nobles gaily joined the conspiracy; and the court was once more obliged to make its escape from Paris, and retire to St. Germain's, in January, 1649.

Strong and extreme measures were at last resolved upon although not prepared with that vigor and foresight that Richelieu would have displayed. Troops, under Condé and the duke of Orleans, prepared to invest Paris, and occupied on either side of the city the bridges of Charenton and St. Cloud; but with only 12,000 men, the utmost of the royalist force, it was impossible to invest the metropolis. A royal order, commanding the parliament to retire to Montargis, was treated by them with contempt. A civic guard was raised, to the number of 12,000; the chief officers, it is remarkable, being lawyers and officers of parliament; the provost of the merchants, however, retained the supreme command. In addition to these, a stipendiary force of 20,000 men was raised in a few days, by means of a house-tax, fixed at so much for every plain house-door, and double the sum for the gate which admitted a carriage. The noblesse did not forget their petty ambition, even in adopting the burgess cause. The duke of Elbœuf had first seized on the chief command, and was reluctant to yield it to the prince of Conti. The duc de Beau fort, however, was the most popular chief, owing to his affable manners and handsome person. He was called the *roi des halles* (the king of the markets). The war, if it can be called such, commenced by the attack of the Bastile, at which the ladies of the party assisted. It surrendered gallantly to these fascinating adversaries. On his side, Condé began to press towards the wall; and some skirmishes took place, in which a few were slain; amongst others, the duc de Châtillon.

Two circumstances soon after occurred, that much altered the views and shook the resolutions of the court. One was the defection of Turenne, who, won over by his brother the duc de Bouillon, promised to march the army, which he commanded on the Rhine, to the support of the Fronde; the other was the connexion of the *frondeur* nobles with Spain, and the public reception by the parliament of an envoy from that power. This savored of the inveteracy of the League. The elder magistrates, and principally Molé the president, indignant at this alliance with the enemies of the country, began to exert themselves to frustrate the violent projects of the young noblesse, and to seek an accommodation with the court. The majority of the parliament, already disgusted with the froward, frivolous, and arrogant behavior of the nobles, came so far into the same views, that Molé himself, with some of his brethren, were dispatched to the queen at Ruel, to essay an accommodation. The court grasped at the opportunity, but still negotiated for advantages; whilst De Bouillon stirred the populace of Paris against the moderation of the parliament, and urged the alliance with Spain. Molé, determined to disappoint the ambitious duke, signed a treaty with the court in haste, on the 11th of March, ere Turenne could arrive, or Spain dispatch its aid.

Great was the indignation of the populace, and of the seditious leaders, at the news of this peace. All cried out treason Bouillon was confounded, and De Retz perplexed. Molé knew that he risked his life by thus balking the seditious ardor of both the nobles and the mob; but the thought gave him courage, not hesitation. The critical moment was that of declaring the treaty to the assembled parliament. A ferocious crowd, crying "Treason! no peace! no Mazarin!" surrounded the palace of justice; and the throng within its walls was scarcely less hostile or less calm. Molé stood up and read the treaty; clamor instantly covered his voice. The prince of Conti exclaimed against a peace concluded without his knowledge, and that of the nobles his friends. "You, then, are the cause," retorted Molé: "whilst we were at Ruel, you were treating with the enemies of France; you were inviting the archduke, the Spaniard, and the foe, to invade the kingdom." "It is not without the consent of several members of the parliament that we took this step," replied the prince, not denying the charge. "Name them," was Molé's instant retort; "name the traitors, that we may proceed to try and judge them."

The firmness of the president at once awed the nobles, and won over the majority of the assembled magistrates to support him. The only hope of the favorers of sedition was in the rabble, which, incensed and tumultuous, had penetrated into the passages and corridors of the palace. Some, with poniards and arms, demanded the head of the president. "Give us up the *grande barbe* (long beard);" so they called the venerable magistrate. Others shouted the word "Republic." Molé heard them with unshaken courage. Those around besought him to make his escape by a postern. "Justice never skulks," replied Molé, "nor will I, its representative. I may perish, but will never commit an act of cowardice, which would give hardihood to the mob." Accordant to this magnanimous resolution, the chief magistrate walked boldly down the principal staircase through the mob, awing the most audacious by his firmness. Even De Retz was lost in admiration; and has recorded "that he could perceive in the countenance of Molé, then threatened by the fury of the multitude, not a motion that did not indicate imperturbable firmness, and at the same time a presence and elevation of mind greater than firmness, and every way supernatural." This is one of the noblest traits of courage which history has recorded.

When the chiefs of sedition saw that they could not conquer, and that the treaty would pass in their despite, each hastened to make his private offers and demands of the court. Bouillon wanted Sedan; Turenne, Alsace; Elbœuf, the government of Picardy; Beaufort, to be admiral. They were not listened to. Angered and resolved to proceed to extremities, they wrote to Turenne to advance, and to the archduke to invade the north. But Turenne's treason was defeated by D'Erlach, commander of the Swiss; himself obliged to fly; and the archduke, his support failing, retreated. Thus the moderate portion of the parliament, supported by the civic guard, succeeded in restoring peace with the court, despite the opposition of the nobles and the mob. The reader will not fail to remark how distinct these several classes kept from each other, even when in alliance and fighting the same battles; a state of society that has not ceased at the present day to characterize France: whilst in England, the blending of the lower ranks of the nobly born with the higher ranks of the industrious and unennobled, effected by the habits and institutions of the country, have rendered the pernicious line of demarcation betwixt castes and classes almost invisible to the historian.

The scene now shifts, and another act of the Fronde commences, displaying the chief actors in altogether new characters and dresses. No sooner was the peace declared than the prince of Condé, jealous of the cardinal, united with the nobles whom he so lately combated: he visited his sister, madame de Longueville, became reconciled to her, and to La Rochefoucault; the duke of Beaufort and the coadjutor being the only two that remained at the same time hostile to Mazarin and jealous of Condé. A few nobles, however, were not sufficient to give weight to the demands of the prince, and Mazarin resisted them. The prince, in consequence, saw the coadjutor, and planned, or pretended to form, an alliance with him and the violent members of the parliament. The court, terrified at the prospect of being so abandoned, and of seeing Condé at the head of the Frondeurs, granted all the desires of the latter, who, ashamed to break with his new allies, yet left without a pretext to continue his quarrel with Mazarin, "changed his mind 300 times in three days." The haughty prince, who hated the parliament and the rabble, at last decided to disappoint the coadjutor; he became reconciled to Mazarin, and of course quarrelled with the Frondeurs, whom he accused of an attempt to assassinate him. The same imprudence, the same haughtiness, petulance, and overbearing temper, marked the prince to whichever side he leaned, and disgusted both. As a friend he was even more troublesome than as an enemy: Mazarin and the queen felt this they could no longer tolerate his insolence; and the presen moment, as he had left himself no friends in any party, seemed the best opportunity for being revenged on him. To arrest and send the prince to prison was the old monarchic mode of treating the froward; but one of the articles stipulated by the parliament, and secured to them in the last treaty, was, that every prisoner should be interrogated in four-and-twenty hours, and delivered over to his lawful judges. To infringe upon this law might rouse the parliament, and re-excite the rebellion of the Parisians. To secure himself against such an event, Mazarin leagued with—whom? The coadjutor himself, and the most violent of the Frondeurs! They, the populace sharing their sentiments, hated Condé for his ancient enmity and his late desertion. De Retz and Mazarin, accordingly, had interviews, the former entering the Palais Royal by night in disguise: the consequence of this secret understanding soon appeared. The prince of Condé, the prince of Conti his brother, and the duc de Longueville, were arrested at the door of the council-chamber, and sent to Vincennes.* The dukes of Bouillon, and La Rochefoucault, the duchess de Longueville and Turenne, succeeded in escaping; the princesses of Condé were ordered to retire to Chantilly. Bonfires, illuminations, and every sign of joy on the part of the Parisians, marked this extreme measure. The popular hatred of Condé, and confidence in De Retz, lulled for the moment their dislike of the cardinal Mazarin.

Two events which mark the spirit of the time, and which occurred previous to the prince's arrest, must not be passed over. The honor of a *tabouret*, or stool at court, was only granted to the ladies of princes of sovereign houses, or to the wives of dukes and peers. Exceptions, however, had been made in favor of the younger branches of the Rohans, the La Tremouilles, and the family of Bouillon. La Rochefoucault pretended to the same distinction: the prince of Condé supported his claim. The noblesse instantly assembled

* January, 1650.

to the number of 800, and formed a protest against such pretensions, which went, they said, to destroy the natural equality that existed amongst all gently born. The dispute led to a discussion of political rights and principles, then the dangerous mania of the age; and some voices clamored for the states-general. The French noblesse are entitled certainy to the credit of having demanded these national assemblies at a time when the judicial body or parliament, in whom the favor and confidence of the people were then centred, deprecated any such proposition. It may be asked why the chiefs of the judicature, and such upright lovers of liberty as Molé, were opposed to the convocation of the states-general. The answer is, that the example of England, then in the mouths and minds of many, terrified them, and made them prefer their own body as a constitutional check, to such a representative assembly as that which, in the neighboring kingdom, had begun with civil war, and ended in regicide and despotism. It must be owned they had some cause for fear. A revolution is bad enough; but an imitative revolution, a parody of such a great event, is to be deprecated tenfold, as incurring all the evils and few of the advantages of the convulsion. Already the people of Paris talked of republics and liberty: the monarchy, they said, was too old, and it was time it should expire. Nay, the duke of Bouillon himself, adopting the revolutionary phrase, proposed on one occasion to *purge* the parliament. The taste for assembling and debating was general. The annuities charged on the Hôtel de Ville were suspended by the troubles: 3000 of these fund holders, chiefly citizens of Paris, met, drew up resolutions, petitioned, and clothed themselves in black, the uniform of the tiers or third estate. Molé instantly rebuked them, as attempting to form a *chambre de communes*, a house of com mons. The burgesses were indignant at the comparison: and this very reproach, that they were imitating the commons of England, had great effect in dissipating their assembly. This is an early instance of the law of repulsion, by which England and France so often react one upon the other in political opinions. The English revolution of the seventeenth century contributed strongly, by its crimes, its abuses, and its extremes, to check the progress of liberty in France, and to give to despotism its strongest plea—expediency. The French revolution of the eighteenth century resuscitated toryism with us, though certainly in an inferior and very ineffective degree.

Principles, however, were soon forgotten in the general sympathy which the misfortunes of Condé excited. The naughtiness, the imprudences, of the hero of Rocroi and Lens were now forgotten; and the nobility began to rally to his cause as their own. The court were at first successful in reducing Normandy, the government of the duke of Longueville; but in Languedoc and the provinces on the Gironde, the dukes of La Rochefoucault and Bouillon soon gathered an army of adherents, and were joined by the wife and infant son of the prince. Clémence de Maillé, princess of Condé, had hitherto commanded little respect either from the world or from her husband, who, having married her merely as the niece of cardinal Richelieu, was ashamed of her humble origin and his own condescension. She now however displayed a heroism and an attachment worthy of the spouse of the great Condé. The princess escaped with her young son, the duc d'Enghien, from Chantilly, and after some delay in a fortified place, joined the dukes of La Rouchefoucault and Bouillon in the south. But the noblesse was not then the predominant order in the state, and she was obliged to seek more powerful protection in the parliament of Bourdeaux. This provincial court of justice was highly incensed against the duke of Epernon, governor of Languedoc; and consequently ill-disposed towards the queen and cardinal, who seconded him. They of course embraced with ardor the new laws established by the parliament of Paris, which gave to the courts of magistracy power to control the measures of government, and which forbade arrests without bringing the accused to speedy trial. They could little comprehend the manœuvres by which De Retz and his violent party induced the parliament of Paris to overlook the imprisonment of Condé. They were eager to take his part, and to admit the princess within their walls; but at the same time had considerable distrust of the nobles who supported her, and who were negotiating with Spain. To satisfy these scruples, the princess entered Bourdeaux alone; but the popular clamor drowning the voice of the magistrates, she soon had the city at her command, and the dukes of Bouillon and La Rochefoucault entered with their troops and took the command.

The queen and Mazarin led the young king, and an army commanded by the mareschal de la Meilleraye, to reduce Bourdeaux. Its first feat was to raze Verteuil, the famous château of the La Rochefoucault family,—a barbarous act, and inconceivable in Mazarin, who loved the arts. Bourdeaux was then invested, and its suburb was carried after a valiant defence, in which La Rochefoucault displayed remarkable gallantry. To gain footing in the town itself was soon found impossible, such was the obstinacy of the armed citizens.

Whilst Mazarin and the court thus lay encamped before Bourdeaux, Turenne had entered the north of France, and was marching without opposition towards the capital, intending to liberate the princes from Vincennes. Condé, confined in the *donjon* of that castle, whiled away his captivity by cultivating the few flowers that the terrace of his window could contain. "Who would have thought," exclaimed he, on learning the resistance of Bourdeaux, "that my wife should be fighting whilst I was gardening!" The princes were removed from Vincennes to the safer retreat of Marcoussy, and Turenne, fearing to indispose the parliament of Paris by appearing at the head of foreign troops, retired again towards the frontier.

The coadjutor and the violent Frondeurs grew weary of their alliance with Mazarin, into which their fear and hatred of Condé had alone induced them to enter. They not only found Mazarin ungrateful and insincere, refusing even to De Retz the cardinal's hat that he demanded, but their popularity, which was their chief force, and their influence over the parliament, were rapidly diminishing from their union with the court. Mazarin, suspecting the intention of the Frondeurs, and alarmed by the march of Turenne, granted peace to Bourdeaux, concluding more a truce than a treaty with the princess of Condé, Rochefoucault and Bouillon. The minister then returned to Paris, where he found the parliament no longer silent as to the arrest of Condé, but prepared to expostulate, and demand his release. Mazarin caused the princes to be instantly conveyed from Marcoussi to Havre de Grâce, where they were still more in his individual power. La Rochefoucault and Bouillon also returned to Paris; and a series of intrigues took place; these partisans of Condé negotiating at the same time both with the coadjutor and with Mazarin for his release. An alliance with either would effect this, and La Rochefoucault was in doubt. The coadjutor, in the habit of a cavalier, came by night to the rendezvous at the house of the princess palatine. La Rochefoucault went in equal secrecy to the Palais Royal. The over-caution of the cardinal lost his cause. La Rochefoucault pressed him at once to conclude the alliance, and give orders that Condé should be set at liberty. Mazarin hesitated. Unprincipled as he was himself, he could not believe it possible that the friends of Condé could unite with De Retz. La Rochefoucault warned the cardinal in parting that the morrow would be too late. Mazarin smiled incredulity and irresolution; and the duke hurrying to the other place of rendezvous, concluded the agreement with the coadjutor. The effects of this alliance were immediately manifest. The majority of the parliament clamored for the release of Condé, and addressed the queen on the subject. It was necessary to yield; and Mazarin saw that, deserted by all parties, he would infallibly be the victim. In his rage he anathematized the parliament before the whole court, called it an English house of commons, compared the coadjutor De Retz to Cromwell and himself to Strafford, and declared that, in sacrificing its minister to popular clamor, the crown would, as in the case of Strafford, sacrifice itself. This conversation, being reported to the parliament by De Retz, raised a storm indescribable, and terminated in an address to the queen, desiring that Mazarin should be banished from her councils, and that the prince should be liberated. Naught was left the cardinal but flight. He took his departure immediately. It was agreed that the queen and young king were to follow him, and that, possessed of Havre and the persons of the princes, they would be able either by open war or negotiation to bring the parliament and the Frondeurs to more reasonable terms. This project however failed through the cunning and activity of the coadjutor, who, learning the queen's intention of departing, raised a mob around the palace, and made her virtually a prisoner there. Cardinal Mazarin alone found himself without authority. He could not even gain entrance into Havre unless unattended. He entered, nevertheless, saw the captive princes of Condé, Conti, and Longueville, endeavored to cajole them, and set them at liberty, without receiving in return a single mark of gratitude or regard. Thus every way disappointed, Mazarin resigned himself to his disgrace, and left the kingdom.

The prince of Condé was now all-powerful: the parliament, the Fronde, the noblesse, the populace, had all rallied to him; the minister was in exile, the queen a prisoner. Many blamed him for not setting aside Anne of Austria, and assuming the regency; but he was totally without the qualities requisite for taking advantage of his position; he was too lazy, too confident, too generous, too rash: and, making not a single exertion, the several parties that had united to compel at once his release and the exile of the minister, were allowed again to fall asunder, and abandon to the court the recovery of its ancient influence. The noblesse at this period were animated with a strong desire to imitate the magistracy, and, by remaining united, to restore or re-establish the influence of the aristocracy, in opposition both to crown and judicature. They assembled in the convent of the Cordeliers (afterwards doomed to hold a club of a very different kind, that of Danton), and formed a house of peers, discussing state affairs, and fixing the privileges of the nobles. The parliament took fire at this, and forbade the assemblies. The noblesse looked to Condé tc head them; but he, without principle or aim, and deeming his interests, as prince of the blood, distinct from those of the aristocracy, held back at this crisis. The noblesse called the assembly of the church, then sitting, to their aid, who protested, and complained that the parliament had altered the ancient constitution of the kingdom, by adding themselves as a fourth and spurious estate to the three established ones of king, lords, and commons. Despite of this, the parliament had force and the popular feeling on its side. The noblesse were obliged to succumb, and dissolved their assembly; not, however, before they had recourse to the queen and the royal authority, who issued a declaration, promising to convoke the states-general for the following September.

Here the queen recovered consideration and authority sufficient to enable her to aim at and grasp more, by allying with the prince of Condé. One of the stipulations betwixt them was, that the marriage should be broken off betwixt the prince of Conti and mademoiselle de Chevreuse. The coadjutor, connected by gallantry and friendship with the family of Chevreuse, was indignant at this, and a quarrel ensued betwixt Condé and the old party of the Fronde. Hence another scene in the drama, which represents Condé insulted by those very men who had been so instrumental in releasing him. De Retz and the prince nearly came to blows in the Palace of Justice; and the former had almost fallen a victim to the passion of La Rochefoucault, who jammed the coadjutor betwixt two folding-doors till he was almost suffocated: the duke at the same time called to one of his friends to stab De Retz, an injunction that was not obeyed, and perhaps not intended to be obeyed. It is, nevertheless, startling to the modern reader to find the courtly author of the "Maxims" engaged personally in the office, and using the language, of the assassin.

The consequence of these dissensions was the recovery of her authority by Anne of Austria, who, in affecting to ally with Condé, was merely enticing him to disgust, and desert, the Fronde. This achieved, she flung off the mask, and Condé found himself as much detested by all parties as a few months back he was their favorite and their rallying word. The prince, thus deserted, endeavored to make common cause with the noblesse, and clamored for the states-general; but it was too late: the parliament united with the court in opposing their convocation, and Condé in despair retired from Paris, obliged to seek support in civil war and in alliance with Spain.

In September, 1651, Louis XIV., then approaching fourteen years of age, was declared to have completed his minority. The day was celebrated with great magnificence. The royal authority remained, however, as before, in the hands of the queen; her only thought was the recall of Mazarin. The attachment borne by Anne to this prelate-minister is inexplicable. She might have reigned supreme, and been the arbiter betwixt contending parties, could she have consented to leave Mazarin an exile. De Retz endeavored to impress this necessity upon her; but power appeared to her worthless without the cardinal; and no sooner had Condé broken with the parliament, and burst into war against the court, than the minister prepared to return. He levied an army, made an attempt on Brissac, and soon after joined the court at Poitiers, taking as usual the chief seat in the council. The rage of the parliament was excessive on learning this: they set a reward on the cardinal's head; and now convinced of the little reliance to be placed either on the queen or prince, the chief magistrates endeavored to form a third or central party, which should make head against both. Mazarin had, however, been gaining friends. He now married two of his nieces, one to the heir of the duc de Bouillon, another to a son of the duc de Vendôme. Bouillon had Sedan restored to him by the cardinal in return for this alliance, which brought over to the court the powerful aid of Turenne.

The mareschal d'Hocquincourt had still the command of the royal army: it was encamped at Blesneau near the Loire. Condé, who was endeavoring to rally Bourdeaux to his cause with little effect, left the south, and suddenly joining his army, surprised Hocquincourt and defeated him. Turenne, who commanded the reserve of the royalists, exclaimed, on perceiving the order and manner of the attack, "The prince is there!" But for Turenne, the defeat of Hocquincourt would have proved fatal to the court; but the former general, though able to rally but 4000 men, contrived to post them with such advantage and skill as to defeat all the efforts of Condé to follow up his victory.

The prince then hastened to Paris, hoping to find the parliament his ally against Mazarin: but the stern magistrates, though firm in their abhorrence of that minister, were not more favorable to Condé, and openly reproached him with his Spanish alliance. From the parliament he did not scruple to appeal to the people, whose lowest class rose in tumult, and threatened the magistrates. The very courts proved no refuge: counsellors and judges were insulted and even beaten as *Mazarins*. On one occasion the mob clamored before the house of Molé; his terrified domestics armed themselves, and barricaded every entrance. The president at length, hearing the tumult, instantly ordered that his doors should be thrown open: the rabble rushed in, shouting and triumphant, till they met, "great beard," as they called the chief judge. They hesitated at his aspect: but when he addressed them in angry tones, and threatened to hang them at his gate, they all fled instantly as from the very sword of justice.

Condé, thus disappointed in the support of the parliament, and of the respectable citizens, could not cope unaided with the royal army. The Parisian rabble, very forward in a riot, could not be made to stand the fire of regular troops. The prince having recourse to the Spaniards, who, busied themselves in the sieges of Gravelines and Dunkirk, induced the duke of Lorraine to march into France and support Condé. The skilful strategy of Turenne, however, compelled this new auxiliary to retreat; and the prince, after a fresh attempt to raise sedition in the capital and control the parliament, was reduced to fight Turenne with far inferior forces. The latter drove him from St. Cloud, and Condé marched to take post at Charenton, when, his rival pressing him closely, as he defiled round the walls of Paris, the prince was obliged to throw himself into the fauxbourg St. Antoine, behind the intrenchments formerly raised for their defence by the inhabitants.

The gate of Paris called St. Antoine was then immediately under the Bastile, the cannon of which swept the three roads diverging from it. Condé, denied entrance into the city, was still secure from attack on this side; and, posted in the central position of the gate St. Antoine, he determined to make head against the royalists, who approached to attack him by the three roads. Mazarin, and Louis XIV. were on the heights, now covered with the cemetery of Père la Chaise, spectators of the ensuing action, the young monarch being most anxious to witness the destruction of this rebellious prince. The triple attack commenced: that on the prince's left, commanded by three sworn and personal enemies to him, was defeated by his valor, the chiefs all perishing. The hero then rushed to defend the central street: he met Turenne in person, and there the conflict was more doubtful. "Did you see Condé during the action?" asked some one of Turenne when the affair was over. "I must have seen a dozen Condés," was the reply: "he multiplied himself."* On the right the action was most bloody: the nobles of the prince's party were almost all slain or wounded there, amongst the rest La Rochefoucault, who,

* I think there be six Richmonds in the field.—*Shakspeare. Richard III.*

struck on the head, was carried off by his wounded son. Turenne was the most powerful; and no chance appeared of Condé's saving himself and the relics of his army, when the gate of St. Antoine unexpectedly opened to receive him, the cannon of the Bastile at the same time sending their fire up the three attacked streets, and thus effectually checking the progress of the royalists.

This well-timed succor came from mademoiselle de Montpensie, daughter of the duke of Orleans, whose sympathy for the heroic Condé, now in distress, was aided by the clamors of the populace, enraged at beholding a rash and imprudent but still generous prince sacrificed to the detested Mazarin. She wrung from the municipal officers the orders for opening the gates; herself directed the firing of the guns of the Bastile; nay, her hand is said to have applied the match. Mademoiselle had aspired to the hand of Condé, to that of the king, and might hope at least to espouse a sovereign prince. But Mazarin observed, on seeing the fire of the Bastile, and knowing who commanded it, "That shot has killed the husband of mademoiselle."

The prince of Condé, who had covered himself with glory as a warrior in the battle of St. Antoine, now blotted his fair fame. The parliament was still opposed to him, and the respectable citizens equally averse to support his resistance. The prince determined to try more forcible means of intimidation than had yet been used. An assembly of burgesses was held at the Hôtel de Ville. Condé repaired thither, accompanied by a mob of his lowest partisans, and demanded permission to raise troops and contributions. This demand being refused, he left the meeting and the Hôtel de Ville abruptly, exclaiming that the burgesses were *Mazarins*. The word was enough for the collected mob, which instantly attacked the Hôtel de Ville. Soldiers in disguise, but armed, joined the tumult, and kept up a constant fire upon the windows and into the apartments. A great number of the citizens perished in the building; others were massacred in the streets. A considerable number fled, and sought refuge in the royal camp.

By this sanguinary act, worthy of the days of the Armagnacs and Burgundians, Condé remained master of the municipal council, and in a little time of the parliament also. The king summoned the magistrates of the latter to repair to Pontoise, and there hold their sittings, until Paris was restored to his authority. The greater number obeyed, and the capital was left destitute of all its principal citizens; but even those who remained preserved their resentment, and were not prepared to stoop before the prince. The latter was unable to reap any advantage from the ascendency which he had gained by crimes. On the contrary, the court gathered influence daily; people began to be reconciled to the absolute power of the monarch, and even of the ministers, which at least secured them from plunder and assassination. The Parisians had now made five years' trial of opposition to the court, and of struggles for liberty. Each class had united, debated, intrigued, and fought for the great boon. The legists had planned and decreed a constitution; but it was found not tenable, nor could the pretensions of the noblesse be reduced to system. Five years of turbulence, of anarchy, of mutual slaughter, had produced no good effect, nor advanced the nation one step towards the goal it sought. England, too, whose example had stirred their emulation, might now serve to deter the French from insubordination. In short, with or without reason, the French of a sudden took a disgust to freedom. They invoked the royal authority as the harbinger of peace, and were prepared to yield to it, making sacrifice of political creeds, and interests, and passions. The noblesse, all save Condé, implored pardon, and negotiated for impunity. They did not even murmur a word of the states-general. The magistrates abandoned their high claim to political right; whilst the mob hailed Louis XIV., on his entry into Paris, as exultingly as if the triumph had been theirs, not his.

The court, however, deemed it necessary to assume the appearance of yielding on one important point. Cardinal Mazarin retired to Sedan. This difficulty removed, few remained. The king published an amnesty, from which the princes and La Rochefoucault were excepted. Condé quitted Paris to join the Spanish armies. The duke of Orleans was ordered to Blois, and the duke of Beaufort accompanied him. Louis entered Paris on the 21st of October, 1652, and held a bed of justice in his parliament on the following day, which was the anniversary of the famous declaration, or constitution it might be called, of 1648. From his throne the monarch declared his will, that the parliament should no more presume to interfere with state affairs, to discuss or oppose them; at the same time he forbade its members to cultivate the acquaintance of princes and grandees. This royal edict, annulling its long and fiercely contested claims, the parliament registered without a murmur; and from that hour the spirit as well as the insurrection of the *Fronde* may be considered as ceasing to exist, at least in the capital. If a proof be needed, it lies in the arrest of the coadjutor, the cardinal De Retz, in a few weeks after, without a symptom of riot, or even chagrin, on the part of a people, of whom he had been the idol and the leader so lately and so long. His great enemy thus removed, cardinal Mazarin ventured to return. The Parisians welcomed and *fêted* him with a fickleness that did them little honor.

Thus ended the *Fronde*, an epoch little understood or developed by historians. Voltaire dismisses it in a few pages, satisfied with recording its *bon mots*. He seems to have looked upon this civil war as merely a pastime, entered into by a few froward youths and their mistresses. He did not see in it the serious, the sanguinary and unhappy struggle of a nation for its liberty.* Even later writers, more profound than Voltaire, have designated the *Fronde* as "the last campaign of the noblesse." It was indeed so. But the noblesse formed not the prominent body. It was the parliament, the magistracy, that put itself forward to represent the commons, of which they claimed and established the privileges for themselves. This was, no doubt, an audacious and hopeless enterprise. The states-general, the ancient representative assembly of the nation, was the form to which they should have rallied. But the extravagance of the English parliament deterred them; and they fixed upon their own body, as a less democratic and dangerous assembly, to participate in legislative power. The scheme was new: it was conceived with boldness, and supported with courage; and if the legists failed in arriving at settled liberty by its means, they may plead that representative assemblies have frequently failed in the same endeavor.

The moral to be drawn from these and similar attempts cannot be too strongly inculcated. This is, the necessity of consulting the traditions, the indigenous institutions, of a country, in any attempt to reform or remodel, or even to direct, its scheme of government. Countries, like men, have their peculiar character, which origin, climate, and fortune decide in the earlier epochs of civilization. Then it is that the political instincts of a nation become manifest; seeking under nature's guiding their true development, and putting forth the roots of a social system, the growth of which man may check or aid, may prune or endow with fresh luxuriance, but which to destroy and re-create at pleasure is as much beyond his power as to put together and build up the oak of the forest.

* Hume calls the *Fronde* "a rebellion unennobled by the spirit of liberty."

CHAP. IV.

1653—1697.

FROM THE TERMINATION OF THE FRONDE TO THE PEACE OF RYSWICK.

A CENTURY has passed in this narration since the reader was congratulated on quitting the annals of despotic power, in which the course of events and fate of countries were decided solely by the personal character of monarchs, the selfish intrigues of their grandees and courtiers, and by the great predominance of chance, the influence of which is ever in inverse proportion to the progress of liberty and enlightenment. At that period, a phenomenon called *principle* began to make its appearance, acting as a motive and as a bond amongst men, and proving at times an obstacle against which all the efforts of monarch and pontiff dashed in vain. Symptoms of this, more or less numerous, endured down to the present time. Civil and religious freedom were understood and prized; various views and tenets of either animated personages and parties, giving a life and a moral interest to the historic scene, which now for a long interval it is again doomed to want.

We re-enter the reign of tyranny, where all the intellect of the nation, as well as its external pride and independence, bows before the monarch's throne; where servitude supplies the place of creed, and selfish vain desires of superiority, not worthy the name of ambition, form the proudest passion of the breast. Again we are to lose sight of the people, nay, of the country itself, to occupy ourselves with a knot of courtiers and their chief. The amours of the latter are to be recorded, and the chronicles of scandal raked, in order to date the reign of his many mistresses. History grows merely personal, —a lewd, a gay and prattling biography, a splendid and empty pageant, magnificent without dignity, glittering without worth. The philosopher's eye disdains to contemplate a scene where the petty motives and acts of private life must be produced on the public stage, and where the fate of empires must be traced to causes better calculated to string together the incidents of a novel.

The events of Louis XIV.'s youth were such as to inspire him not only with high ideas of his kingly rights, but to prove to him the necessity of absolute power in the monarch. In the great English rebellion, and in the *Fronde*, he had seen freedom under its most hideous aspect, and followed by the vainest of results. We can scarcely then blame him personally for his despotic propensities, which, moreover, his manly and ambitious character tended to increase. The young king and his brother Philip, then called the duc d'Anjou, were educated in the privacy of the palace. The nieces of the cardinal were their playmates; and Louis formed successive attachments for two of these young ladies, especially for Maria Mancini, afterwards the wife of the constable Colonna. So intimate was the connexion betwixt Mazarin and Anne of Austria, that many were persuaded of their marriage. Certainly her attachment to him was personal and tender. At the same time, the gallant notions of Louis XIII.'s reign resembled much those of chivalry, in devotion chastely borne by many a lover towards his mistress. It was not until these dangerous connexions, and the stilted sentiment which preserved them pure, were made the subject of general ridicule, that the love intrigues of the court became scandalous, and its morals corrupted. Louis XIV. always preserved for the cardinal a sort of filial reverence; he may be said to have learned in the school of implicit obedience how to be himself despotic. At intervals, however, the imperious temper of the young monarch burst forth, and betrayed itself. In 1655, the parliament, after registering certain fiscal edicts, thought proper to re-examine them, to complain, and show symptoms of their ancient independence. Louis was at Vincennes, engaged in the chase, when he heard of their conduct. Instantly, without consulting the cardinal, or even tarrying to change his dress, the young monarch gallopped to Paris, entered the Palace of Justice and the Hall of the Parliament in his hunting habit, booted, and with whip in hand. "Gentlemen," said Louis to the astonished legists, "every one is acquainted with the ill consequences of your former assemblies. Their recurrence must be prevented. I command you instantly to cease busying yourself with my edicts. And you, Mr. President, I forbid either to call or suffer such assemblies." This bold assertion of the royal will from the mouth of a stripling, proved sufficient to crush the reviving spirit of the magistracy. It was silent, and obeyed.

The great Condé, in the mean time, reduced to command a division of the Spanish army, was vainly endeavoring to make progress in France. Turenne barred the road, and defeated all his attempts. In 1654, the archduke and the prince formed the siege of Arras. Turenne attacked them; forced their lines; and defeated the Spaniards, whose retreat was covered and effected by the exertions of Condé. It was this year that Louis XIV. made his first campaign, showing that he did not want personal courage. He was frequently in the trenches, and exposed to the fire. In 1655 and 1656, Turenne assumed the offensive, and besieged Valenciennes. Condé repulsed and forced him to raise the siege. Generals and armies were too equally matched to admit of a decisive action; and both looked to strengthen their side by fresh alliances.

France and England had been for some time at variance, if not at war, owing to the reception granted by the former to the exiled king. Dunkirk had been lost owing to this, the English having blocked the port, whilst the Spanish besieged it. But now Charles was compelled to retire from Paris, and an alliance with Cromwell was solicited by Mazarin. Spain was equally solicitous to form a league with the usurper. She offered to aid him in conquering Calais. Her rival proposed that Dunkirk should be recaptured, and retained by the English. Cromwell decided for the French alliance; Spain, with her colonies and richly-laden fleets, being a more rich and less powerful enemy to prey on. Six thousand English joined the French army in Flanders, which, in 1658, laid siege to Dunkirk. The Spaniards under Don John, seconded by Condé, advanced to raise the siege; and the battle of the downs of Dunkirk was fought betwixt them. The prince of Condé dissuaded the attack; and, on finding his advice disregarded, he prepared for action, observing to the duke of York, that "if he never saw a battle lost, he would now enjoy that sight." Condé was victorious on his side at first; but the English, accustomed to their civil wars, charged and fought more "like incarnate devils than men," so that the Spaniards suffered a complete defeat. Louis XIV. entered Dunkirk, and gave it up to Cromwell, whom Mazarin at the same time styled in his letters "the greatest man upon earth"

The king soon after fell dangerously ill at Calais: his life was despaired of; and Mazarin was already in alarm, making preparations for flight, when an emetic was proposed as a remedy. It was a thing then unknown, and looked upon as unnatural and dangerous. It was administered, however; and Louis recovered, to the great joy of his minister. France in the mean time, though victorious, was anxious for peace. Cromwell's death rendered the alliance of England little profitable, and the finances of the kingdom were in a state of disorder and debt. Anne of Austria's desire was that he should espouse the infanta; but as there was a probability of this princess becoming the heiress of the monarchy, the king of Spain was reluctant to have his rights confounded with those of the house of Bourbon. The future proved the justice and sagacity of his reluctance. Still, Spain had even more need of peace than France; and when Louis moved to the south of his dominions, and affected to pay court to a princess of Savoy, Don Louis de Haro, the Spanish minister, alarmed lest the sole opportunity and bond of peace should be destroyed by a marriage with Savoy, dispatched a private emissary to Mazarin, proposing the hand of the infanta, and negotiations for peace. The king at that time, it is said, preserved a lingering attachment for Maria Mancini; and the cardinal was not averse to see his niece queen of France. Anne of Austria, however, would not make this sacrifice to her friend and minister. She was peremptory; and the demoiselles Mancini were sent away from the court for a time.

The conferences for the peace commenced in August, 1659, and did not terminate till November. They were held in the Isle of Pheasants, in the midst of the Bidassoa, which divides both kingdoms; Mazarin and Don Louis de Haro acting personally as negotiators. The territorial arrangements were as follows:—The frontier line of France on the north commenced at Gravelines, including it, then ran south to Lillers, shutting out St. Omer and Aire: Landrecies and Quesnoy, Marienburgh and Philippeville, marked the boundary in Hainault.* To the right of the Meuse, Montmedy and Thionville were the extreme fortresses of the French. Lorraine became virtually French, although its duke was nominally restored; and Alsace was finally ceded to them. On the south-east, France gained the fortress of Pignerol, on the other side of the Alps, which secured it a passage into Italy. In the south-west, the Pyrenees became its boundary by the acquisition of Roussillon. Thus France assumed almost its present form and extent at the treaty of the Pyrenees in 1659. Its subsequent acquisitions have been Franche-Comté and French Flanders.

The remaining articles of the treaty related to the marriage which was agreed upon betwixt the French king and the infanta, and to the restitution of the prince of Condé to his rank and possessions. This was the point most difficult to settle, Mazarin remaining firm against concessions to the prince. Don Louis threatened to form for Condé a principality of Rocroi, and other towns on the Flemish frontier; a

* Mazarin, according to Brienne, did not insist on having Cambray, on the condition that Spain was to support his pretensions to the popedom.

proposition that might well alarm the French minister. But Condé facilitated his return, by yielding certain of those towns to France, and making full submissions. At this price, he was restored to his rank and estates, as well as to the government of Burgundy. To the article of the royal marriage was coupled a stipulation, that the infanta, on becoming queen of France, should solemnly renounce, for herself and her heirs, all right of succession to the crown or possessions of Spain; and Louis himself was required to join in the renunciation.

The espousals were celebrated in June of the following year (1660), with unusual magnificence. The courts and monarchs met in the Isle of Pheasants. Condé was received and pardoned. The weak Gaston duke of Orleans dying about this time, Louis XIV. granted his appanage and title to his own brother Philip, hitherto duke of Anjou, from whom is descended the reigning house of Orleans. Mazarin might now be said to have completed his career, or, in a political view, to have completed the career of Richelieu. Every great object of policy proposed by the latter had been gained: the nobles were humbled; the house of Austria weakened; and France, enriched, in territory at least, at her expense, had attained compactness and a powerful frontier. In his private fortune, Mazarin had been as successful: he married his nieces to the first nobles of Europe, who, though prizing high blood, did not think it derogatory to ally with power, however upstart. The pecuniary wealth, the valuables and pictures, of Mazarin, were immense. He was fond of hoarding,—a passion that seized him when he first found himself banished and destitute. His love of pictures was as strong as his love of power—stronger, since it survived. A fatal malady had seized on the cardinal, whilst engaged in the conferences of the treaty, and worn by mental fatigue. He brought it home with him to the Louvre. He consulted Guenaud, the great physician, who told him that he had two months to live. Some days after receiving this dread mandate, Brienne perceived the cardinal in night-cap and dressing-gown, tottering along his gallery, pointing to his pictures, and exclaiming, "Must I quit all these?" He saw Brienne, and seized him: "Look!" exclaimed he, "look at that Correggio! this Venus of Titian! that incomparable Deluge of Caracci! Ah! my friend, I must quit all these. Farewell, dear pictures, that I loved so dearly and that cost me so much!" His friend surprised him slumbering in his chair at another time, and murmuring, "Guenaud has said it! Guenaud has said it!" A few days before his death, he caused himself to be dressed, shaved, rouged, and painted, "so that he never looked so fresh and vermilion" in his life. In this state he was carried in his chair to the promenade, where the envious courtiers cruelly rallied, and paid him ironical compliments on his appearance. Cards were the amusement of his death-bed, his hand being held by others; and they were only interrupted by the visit of the papal nuncio, who came to give the cardinal that plenary indulgence to which the prelates of the sacred college are officially entitled. Mazarin expired on the 9th of March, 1661.

The first act of Louis XIV. on the death of his minister was to summon the council, and communicate to it his resolve, to govern henceforth alone, commanding the chancellor and the secretaries of state strictly to sign no paper but at his express bidding. The disgrace of Fouquet, superintendent of finance, was the first act of the king's authority. Fouquet was an expensive, prodigal, and licentious character, most unfit to have the management of a treasury, which he often converted to his personal grandeur and indulgence. Louis wisely preferred Colbert, stern, economical and orderly. But to disgrace or supplant a minister in those days required address and dissimulation even in a monarch. In the midst of a fête "outrageously" splendid, given by the superintendent to Louis, the latter was tempted to arrest him. The measure was only deferred till Fouquet's fortress of Belleisle could be seized simultaneously with his person. His process and his papers, in which so many were mentioned and implicated, threw the court into a ferment. He was condemned to perpetual imprisonment, and seems to have merited his fall; although his want of honesty as treasurer was redeemed by such traits of generosity and worth, as had won the attachment of La Fontaine and the sympathy of madame de Sévigné.

The best proof of the disorder of the finances under Fouquet is, that for the last four years of his administration no accounts whatever were forthcoming of the revenue or the expenditure. In a series of years taxes had been heaped on taxes, the receipt not increasing. The customs especially had been so severe that regular commerce was sacrificed completely to the contraband trade; the product of the duties diminishing as the duties themselves mounted up; and agriculture had been treated with an equal lack of mercy and of wisdom. Colbert, the new finance superintendent, found matters in this state, with arrears and debts amounting to twice the ninety millions of livres at which the year's revenue was computed. A chamber of justice or commission examined the accounts of the farmers of the taxes discovered their frauds, and forced them to disgorge much of their gains. And Colbert, by the sole means of simplifying the public accounts, was enabled to relieve the people of three millions of the *taille*, with many vexatious restrictions on commerce, to pay off at the same time the onerous debt of the Hôtel de Ville, and yet, without the substitution of a single new tax, to show n amount of revenue increasing every year. Thus, in lieu of such an account as that of 1661, which presented eighty millions of livres revenue, from which fifty millions charges and expense of raising were to be deducted, Colbert in 1671 raised a similar sum of eighty millions, free of all expense of levy, and from taxes felt less by the people. If the great enterprises and efforts of the monarch and the minister be at the same time taken into consideration,—the purchase of Dunkirk from England, the establishment of the Gobelins, and so many new manufactures, the commencement of the canal of Languedoc, the building of the Louvre, the Invalides, and Versailles,—we have cause to admire the miracles that mere economy can work in finance. This was Colbert's only principle, as no progress had then been made in finance or political economy as a science: and of this the administration of Colbert, especially in his laws respecting the commerce of grain, offers ample proof.

As long as Anne of Austria lived, France preserved its amicable connexions with Spain, and remained universally at peace; the slight aid afforded to the Dutch, in their naval war with England, scarcely forming an exception. This period is chiefly filled with the amours of the monarch. The first, at least the first principal, object of his affections, was mademoiselle de la Vallière, maid of honor to madame, wife of the king's brother. La Vallière's character for tenderness and softness of heart, reflected and expressed in her lovely countenance, has become proverbial. She became publicly acknowledged as the king's mistress, and their children, styled M. de Blois and mademoiselle de Vermandois, were reared with all the care and honors of the blood royal. But the king was still fickle. Mademoiselle de Mortemar, another maid of honor, soon caught his attention. She had won the good graces of the queen by her affected devotion. She also insinuated herself into La Vallière's favor, and thus obtained a full opportunity of playing off her fascinating arts upon Louis. This lady, better known under the name of madame de Montespan, was beautiful in person, her beauty being of a sterner cast than that of her rival. But her wit, which she loved to exercise at the expense of her unsuccessful gallants, was what chiefly attracted the king. Such charms were most likely to wean a quick-spirited lover, and one not without taste or talent, from La Vallière, who was without vivacity or intellect. The inconstancy of the king became manifest in 1667. La Vallière perceived it, and fled in despair to a convent at Chaillot. This roused remorse in the king's breast, though it might not awaken his former love. He sent Lauzun and Colbert—an awkward mission for a financier—to induce her to return. She consented reluctantly, and returned, to support the rank of mistress in shame and sorrow, to which both her hurt affections and religious scruples gave poignancy.

The death of Anne of Austria occurred about this time, and "caused little change in affairs, though much in the aspect of the court. This princess, who knew the world," says the marquis de la Fare, "was skilled in duly appreciating the birth and merit of each person, and knew how to make distinctions. Proud and polished at the same time, none could so well hold a court; and though virtuous, she suffered with pleasure that degree of gallantry necessary to render society agreeable, and without which there is no politeness. After her death manners became changed. Passions produced indeed the same effects, which were not concealed by the same reserve. In the days of Anne of Austria, no young man made a daily habit of drunkenness; no coarseness was allowed in pleasantry: good and bad company were never mingled. There was a deference in those who were but entering life, and a high place in society was not to be acquired in a day. But Louis, after his mother's death, prized neither merit, character, nor wit in a courtier; no perfection, in short, but that of being devoted, attentive, and observant of etiquette. He passed his life, for the most part, in the country, by which his court lost by degrees all the urbanity and politeness of towns. The king himself made no distinction between men; and, being naturally pedantic and austere, he established a severe etiquette in the intercourse of the sexes, which, instead of increasing the prudence and virtue of women, gave them merely effrontery."

"Despotic authority," says the same writer, "is incompatible with the development in a state of either great talents or great virtues." This, indeed, may now appear a truism. But it is rather startling to find despotism, and, above all, the despotism of Louis XIV., unfavorable to politeness, and to female charms and character, as well as to those urbanities which it was supposed to have produced in perfection.

The French king now began to awake to projects of ambition. Hitherto he had observed the treaty of the Pyrenees, except in dispatching secretly some feeble aid to Portugal.

But the king of Spain's death, by which the crown devolved upon a sickly infant, opened hopes to Louis of profiting by the claims of his queen as a Spanish princess. It was true that she had solemnly renounced all such rights of succession; but then the dowry stipulated as the price of this renunciation had never been paid; and casuistry went to work to set aside or allow an escape from this renunciation. Louis pretended that certain of the Spanish provinces of Flanders descended in the female line, and therefore belonged to his queen, daughter of the late king of Spain by his first wife, rather than to the present king, his son by a second wife. Securing the neutrality of the emperor, who thus deserted the interest of the house of Austria, Louis marched into Flanders at the head of a numerous army, and took possession of what is called French Flanders, Lille, Tournay, Mons, and Charleroi, almost without spilling blood. Foreign potentates seemed to shrink before his sovereign power almost as completely as his proud nobles had done. There was magic in his ascendency, and superiority in his name. There was also a new spirit in the administration. Discipline and order were restored to the army. Ample magazines of provisions, of ammunition, of all the materials of war, were provided by Colbert and Louvois. But the Spanish monarchy was also in a state of decay; and peace seemed to complete its ruin even more rapidly than war. A proof appeared in the easy and immediate surrender of so many fortresses. Brussels and even Antwerp thought of submitting. Louis, however, deemed it wiser to secure a province than to overrun a kingdom. He checked his career of conquest, ordering Vauban to fortify the captured towns. That engineer exhausted his art in constructing the bulwarks of Lille.

Such facile success encouraged Louis to turn his arms towards another quarter. The county of Burgundy, or Franche-Comté, was, as the reader may remember, separate from the duchy, and had fallen along with Flanders into the possession of Charles V. It still appertained to Spain, though from its distance and isolation under but a nominal rule. It was on this province that Louis cast his ambitious eye. The prince of Condé, who was said to have advised and undertaken this enterprise in emulation of that of Flanders by Turenne, entered upon it in the month of February, 1668, and in three weeks the whole province had submitted. This new conquest alarmed the Dutch, then the most politic and stirring power in Europe. They feared lest all Flanders should be swallowed up by France, and thus leave no separation between Holland and that ambitious country. England, which had glimpses of wisdom in the reign of Charles II., joined in the fears of the Dutch; and betwixt De Witt, Sir William Temple, and the Swedish ambassador, was in a few days concluded the Triple Alliance, formed to put a check to the ambition and conquests of France. Louis receded before this menacing league. He offered to restore Franche-Comté, which he knew could at any time be conquered, at the price of preserving Lille and the principal part of his Flemish conquests; and the triple alliance consented. On these terms was concluded the treaty of Aix-la-Chapelle, in May, 1668.

In each interval of peace some new subject was started, often of trivial importance, but which, by the interest, the zeal, the parties, and the feuds, excited by it at court, comes to occupy a place in history as grave as an invasion or a victory. Jansenism at this time was the point in dispute. Jansenius had broached some opinions favorable to predestination. The Jesuits controverted them; and there the matter might have rested, had not a learned community, a kind of monastery of lettered and reflecting men, called of Port Royal, the name of the house which they inhabited, thought proper to take up the quarrel of Jansenius. The Jesuits then monopolized the authority and influence of the church, whose spirit and moral code they attempted to modify, and adapt to the present courtly and despotic times. The studious, reasoning, and ascetic brethren of Port Royal saw the tendency of the Jesuit preaching, the false and worldly basis of their creed. It was on the subject of Jansenism that the Jesuits had declared themselves, and had come forth in the arena of argument. The pious wits of Port Royal seized the opportunity, took up a cause sufficiently absurd in its fundamental dogmas, but which they were enabled to support by battering the still more absurd outworks of the Jesuits. The latter won the pope to their side, and obtained from the head of the church a condemnation of the tenets of Jansenius. The polemic writers of Port Royal bowed to his holiness, confessed that he was infallible as a high-priest, in condemning such and such belief, but most fallible as a critic, since not one of these propositions, so lustily condemned, were to be found in Jansenius This ingenious effrontery succeeded; for, under color of disputing about such abstractions, Pascal and Arnaud attacked their enemies in more vulnerable points,—in their moral laxity, their sophistic logic, their worldliness, courtliness, and servility. Louis XIV. took the Jesuit side. Many of the courtiers, who dared no longer draw the sword of rebellion, ventured to move the tongue, and exercise thought at least in independence. Amongst the most distinguished sectaries of

Port Royal, was the duchess de Longueville, sister of Condé, the famous partisan of the *Fronde*, and mistress of La Rochefoucault. Her hôtel, once the resort of the coadjutor and his party, of the hot cavaliers that drove the court from Paris, was now the lurking-place and concealment of the Jansenists. She braved the royal authority at all times, whether in the cause of the noblesse or of religion; gallant and dissolute in the *Fronde*, in Jansenism rigid and devout. "She was Jansenist in truth and heart," says Brienne, "just as she had indulged her gallantries with the same sincerity, and always drums beating" (the expression means openly and boldly): "a princess of the blood need fear nothing; and madame de Longueville marched on her way with head erect." Although the Jansenism of Pascal and of Arnaud was the protestation of reason, common sense, and deep religious feeling, against the corruptions of the Jesuits, that of madame de Longueville and her class must be considered as a kind of covert opposition to the court, and to the despotic will of the sovereign. The froward love of independence, that could no longer exercise itself in political intrigue, found more harmless vent in criticism and polemics.

Louis XIV. in the mean time had kept his ambitious thoughts turned towards Flanders. Of the members of the triple alliance, the Dutch, its originators, were the chief objects of his resentment. He had been always allied with them against Spain; and to find these republicans, mere merchants, turn against and thwart him in his first enterprise, was outrageous to his pride as well as interest. The endeavors of Louis were first employed in detaching England from the alliance; no difficult matter with Charles and his ministers, both bent on re-establishing despotic power, and both at the same time too profligate and corrupt to have any scruples in accepting French gold. To make sure of the inconstant king of England, Louis made use of every means. The duchess of Orleans, sister of Charles, proceeded to England, and not only used her own exhortations to establish a close connexion betwixt the two countries, but employed the charms of one of her attendants, mademoiselle de Querouailles, a Breton beauty, to fix the inclinations of the monarch. This lady, better known as the duchess of Portsmouth, perfectly fulfilled her mission, in fascinating Charles, and preserving his inclinations in their bias towards France. The sudden death of the duchess of Orleans on her return to St. Cloud, strongly suspected, though never proved, to have been caused by poison, brought no delay to the signature of a treaty, by which England and France united their forces by sea and land to make war upon Holland. Louis not only subsidized England on this occasion, but bought also the neutrality of Sweden and the neighboring princes of Germany. The emperor continued tranquil, owing to his secret agreement with France respecting the succession to Spain.

The treaty with England had been concluded in December, 1670. Louis consumed the entire of the following year in preparations, which the free and divided government of Holland allowed it to imitate but feebly, It was not until the month of May, 1672, that the manifestoes of England and France appeared, accompanying their declaration of war against the Dutch. One complained of an offensive medal, another of a picture representing ships on fire in the Thames. This was the wolf's quarrel. To the 130,000 soldiers composing the army of Louis, and commanded by Condé, Turenne, and Luxembourg,* Holland had to oppose but 30,000 men, commanded by a young prince as yet unknown to fame: this prince, however, was William prince of Orange. The characters of the two chiefs were as contrasted, as their fortunes rivalled each other: William was weak, and of no commanding stature, though his countenance bespoke the firmness and sagacity of the hero: he was grave, taciturn, phlegmatic, thoughtful; but the disciple of De Witt, as the statesman and the soldier, had far more talents and resources than the purple-born son of Anne of Austria. William had need of this superiority in the unequal struggle to which the ambition of Louis forced him.

The French armies marched northward through the countries betwixt the Meuse and the Rhine, thus avoiding the Spanish Netherlands. Four or five towns were besieged at once, and made no resistance. "A panic seized the Dutch troops, good soldiers enough, but wretchedly provided with officers who had never served, and who were for the most part the sons or relations of burgomasters."† In June took place the passage of the Rhine by the French army; a feat so celebrated by the poets, the historians, and the painters of the day. It was nevertheless effected with scarcely either opposition or danger. A band of a few hundred horse merely hovered on the opposite bank. The young duke of Longueville foolhardily advanced, discharged his pistol with bravado and was slain. Condé was wounded in the wrist. After this no obstacle presented itself to the advance of Louis: province

* Head of the Montmorency family; being son of Montmorency Boutteville, beheaded in the last reign for fighting a duel.

† La Fare.

after province, town after town, submitted. Utrecht received the king as conqueror. Naerden, within a few leagues of Amsterdam, fell into the hands of the French; and although the waters, let in by the breaking of the sluices, surrounded and secured Amsterdam, even that metropolis meditated submission also. One project of the inhabitants was to embark, like the Athenians, on board their fleet, sail for their East India settlements, and abandon their country to this modern Xerxes. Thus, what all the power of the Spanish monarchy could not accomplish, excited against the religious freedom and the independence of Holland, the arms of Louis XIV. were enabled to effect over the country enervated by peace. Yet the De Witts had ruled in the interval. These statesmen, however, had bent their minds to the foreign politics of their land, to its alliances and relations; forgetting to keep up the vigor of its internal state. They fell victims now to their want of wisdom, or want of success; being torn in pieces by an incensed mob, who, partisans of the prince of Orange, and seeking to elevate him to supreme power, complained that De Wit had sacrificed the independence and honor of the country to the preservation of freedom in its form of government.

The French king, in the mean time, in answer to the Dutch deputies who sought for peace, (Grotius was of the number,) demanded for himself the limit of the Rhine, and the re-establishment of the Catholic religion in Holland, besides satisfaction to the demands of the English. The Dutch magnanimously refused such terms. The capital was for this year secure behind its waters; the French army being weakened by garrisoning so many towns. Condé pressed the monarch to dismantle these towns, and unite the army to reduce Amsterdam; but Louvois, minister at war, biassed by his peculiar pursuits, would not consent to the demolition of a single bulwark. The consequence was, that nothing more could be effected, and Louis returned, to enjoy the congratulations of his capital and the flatteries of his court.

Whilst the French armies thus wintered triumphantly in the conquered provinces, the envoys and complaints of the Dutch roused Europe against the ambition of Louis. The people of England were above all struck with compassion and sympathy for a nation free, Protestant, and commercial, like themselves; but their corrupt and anti-national government, bribed by French gold, still maintained their disgraceful alliance. The emperor, the king of Spain, and the elector of Brandenburg, were more alive to the true interests of Europe, and prepared to send troops to aid the Dutch. The latter, called the Great Elector, being the founder of the Prussian monarchy, was the first who declared himself, marching from Westphalia against the invaders. Turenne, however with a far inferior force, succeeded, by his skilful manœuvres, in preventing the elector from passing the Rhine, and even forced him to a temporary treaty. Resistance now began to awaken, and enemies to thicken, against the French. The imperalists advanced on one side; the prince of Orange made his appearance at the head of a formidable army; and the French were obliged, in order to concentrate their forces, to evacuate the Dutch provinces, and retreat towards France. The army before Amsterdam, commanded by the mareschal de Luxembourg, signalized itself by a vain expedition, followed by the plunder and destruction of two inoffensive towns. The capture of the strong town of Maestricht, in the campaign of 1673, compensated Louis for his retreat.

In the commencement of the ensuing year, the English king was compelled by his refractory parliament to break with the French, and send orders for the recall of his troops. Despite of this, we find Churchill, afterwards duke of Marlborough, distinguishing himself as a promising officer under Turenne, and attracting the notice of that general. Louis commenced the campaign, before the close of winter, by the conquest of Franche-Comté, which he for a second time easily effected: Turenne keeping off the duke of Lorraine, who menaced on the side of Alsace. This is considered one of the most brilliant campaigns of Turenne; though, according to his custom, he neither won nor ventured a general action. Aware of his talents, the court gave him very few troops: "knowing him," says Villars, "to be capable of every thing, they reduced him to the inability of doing any thing." The jealousy and hatred of Louvois, too, deprived him of the means of victory. Still, with a diminished force, the activity and skill of Turenne enabled him to prevent the imperalists from fixing themselves on the left of the Rhine. He first crossed that river, and unexpectedly attacked a division of them at Sintzheim. Turenne acted the bold part of Condé on this occasion, leading on his troops in person to assault the enemy in a lofty and fortified position. He drove them from it, and defeated them. This opened the Palatinate to the French, which they ravaged and laid waste in the most barbarous manner. A continuance of war hardens all who carry it on, from the soldier in the field to the minister in his cabinet. This was the first trial of the ravaging system, which laid a country waste, to prevent its being made the seat of war. His cruelties on this occasion form a blot on the memory, as well as on the campaign, of Turenne.

Condé commanded in Flanders against the prince of Orange. An action took place at Senef betwixt these generals, that proved more the valor than the skill of either. Condé attacked the rear-guard of the Dutch and Spaniards as they crossed the rivulet of Senef. Villars, then a young man, was at his side, and exclaimed, "There is what I have longed to see, the great Condé charging sword in hand!" He routed the rear-guard; but, not content with this partial success, he would persevere, and, without waiting for reinforcements, charged the mass of the enemy, which the prince of Orange had drawn up on a height. The French were driven back; but the rest of their army, arriving, attacked indiscriminately. Both generals gave proofs of valor: but there were no traces of that skill which secures decisive advantage, sparing at the same time the soldier. Senef was a carnage. Military writers deny it the name of a battle; and yet upwards of 20,000 dead strewed the field. The prince of Orange lay under the disadvantage of never having served under a general of renown. He was unfortunately obliged, like the chess-player, to learn experience in defeat. Victory at Senef inclined somewhat to the side of Condé.

Turenne could not afford to win such victories as this. Though triumphant at Sintzheim, still two armies menaced him from north or south; or rather, that in the north menaced to invade the kingdom through Lorraine. A dispatch from court summoned Turenne to abandon his position in the north of Alsace, and to hurry to the defence of Lorraine. Turenne refused; marched south; and beat one enemy in the neighborhood of Strasburg; then, pretending to enter winter-quarters, he made a forced and sudden march in the month of January; and the elector of Brandenburg was astounded to find the French in the midst of his quarters in Lorraine, whilst he thought they were quiet, at least for that season, in Alsace. Turenne, aware of the panic that his surprise was calculated to create, instead of offering a drawn and regular battle, attacked the elector in the close of the evening. The darkness added to the disorder of the imperialists, and the facility of their rout. The effects of the campaign were trophies worthy of the greatest commander; there was no brilliant victory to catch the popular ear. Turenne was the general a king might prize: Condé more apt to be a nation's vaunt. Marlborough, who served his noviciate in these campaigns, learned to combine the military virtues of both.

In the following year, the enemies of France, perceiving the danger of opposing inferior generals and divided forces to Turenne, gave the command on the Rhine to the famous Montecuculi, a veteran general, the worthy rival of his antagonist. The imperialist commander sought to pass the Rhine t Strasburg; Turenne's object was to prevent him; and weeks of profoundly skilful manœuvring passed in vain. Th French were always strongest on the threatened point; the great art of defensive war. Montecuculi gave up the attempt, retired south along the Rhine, and posted himself at Salzbach. Turenne followed him, and at length began to entertain hopes of attacking his wary antagonist at an advantage. He was engaged in reconnoitring for this purpose, when a cannon-ball, somewhat spent, carried off the arm of the marquis of Saint Hilaire, general of the artillery, and then struck Turenne. It did not penetrate his body; he even supported himself for an instant or two on horseback, and then fell lifeless. The son of St. Hilaire ran to support his wounded father, for whom he naturally enough reserved his sympathy "Weep not for me, my son," exclaimed that general, "but for this great man!" Turenne was mild, simple, magnanimous. His seeming want of principle in changing, now for the court, now for the *Fronde*, is explained by his being the brother of the duc de Bouillon, who considered himself a sovereign prince. "The successes of monsieur de Turenne," says the president Henault, "resembled his character: they were solid and unostentatious. They were not drawn battles, which often make more noise than they produce solid advantages; but useful combats, that preserved his country. One might say of him, as was said of Cæsar, that he made war, not as it pleased fortune, but as it pleased himself." Turenne was one of those Protestants whom the commands of Louis XIV. converted to Catholicism. The constable's staff was said to be the object of his ambition; but the arguments of Bossuet afforded a motive, or a pretext, more honorable.

With the death of their general ceased the superiority of the French. They instantly resolved on retreating beyond the Rhine, pursued by Montecuculi, "whose great age," says Villars, "alone prevented him from routing it." Both armies passed the Rhine, and the theatre of war was transferred to Alsace. Condé soon after came to take the place of Turenne upon the Rhine, whilst the mareschal de Luxembourg succeeded him in Flanders. But the campaign was afterwards marked by little that was memorable, except perhaps the circumstance of the *ban* and *arrière-ban*, the old feudal force of the noblesse, being ca ed out for the last time. This was the last year that either Condé or Montecuculi appeared at the head of armies. Age and the gout had disabled the former, and he now retired to the solitude of Chantilly.

The war had burned its brightest flame; the embers but remained to rake. The king created six new mareschals, and was said "to have changed his louis-d'or (Turenne) into five sous pieces." Crequi was beaten by the old duke of Lorraine, nd taken prisoner. The following year the king suffered double mortification, in missing himself a good opportunity for attacking the prince of Orange, and in his brother's redeeming the lost opportunity by defeating the prince near St. Omer. Whilst the valor of France thus slumbered on land, or remained but on a par with that of her enemy, her fleets began to acquire glory on another element. In the frequent combats betwixt the Dutch and English, the French had borne an honorable part, although their admirals are accused of having had orders to spare their infant navy. A little experience had sufficed, however, to give them the confidence and skill requisite to second courage. A seaman of talent and heroism sprung up in Du Quesne, who fought the Dutch with success in several battles. In one of them, off Sicily, the famed De Ruyter perished. Under a grateful monarch, Du Quesne would have become great admiral of France. His reward was, to be reproached for being a Protestant. The bigotry of Louis was growing with his years. "When I fought for your majesty," replied the blunt sailor, "I never thought on what might be your religion." His son, driven into exile for adhering to the reformed faith, brought the bones of his father with him, determined not to leave them in an ungrateful country.

Conferences, in the mean time, took place at Nimeguen, under the mediation of England, for the conclusion of peace. All parties were sufficiently weary of war. Even Louis longed for repose. But it was always his aim to strike an important blow previous to treating. He with this view laid siege at once to the three principal towns in Flanders, St. Omer, Valenciennes, and Cambray; and so great was his reputation, so ample his materials for this his favorite kind of warfare, that all three surrendered to his arms. The marriage which took place in this year, betwixt the prince of Orange and the princess Mary of England, delayed the peace, however, by altering the balance of the respective parties. The prince hoped, by the support of the English king, to bring Louis to more reasonable terms. But the fickleness and weakness of Charles, and the jealousy of the Dutch, marred his scheme. In January, 1678, Louis was again in the field, and made himself master of Ghent; whilst Charles was engaged with the animosities of his parliament on one side, and the insidious offers of the French monarch on the other. The Dutch, seeing the English not to be depended on, accepted the proposals which Louis now made. This their high mightinesses did with more alacrity, seeing that the acquisitions which the conqueror proposed to keep had been won from Spain. Louis offered to restore Ghent, Oudenarde, Charleroi, and Limberg; retaining St. Omer, Cambray, Valenciennes, all French Flanders in fact, as well as Franche-Comté. The difficulty of such a treaty was to obtain the consent of Spain, at whose expense it was concluded. But the imbecile monarch of that country did not know what towns belonged to him, or where was the frontier line; and those who governed for him were more interested in securing a part in his succession, than in preserving the dominions of the monarchy entire. Spain, in short, consented; and all appeared terminated, when the French made fresh demands of a restoration to Sweden of Pomerania, and that the Dutch should send a submissive embassy to their monarch. Hereupon all was again broken off. The Dutch would not yield, and the days passed in vain negotiations. The 10th of August was the last day fixed for the duration of the conferences; and just before midnight on that day, the French, who had been but shuffling to enhance their bargain, signed the treaty of Nimeguen, in 1678. In four days after the prince of Orange, either in ignorance or disregard of it, attacked the mareschal de Luxembourg at Mons, and sacrificed several thousand soldiers in a bootless engagement. Spain signed the treaty soon after. Peace betwixt France and the empire was concluded in 1679. "Here may be seen," says Voltaire, "how little events correspond to projects. Holland, against which the war was undertaken, and which had nearly perished, lost nothing, nay, even gained a barrier; whilst the other powers, that had armed to defend and guaranty her independence, all lost something."

The years which followed the peace of Nimeguen were the most prosperous and glorious, the most elevated one may say, of the reign of Louis XIV. Success had more or less crowned all his enterprises. The renown of his name was even greater than his power. England was his tributary; Spain yielded him precedence. The least insult offered to his representatives, or failure of etiquette, was sure to bring down signal vengeance. Algiers was bombarded,—a new mode of warfare. Genoa was brought to a sense of the French king's dignity by the same means, and its doge compelled to repair as a suppliant to Versailles. At times, it must be owned, the pride of the monarch partook of the unjust and ungenerous domineering of the grown school-boy. Thus he opposed some salutary regulation, by which the pope, to secure the tranquillity of his own city, had infringed upon the licentious privileges of the ambassadors at his court. Not content with the just pride that might well become his power, Louis XIV. swelled into a kind of royal bully, blustering on all occasions, showing an utter disregard of others' rights or independence, or even of his own stipulations. He pretended to appoint an archbishop and elector at Cologne. His new conquests were governed in the most arbitrary way: all the German princes who possessed properties therein were expelled without scruple. The important town of Strasburg was seized and appropriated. Even in the midst of peace, French marauding parties devastated the Spanish provinces, and penetrated to the gates of Brussels. This produced a short renewal of hostilities in 1684.

To paint, however, the chief glories of the reign of Louis belongs to the historian of literature and the arts. Molière, Racine, Boileau, La Fontaine, were now shedding on the monarch and the land all the radiance of their fame. Bossuet, Massillon, and Fénélon, adorned the pulpit and the episcopal seat. The Academy was installed in the Louvre. Men of letters and of wit came almost to form another estate, rival with the magistracy, and one which, in the next century, had more influence than any other order, first on the spirit and opinions, then upon the fate, of the monarchy.

There is scarcely space in these volumes for the mere anecdotes of the times, or those unconnected with the progress of events. The adventures of Lauzun, and the imprisonment of the mareschal de Luxembourg, must, nevertheless, at least be alluded to. Lauzun, a young favorite of the king, diminutive in person but fascinating in his character and manners, had gained the affections of mademoiselle the courageous daughter of Gaston. She espoused him in secret, and Louis, by tenderness for his favorite, was carried away from his natural character so much, as to give permission for their being publicly married; the princess conferring on her humble husband the titles and rich succession of the house of Montpensier. One of the liveliest letters of De Sévigné announces this event. Never was the proverb of the cup and the lip verified with greater mortification to an expectant than in the present instance. The jealous princes, *Monsieur* amongst the rest, represented to Louis the shame accruing to the dignity of the royal blood by its alliance with a Peguillon, such was the name of the duc de Lauzun. The marriage was accordingly countermanded, to the equal despair of bridegroom and bride. The former, showing some time after a very natural discontent, was sent prisoner to Pignerol, from whence he was liberated some years after, and promoted to a command in Ireland. The other circumstance that excited equal interest at court was the arrest of the mareschal de Luxembourg for associating with sorcerers, in other words, frequenting fortune-tellers. It was a singular crime for a hero. But heroes are not always exempt from superstition: on the contrary, the children of fortune are most given to worship and consult their parent. Luxembourg was liberated, after having suffered severe imprisonment in the Bastile from the enmity of Louvois; the mareschal reappeared in his place at court, whilst his accomplice the sorceress expiated her fault at the stake in the Place de Grève.

Madame de la Vallière had finally retired from court in 1674. The king no longer opposed her resolution of shutting herself up in a convent; nay, he approved a sacrifice that removed from his view an object of remorse. She became a nun of the order of the Carmelites in the rue St. Jaques. But thirty years of age at the period of her vows, she lived thirty-six in exclusion, endeavoring to efface by her tears the crime of having shared a monarch's passion. When the news of the premature death of her son was conveyed to her, she exclaimed, "Alas! must I weep for his death before my tears have sufficiently expiated his birth!" The station of the monarch could not prevent him from sharing her religious scruples. The prelates, the only class of courtiers who preserved the liberty of expostulation, censured his life of adultery; and he, before whom all Europe trembled, humbled himself with laudable piety before his confessor. The struggle was long and doubtful betwixt his love of indulgence and his virtuous resolves. More than once he determined to see De Montespan no more except in public. But even these interviews produced tenderness and reconciliation. At length a transitory passion of the monarch for a new object, young and lovely, who perished shortly after, stricken at once with malady and contrition, gave a strong revulsion to his feelings, and madame de Montespan herself was dismissed from favor. Her proud heart vainly endeavored to find that consolation in penitence and religion which La Vallière had formed. As for Louis, he was alone. His queen was dead. He had ministers, attendants, courtiers, but not a friend; and he found that man may be left as desolate and abandoned upon a throne as in the lowest grade of fortune,—one of the strongest proofs of that equal distribution of happiness which the humble find it so difficult to believe. Louis looked around, and, selecting no longer with the eye of passion but of reason, took for a wife the governess of his illegitimate children. This was madame Scarron, the widow of the celebrated comic writer. Though no longer young, she was comely, pious withal, and humble; bred in the school of adversity, not in the gaieties of the court, which Louis already began to despise. The proud and imperious monarch chose, in fact, the humblest individual of the sex, with whom his dignity allowed him to come in contact; and another moral might be drawn from this contrast. The king conferred on her the title of De Maintenon; and a private marriage, kept profoundly secret, was celebrated betwixt them about the year 1685.

This period of the monarch's penitence and remorse was the date of his bigotry also. Satiated with love, with conquest, fame, and grandeur, he exclaimed with Solomon, "All is vanity!" and he now gave himself to what he deemed religion, with the same excess that had marked his pursuit of pleasure. His confessor, La Chaise, obtained great influence over him, as did the chancellor Letellier and his son Louvois. Colbert was a minister liberal in his way of thinking. He leaned towards the Huguenots, whose superior industry, enlightenment, and aptitude for naval service, won him. This minister had many of the Protestants in employ, and he supported them in the good opinion of Louis. Louvois and Letellier, on the contrary, hated the reformers, and, as much from dislike to Colbert as from natural bent, leaned to the exclusive doctrines of intolerance. Colbert was now dead; and the monarch was left altogether under the influence of his bigoted counsellors.

The mind of Louis XIV. was one however that reasoned, and concluded its own resolves. Of what advantage was this? He knew of man nothing beyond a court; and he was forced to reason from what he saw there. His experience showed him that every Protestant noble or courtier had been induced, by his persuasion or command, to recant and be converted to Catholicism. If interest therefore, or the monarch's will, brought unanimity in the religious opinions of the first class of the state, the most proud, the most powerful, the most enlightened, surely the same motives must have tenfold effect upon the mass of the ignoble. This reasoning was just: pity, the example from which it was drawn, instead of being the rule of human nature, was but the base exception. Louis appointed emissaries and missionaries, charged with ample sums and promises of favor, to convert the Huguenots. They returned ample lists of converts. The mode, however, was found expensive. Severity was suggested by Louvois as a cheaper and more expeditious method. It was tried. The Protestants were excluded from public employ, from divers communities. Their children were allowed to recant at seven years old, and were easily enticed to do so, the penalties against relapse being severe. This was soon after the peace, and these first measures occasioned a considerable emigration.

Religious persecution in rulers is like profligacy in individuals; one step inevitably draws on the next, and, with the best intentions and resolves of moderation, both soon reach the extreme. The emigration, especially of seamen and artisans, was soon felt to be prejudicial to the state. To check it, the pain of death was enacted against those attempting to emigrate, and all sales of property made by those who afterwards exiled themselves were declared void. The next step was to pull down the Protestant churches. This was done at Montpellier. It was purposed, at the same time, to have public conferences and disputes with the Protestant pastors, in order to convince them; but the governor wrote back to court that the Catholic clergy were too ignorant, and quite unable to dispute or convert. They asked for a supply of dragoons as more efficient; and these licentious soldiers, quartered on the Protestants all through the south, devoured and plundered their substance; took away their children, to save them from being heretics; hunted the clergy like wild beasts; and destroyed all the churches. Upwards of 700 places of worship were overthrown before the revocation of the edict of Nantes. As Languedoc threatened to revolt under this oppression, fresh treaties and fresh edicts were poured upon them. The penal laws were precisely the same as those which were inflicted by the English Protestants upon the Irish Catholics. The British had but to copy the edicts of Louis XIV., merely abating their barbarity; and no doubt the spirit of retaliation dictated in a great degree their savage measures. A day was appointed for the conversion of all the Protestants of such a district, the dragoons taking possession on that day. The refractory were hanged, and their chiefs broken on the wheel. St. Ruth was one of the leaders of these military expeditions, called the *dragonnades*.*

* Mild measures might possibly have produced more effect. The Protestants of Saintonge received Fénélon in friendship, and regretted his departure. "We would willingly agree with you," said they: "why do you quit us? When you are gone, we shall be at the mercy of the monks, who preach nothing save Latin, indulgence, and *friaries*. We shall no longer hear the Bible read or explained. They will make use of no argument but menace."—*Fenelon's own account.*

At length, in the year 1685, appeared the famous ordonnance, very vaguely and incorrectly styled the revocation of the edict of Nantes. This latter edict has been before censured as untenable, as organizing anarchy, and establishing one empire within another. But all these objectionable or anarchic regulations were destroyed and annulled by Richelieu. Nothing of it remained to repeal but tolerance of the religion, and even that confined to certain towns and districts. The ordonnance of 1685 revoked this tolerance; forbade all assemblies or exercise of the reformed religion; banished all their ecclesiastics from the kingdom in fifteen days; offered to such of them as would recant, their pensions, augmented by a third, which was to be continued to their wives; compelled the baptism of all infants in the Catholic church; and condemned to the galleys all except the pastors who should attempt to expatriate themselves. This, instead of being merely the revocation of an edict, was an enactment of new and unheard-of severity; and, as usual, it induced amplifications still more severe. In 1686, a Protestant pastor, French or foreign, was punished with death if taken. Men who assisted or harbored them were to be sent to the galleys; women, to be shaved and confined: 5500 livres reward was set upon each of their heads. Death was the penalty for a Protestant taken in an assembly or act of public worship. All these details are from Catholic writers, justly touched with horror at their enormity. "Twenty of the religionists were put to death at this time," say the memoirs of Noailles. "The fugitives who assembled on the mountains were pursued. A premium was offered to each parish that would give up twelve; and three or four pistoles to each soldier that brought in one. *Battues* were made through the country by the troops, just in the manner of chasing wild beasts."

It is supposed that 50,000 families emigrated from France at this time, in despite of the sanguinary prohibition.. They were the most industrious part of the population, proved by the circumstance of their thriving in every land that received them, and enriching it as the price of their welcome. England received an immense number, principally silk manufacturers. The north of Germany profited by the same act of expatriation. The bigotry of Louis gave a greater blow to the industry and wealth of his kingdom, than all the unlimited expenses of his pride and his ambition.

From the time that Louis XIV. became a religious persecutor, his power and prosperity began to decline; but this can be accounted for on other than superstitious or providential grounds. There are two kinds of wars: one purely and merely ambitious or interested, undertaken to gain or defend a province, acquire a frontier, or win commercial advantages; the other is a war of principle, where a love or hatred of certain political or religious dogmas is the actuating motive. The former runs into the latter, and partakes of it, when the independence of a nation is threatened; but in general they are distinct, and differ essentially. A war for material interests, interests not vital, is languid, a thing of art or combat, in which are emulation, and honor, and courage, but no greater passions. A war of principle is animated by altogether another spirit. It is rancorous, bitter, merciless, and bloody. Civil wars are generally of this kind. The past conquests of Louis were wars for aggrandizement merely. They awoke the jealousy and enmity of Europe, but not its passions. Henceforth he had to endure a war partaking much of principle. His cruelties to the Protestants had roused the hearts of Germans, Dutch, and English against him. The prince of Orange became the soul and the leader of this association, united in sympathy and feeling. A league was concluded at Augsburg, betwixt the German princes, England, and Holland, against Louis. Spain joined, excited by jealousy of a domineering neighbor; the emperor also, who had seen the important town of Strasburg acquired by the gold of the French king in full peace.

Louis anticipated his enemies, and was the first in the field; sending an army to the Rhine in 1688. It was commanded by the dauphin, who laid siege to Philipsburg. The prince of Orange was then meditating an important enterprise that momentarily distracted his attention from the continent. This was his invasion of England. The reader must be well acquainted with the circumstances of this event, which struck France a more decisive blow than if William had penetrated to the walls of Paris. Louis received with princely generosity the monarch whom his bigotry and pusillanimity had exiled, assigned him a palace and a revenue, fitting out at the same time a fleet and an army which in the same year transported James II. to Ireland.

In the mean time the dauphin had taken Philipsburg, and the king's orders obliged his son to commence the war by an unequalled piece of barbarity. "Some one had persuaded Louis," said Villars, "that the safety of the state consisted in putting a desert between our frontiers and the armies of the enemy. From this idea, against our own interests and the reasons of war, he ordered the great towns of Treves, Worms, Spire, and Heidelberg to be destroyed." The elector's ancient palace, together with the cottages of his meanest subject, per shed in the flames. "The very cellars were blown up, nor was a church spared." The king's increased piety seemed to have taken from him the quality of mercy. This barbarous scheme failed to serve the French. On the contrary, fortune turned against their arms. The young duke of Lorraine drove them beyond the Rhine, took Bonn and Mayence, and gave promises of generalship, when he was cut off by disease. The mareschal d'Humieres was equally unsuccessful in Flanders against the prince of Waldeck, who had under him an auxiliary army of English commanded by lord Churchill. Despite of the six armies and 450,000 men kept on foot by Louis, the French had the worst of this first campaign.

Louis rightly attributed his defeats to the inferiority of his generals. The enmity of Louvois had deprived the mareschal de Luxembourg of command. He was now placed at the head of the army in Flanders, independent of Louvois, and corresponding directly with the king. Catinat, chosen with equal sagacity, was sent to Italy. Luxembourg was a general of the school of Condé, of a quick eye, decisive and skilful in the moment of action, though too indolent and light for the whole conduct of a campaign. It was now incumbent on him to support his character. He advanced to cross the Sambre and attack Waldeck, about the very same time that king William was drawing near to his competitor at the Boyne. The prince of Waldeck was encamped on the plains of Fleurus, not far from Namur, watching the course of the Sambre. Learning, however, that Luxembourg was inferior in force, he allowed him to pass the river, and found his mistake too late; the mareschal, by a temporary reinforcement, being pretty much his equal. Luxembourg won the battle by a successful manœuvre. His right as he advanced being hidden by a rising ground neglected by Waldeck, the marshal threw all his disposable force on this side, by which he was enabled to attack the Dutch left in front and flank. The German horse was broken; but the Dutch infantry made a most valiant resistance, only equalled by the celebrated Spanish phalanx when hemmed in at Rocroi. Yet these Dutch were the very soldiers who had fled before Louis XIV. in the last war without striking a blow. So stubborn was their valor that, although the French were victorious, the loss on both sides was considered as nearly equal.

Catinat in the same campaign gained a victory still more glorious over the duke of Savoy at Saluces, but productive of not more real advantage. The French armies were no less brave, and no less ably conducted than of old, but their enemies had acquired equal confidence, equal skill, and were buoyed up by religious hate. The Protestants of Savoy were found useful by the duke in repelling the French. The spirit of the Dutch was awakened by the same cause. It was on the ocean that the chief trophies of the French were this year won. Tourville, with an immense fleet of upwards of seventy sail, encountered the combined squadrons of England and Holland, amounting to no more than fifty-six, off Beachy Head. The Dutch began the action, but were for a long time weakly seconded by Torrington, the English admiral. The Dutch were thus defeated ere the action became general: they lost two admirals, and six of their best ships. The loss of the English was proportioned to their honor on this occasion. Torrington fled into the Thames; and the French admiral proceeded to insult the coast of England. They even made a descent, and burned the town of Teignmouth.

The following year, Louis commenced by the siege of Mons, which surrendered in a few days. The king of England, who had resumed the command in Flanders, in vain endeavored to relieve it. There was a sharp combat towards the close of the season betwixt Waldeck and Luxembourg, but nothing decisive. On the side of Spain, however, the French, under the mareschal de Noailles, made progress: Urgel was taken, and Barcelona bombarded. The minister Louvois died this year, in time to avoid dismissal. He had opposed the king's marriage with madame de Maintenon; and this lost him the king's confidence. The cruel measures of Louis, especially his ravaging the Palatinate, and his new plan of bombardments, were attributed to this minister. Louis, however, was unable to find a successor of his talents; and, as from the death of Colbert dated the decline of the finances, victories ceased soon after the loss of Louvois. His son Barbesieux succeeded to his office, and soon proved himself inept. Could talents be made hereditary, like wealth, much of the embarrassment of kingly rule would be removed.

It seemed to be part of court etiquette that the monarch should besiege and take a fortress each spring. In 1692, he invested Namur; whilst Luxembourg, with an army, occupied the course of the Mehaigne, and kept the enemy from advancing to its succor. Vauban commanded the attack; Cohorn, a rival engineer, managed the defence. Namur succumbed. During the progress of this siege, a naval action was fought off Cape la Hogue, that for ever decided the fate of the Stuarts. Tourville commanded the French, no longer so numerous, a portion of their fleet being in the Mediterranean. He was preparing to convey James, with a fresh army, to Ireland, when he was attacked by admiral Russel, and defeated; the English pursuing the French ships to shore, and burning them. James, as he viewed the ruin of his hopes, could not but admire the gallantry of his countrymen. He then retired to his little court of St. Germain's, where he died in the last year of the century.

The loss of Namur, a fortress important from its situation at the confluence of the Meuse and the Sambre, as well as for its strength, angered king William. In the first days of August the armies lay near Steinkirk, separated from each other by hills and defiles, little apt for a general engagement. Luxembourg, naturally indolent, and at the moment indisposed, suffered himself to be deceived by the information of a spy, who had been discovered by William, and compelled to write what was dictated to him. The mareschal being lulled by this false intelligence, the English king was enabled to surprise him and rout a body of his troops, ere the mareschal was aware of the attack. The French rallied however; and a valiant troop of nobles, headed by the princes of the blood, the duc de Chartres, the duke, and the grand prior of Vendôme. The princes of Condé and Conti charged with such constancy and fury as to drive back the Dutch and to defeat king William. Steinkirk did great honor to the young French noblesse. Young Turenne was killed there. The duc de Chartres, son of the king's brother, duke of Orleans, was wounded in this engagement, as well as in the ensuing one of Neerwinden. He will be afterwards known to the reader as the regent duke of Orleans. It was in this year that the king, in order to reward the prowess or excite the emulation of his officers, instituted the order of St. Louis.

The French monarch and his court appeared for the last time, in 1693, at the head of armies. With very superior forces he pressed king William near Louvain, and must have defeated him had an attack been ordered; but, from some unaccountable weakness or whim, Louis resolved to quit the army and return to Versailles. Some attribute this to madame de Maintenon, and her fears of the monarch's person and health; others to his jealousy of his brother, who was scattering money to the peasantry of the kingdom, then oppressed by famine. The mareschals and general officers were indignant, and supplicated: Louis was peremptory, and left the seat of war for Versailles with the ladies of the court. It was not until several weeks had passed that the mareschal de Luxembourg could repair this blunder, and make use of his superior forces against king William. The latter was surprised in no very advantageous post by the celerity and manœuvres of his enemy, who threatened Liege as a feint.

William, with a motley army of Dutch, Danes, Hanoverians, English, and refugee French, occupied the two villages of Landen, and Neerwinden; the river Ghette was behind him, rendering defeat perilous, whilst he had not time to cross it now without endangering his rear-guard. He made the most of his time, however, in throwing up intrenchments before the villages and along the line which joined them. On the morning of the 29th of July, the French attacked both villages, and were repulsed: one of their generals was killed another, the duke of Berwick, taken. In vain did their cavalry attempt to charge and get over the intrenchment in the centre; they were beaten off in the whole line. But William, wanting sufficient force, and perhaps wanting that master talent that never allows a routed enemy to rally, waited quietly in his intrenchments. The French renewed their efforts, the prince of Conti heading those against Neerwinden. Then, and not till then, William advanced his cavalry, consisting of his guards and some English regiments, from behind his intrenchments: they were momentarily successful; but it was too late. The French had rallied, concentrated their forces on Neerwinden, and carried it after an obstinate struggle. The victory thus declared for Luxembourg; king William abandoning the field, but showing himself, as usual, formidable in defeat.* One of the corps that disputed the victory longest was that of the refugee Huguenots. The French in their king's ranks respected the inveterate gallantry of these exiles, whose commander, Ruvigny,† was once taken prisoner and instantly released with honorable generosity. Except the capture of Charleroi, that closed the campaign, little advantage accrued to Louis from the battle of Neerwinden: still it was a fortunate year for the French. Catinat defeated the duke of Savoy at Marsaille in a general engagement; Noailles still made progress in Spain, and took Roses; whilst on the ocean Tourville disputed the superiority with the English and Dutch, and severely handled a squadron and convoy under Sir George Rooke.

It was seen how Louis XIV., from some unaccountable apathy or disgust, quitted his army with every prospect of victory before him. This feeling gained upon him: he was not a monarch to be contented with slight advantages; and

* We have heard on good authority, that the greatest captain of this age considered king William the greatest captain of *his*. Without daring to controvert so high an opinion, uttered after all perhaps but in casual conversation, we may state the opinion of his contemporaries to have been, that William of Orange had all the materials of a great general, but, for want of masters and right experience, never became one.

† Father of lord Galway

even victory, justly enough, appeared to him idle when conquest did not follow: he therefore made indirect overtures for peace to Savoy and to Holland: they were unattended with effect. The campaign of 1694 opened; but the monarch was no longer to visit the army in person, and the activity of the war-office accordingly relaxed; so much so that the mareschal de Luxembourg was enabled, merely by skill and countermarches, to keep honorably on the defensive. It proved the last campaign of this celebrated commander, who was soon after carried off by apoplexy. The French were, the same year, repulsed from Barcelona by the co-operation with the town of an English fleet.

The enormous exertions of Louis XIV. against such a combination of enemies, began now to bring their pernicious consequences. The commerce of the kingdom was destroyed; its ports were bombarded and burned; the country was exhausted of men, of money, and of money's worth; and famine, occasioned by an inclement season, had added to the general state of discontent. Colbert was dead. The economy of the minister of an absolute government is productive of little durable effect, perhaps of as much evil as good. That of Sully had merely laid by a store, which the ambition of Henry IV. was about to lavish in vast schemes of war, when death cut him off, and left the hoarded materials of extravagance to his queen. In the same manner the resources husbanded by Colbert served to swell the pride of Louis XIV., and to impel him upon that career of conquest and aggression which had at last surpassed all means of supporting it. The expenditure, which, when last stated, fell far short of the 80,000,000 of revenue, now doubled that sum. The most disastrous and decried expedients were had recourse to, in order to meet the exigencies of the time. Letters of noblesse were sold; a recoinage, that increased the nominal value of money at the rate of two sous for every livre, brought in 40,000,000 to the treasury; and at length a capitation tax was established in 1695, in a graduated scale of twenty-two classes. The ignoble orders seemed to pay with alacrity a tribute which the nobles shared with them. The king set the example by having himself placed first on the capitation list, an illusory but not unwelcome compliment to the commons.

The campaign of 1696, in Flanders, was at first "nice chess playing," to use the characteristic expression of St Simon. King William chose his time, and laid siege to Namur; the mareschal de Boufflers threw himself into it. The comte de Vaudemont protected the besiegers against the mareschal de Villeroy: the latter made every preparation for attacking Vaudemont. Unfortunately, the duc de Maine, illegitimate and favorite son of the king, was in command of the left wing, the post of honor, and the column of attack: Villeroy sent him orders to commence, and was obliged to repeat them, whilst the prince sedulously busied himself in reconnoitring, in confessing to a priest, and in ordering the ranks of his division. Thus the precious time was lost; Vaudemont retreated from his awkward position, and Namur surrendered to king William.

When Louis learned the pusillanimous conduct of his hopeful son, which he did through other means than Villeroy's dispatches, nothing could equal his chagrin. He had been made to expect a victory. So great was his irritation, that he lost sight even of his dignity, which he forgot so far as to beat with his own hands a valet for pocketing a biscuit at dinner. Whilst flustered with this feat, the monarch met his confessor, Père la Chaise, and cried, "I have beaten the rascal well, my father, and broke my cane upon his back; but I hope not to have offended God in the act." The disgrace of the illegitimate prince delighted the high nobles of the court as much as it vexed the king.

Conferences commenced in 1696 for peace. Louis took, however, the speediest way to procure it, by giving numerous forces to Catinat, that he might overwhelm the duke of Savoy, and with these full powers to treat. The duke, knowing that a general peace was near, and fearing for Turin, made a separate accommodation, which he obtained on the most advantageous terms. The French king gave up Pignerol and his conquests on the other side of the Alps, paid 4,000,000 livres, and concluded a marriage agreement betwixt the young duke of Burgundy, eldest son of the dauphin, and a princess of Savoy. At this price Louis not only detached from the confederates, but gained to himself, an important ally.

This should have rendered peace still more desirable to the confederacy. The plenipotentiaries of the several powers assembled at Ryswick near the Hague, in the beginning of 1697. Louis made ample offers of concession; but Strasburg, which he refused to yield, occasioned difference and delay. The allies demanded a truce: Louis denied it; and soon after arrived tidings that the duc de Vendôme had taken Barcelona. This conquest brought down the pretensions of Spain, and Strasburg was no longer insisted on. Despite of this, negotiations might have dragged on interminably, had not the two kings held confidential communications through a more frank and immediate channel than their plenipotentiaries. Bentinck and Boufflers had several meetings, at which William and

Louis came to an understanding to make peace, even without the emperor, if that were necessary. The treaty or treaties of Ryswick were, in consequence, signed in September, 1697. England gained merely the recognition of the monarch of her choice. The French frontier in Flanders was agreed to be that established by former treaties. Mons, Charleroi, Courtray, and Luxembourg, were to be restored to Spain. The cession of the latter fortress, and of Barcelona, was made as a kind of compensation for Strasburg, which France now finally kept. Lorraine was restored to its duke, who was forbidden to fortify his towns, a stipulation that rendered him totally dependent. But that part of the treaty, which concerned the emperor, was not concluded for upwards of a year France, in the treaty of Ryswick, appears to be the purchaser of peace: she yields. But the war, though not so brilliant as preceding ones, had still attained its aim: Louis kept the new frontier that he had first chosen in Flanders, whilst the possession of Strasburg fixed him on the Rhine. He had baffled the most powerful European league; and, whatever were the internal sufferings and weakness of the country, France still preserved, over surrounding nations, the ascendency that Richelieu had founded, and that Louis XIV. had proudly raised.

CHAP. V.

1697—1715.

FROM THE PEACE OF RYSWICK TO THE DEATH OF LOUIS XIV.

THE period just terminated is the "palmy state" of the French monarchy: it had then reached the zenith of its splendor, of its internal authority and external power. Never was Oriental monarch surrounded with more wealth, or worshipped with more devotion. The nobility, forced into obedience to the crown, hoped that all those selfish goods which they had sought from independence, might be as effectually secured by servility. They formed at once a close alliance with the throne, and accepted the maxim, that all honor and power and liberty emanated thence, taking care at the same time so to throng around it, as themselves to intercept its every ray. The mass of the people, less interested, rallied with equal enthusiasm to their king. Recollecting the weakness, anarchy, and public misfortunes that had attended past struggles for that unattainable boon, freedom, they hailed the monarch's absolute power as the guarantee of security and peace. Attachment to the king became a second religion, and every class discarded all the old spirit and prejudices that offended against the creed of royalty. The noble sacrificed his independence, the magistrate also; both waiving those undefined political rights which they had in vain endeavored to establish. The people applauded this humbling of their superiors; and when the first effects appeared in the greatness and glory of the monarchy under Louis XIV., all hankerings after freedom were instantly discarded in admiration of a form of government so simple, so natural, so ascendant.

This universal opinion, assumed with such confidence, entertained with such devotion, was not of long duration: Louis XIV. himself was destined to outlive it. Even with him, its founder, the system of unlimited monarchy was not formed to prosper: the old state maladies, which it had for a moment removed, returned tenfold. Even the gilding of national glory, so lately laid on, and so dearly purchased, began to tarnish; sentiments began to waver: those of the people gathering into that hate towards the monarch which afterwards poured scandalous execrations on his bier: those of the nobles, who found themselves by no means possessed of the advantages which were to recompense their submission; but above all, those of the thinking class, the men of intellect and letters,—those pioneers of civilization, who go before to clear the road of its march. This, however, is but anticipation; the monarchy was yet culminant, or but in the very commencement of its decline. We are about to enter on the first causes that precipitated it into military reverses and financial distress.

The Spanish branch of the house of Austria threatened to become extinct. Charles II., reigning monarch of Spain, was childless, and of a sickly constitution. Who was to be his successor in the monarchy, was a question of the first importance. His father Philip IV. had left two daughters, the elder married to Louis XIV., the younger to the emperor Leopold; but as the queen of Louis had solemnly renounced her rights to the Spanish succession, the claim of her sister the empress was predominant. She, however, had had but a daughter, married to the elector of Bavaria, whose son, the electoral prince, showed, the renunciation of France remaining valid, the best title to the Spanish crown. Charles, in fact, made a testament in this young prince's favor, in the year 1696.

This certainly would have been the fairest and happiest mode of settling the succession; the crown of Spain passing to a new race, unentangled, in the ties of blood, with the quarrels or policies of other countries. It was mortifying however, to the house of Austria, to see so rich a kingdom pass from under its name and rule. Although the young prince of Bavaria was of its blood, still an Austrian archduke was considered by the emperor as a far more fitting heir to the Spanish throne. Both Austria and France had claims independent of the daughter of Philip IV.: Louis XIII. had married an infanta of Spain; the emperor Ferdinand, fathe of Leopold, had espoused her sister. Here again were jarring rights; but the house of Austria prevailed; and Charles II. was induced, some time previous to the treaty of Ryswick, to destroy the testament in favor of Bavaria, and to promise that his bequest should fall upon an archduke, the son of Austria.

During these intrigues, France, being at war with Spain, had no opportunity of acquiring influence with the monarch or the nation, or of furthering its claims to the succession. No doubt this consideration was one of the motives which rendered Louis so anxious for peace. As soon as it was concluded, he dispatched the marquis d'Harcourt to Madrid, in order to learn the state of the court, of the king's mind, the nation's leaning, and to make the most of any advantage. Harcourt though an intriguing, able, and winning negotiator, could gain no footing. The queen was Austrian in heart, and monopolized all influence. The ambassador was thus obliged to use threats, and so keep the Spanish monarch from declaring openly in favor of either an Austrian or Bavarian prince.

In 1698, the duke of Portland came on an embassy to Paris. He was an accomplished personage, and won so much on the French court, that it became the rage to know and entertain him. Even Louis was fascinated, and forgot the usual haughtiness with which he treated foreign envoys. Portland suggested the difficulties of the Spanish succession. They were discussed; and it was agreed that a treaty of partition, for dividing the Spanish monarchy after the death of Charles, was the only means for preserving peace. There is much that is inexplicable in the negotiation of this treaty, as given by De Torcy. According to that writer, Louis first put forth boldly his grandson's claims to the Spanish crown; and king William did not object, provided the dominions in Flanders and Italy were separated from it. And yet in a little time after we find the French king no longer insisting upon either Spain or Flanders, but contenting himself with Naples as the French share of the spoil. Was Louis insincere in this, merely amusing William, whilst Harcourt was pushing his advantages? or had the spirit and hopes of the French monarch fallen so low, that he determined to avoid war at all hazards? Certain it is, that the partition treaty was concluded, which gave Spain and the Indies, as well as Flanders, to the electoral prince of Bavaria, and Milan to the archduke Charles, reserving merely Naples for the prince representing the rights of France, namely, the duc d'Anjou, second son of the dauphin.

This treaty, despite of all concealment, reached the ears of the king of Spain. Austria, excluded by its stipulation, had too great an interest in acquainting him. Alive to his country's dignity, and fired with the insult offered to Spanish pride in thus dismembering the monarchy, and to himself in dividing his spoils without consulting him, and in his lifetime, Charles II. made a will, bequeathing the undivided empire to the prince of Bavaria. In three months after (February, 1699), this infant died, and the work both of the partition treaty and the testament had to be renewed.

Louis XIV. showed the same apparent disinterestedness and moderation. Another treaty was concluded betwixt him and king William; by which the dauphin, in addition to Naples, was to have Lorraine, the reigning prince of that duchy getting Milan in lieu; whilst the archduke Charles, second son of the emperor, was to succeed to Spain and Flanders. This second treaty of partition leads one, even more than the first, to doubt the sincerity of Louis, whose object in thus playing Machiavel must have been to lull the vigilance of Dutch and English, as well as to irritate Charles II. It was hoped, perhaps, that the Spanish king and nation, angry with all parties, would have taken the surest mode of preventing the dismemberment of the monarchy, by bequeathing it to a prince of France, which court was most capable and most at hand to enforce such a claim. With this view, however, it was necessary that the emperor should join in the treaty of partition; an act of abandonment that must have alienated the Spanish king from the house of Austria. Hence came Austria's large share in the partition; a bait to insure her adhesion. The emperor, however, equally insincere, encouraged France to conclude the treaty, knowing how the circumstance would indispose the king of Spain; and, upon learning its conclusion, hesitated to accept it himself, making objections to gain time. In the mean time, his envoy pressed the king of Spain to make a testament in favor of the arch duke. The king was at the moment not unwilling; but the emperor failed to act boldly and frankly, to send his son or to provide troops; and Charles, who saw the weakness of Austria both in council and in resources, recurred to the thoughts of a French prince for his heir. Harcourt had, in the mean time, gained the principal noblesse to support the French interest, and, above all, the papal nuncio and the pope himself exerting themselves for the house of Bourbon, the dying Charles followed their injunctions, and by a written testament bequeathed his dominions to Philip duke of Anjou, second son of the dauphin of France. In a month after this act, Charles expired, on the 1st of November, 1700.

The only doubt now remaining was, whether Louis XIV. would accept the will of the late king of Spain in favor of his grandson, or whether he would adhere to the treaty of partition. There was a long debate respecting this in his council, which council consisted but of three ministers, the chancellor Pontchartrain, the duc de Beauvilliers, and Torcy. They were divided in opinion; but the dauphin, "drowned as he habitually was in apathy and fat," says St. Simon, gathered warmth and energy on this occasion, and spoke eloquently in behalf of his son's rights. Madame de Mainenon, who had also a voice in this council, adopted the same views; and Louis decided. The young duc d'Anjou instantly occupied a chamber of state; had his train borne up; assumed the golden fleece, thus taking the insignia of monarch of Spain; the court and king acknowledging him as such. In December he departed to take possession of his new kingdom.

The emperor's indignation, in the mean time, burst forth. King William, equally mortified, but calm in his measures as in his demeanor, demanded explanations. He was hampered by the prevalence in parliament of the tories, who deprecated continental connexion or war, and who were loud in their clamors against the partition treaties. In February, 1701, the mareschal de Boufflers surprised the principal Spanish towns in Flanders, making prisoners such of the garrisons as happened to be Dutch. This was effected through the connivance of the elector of Bavaria, governor of these provinces. It was the subject of fresh alarms to Holland. But England, under tory influence, still hesitated, and seemed to view the aggrandizement of the house of Bourbon with a culpable indifference. A piece of fatuity in Louis destroyed this apathy of England, so vital to him in the present circumstances, and so galling to William. James II. dying about this time at St. Germain's, his son was acknowledged king of England by the French court. This was an insult and a defiance to Great Britain; and Louis showed in it as much idle and imprudent hardihood, as in the partition treaties he had displayed a want of pride, supposing them not to have been dictated by dissimulation. The consequence was, that the national animosity against France and Louis was aroused in the English mind; the tories, unable to stem the tide, went with it; and king William, though bowed in spirit by disease, still rallied under the influence of his old anti-Gallican zeal, and set himself strenuously to the work that he most loved, the formation of a league against the ambition of France. Still, his demands were not exorbitant: he required chiefly, that the French garrisons should be removed from the Spanish towns in Flanders; that Ostend and Nieuport should be put as sureties into the hands of England; and that, by a solemn treaty, it should be declared, that none of the present dominions of Spain should ever be annexed to France. These proposals, so modest, when considered as but replacing the provisions of the partition treaty that Louis had agreed to, were nevertheless rejected with contempt by that monarch, and styled insolent and arrogant. The good fortune of the Spanish succession had resuscitated his ancient pride. He forgot the enfeebled state of his kingdom, which had made him stoop to Savoy, rendered him eager to accept terms at Ryswick, and even humble in endeavoring to preserve peace since. Spain was necessarily detached from any new alliance against him. With England, Holland, and the empire, he thought himself, maugre his financial distresses, not unequal to compete.

Thus commenced the war of the succession, "the only *just* one," says Duclos, "that Louis ever undertook. The emperor, no longer occupied by hostilities with Turkey, was now much more formidable than before. The duke of Hanover, elevated some years since to the electorate, was grateful for the favor. The elector of Brandenburg was honored with the title of king of Prussia, and these two German princes joined against France, which numbered amongst its allies the electors of Bavaria and Cologne. The emperor began the war in 1701 by pouring a large army into Italy, under the command of prince Eugene. This young prince of the house of Savoy had been destined to the ecclesiastical state. He asked an abbaye of Louis, who refused him; a circumstance that the French monarch had ample cause to remember and regret. Eugene flung off his demi-ecclesiastical habit, and, entering the military service of the emperor, distinguished himself in those wars of Austria against the Turks which ended with the peace of Carlowitz. Mareschal Villars had been his comrade in the imperial ranks. Eugene marked his first campaign in Italy by defeating Catinat, and taking Vileroy prisoner in the town of Cremona.

King William, the soul of the confederacy against France, was preparing to take the field. Already, however, his health was sinking. Meeting with a fall from his horse, a fever was the consequence, which carried him off, at his palace of Kensington, in May, 1702. The chief reproach brought by the French against him was, that he showed no religious feeling in his last moments, and this because of the absence of the army of prelates and confessors, the pride, pomp, and circumstance of popery, with which Louis thought it necessary to redeem a life of dissoluteness. The English tory writers more inveterate, have shed upon William all the gall of faction. They upbraid him with the unamiableness and reserve of a weak constitution. They accuse him loudly of tolerance, and cannot forgive him for having saved the liberties of England, and breathed his last breath in defending those of Europe.

The mantle of William fell, however, upon the duke of Marlborough; a general bred in the best school of warfare under Turenne, and who was as superior to the monarch in military talent and political address, as he was inferior in lofty, generous, and disinterested views. Intrusted with the chief command by queen Anne, Marlborough roused the spirits of the Dutch, who had not yet recovered the loss of their prince, and entered on the campaign in Flanders. Even in that early part of his career, he would have stricken one of those master blows which afterwards distinguished him. He proposed attacking the mareschal de Boufflers at Beringhem; and Berwick allows that, had Marlborough had his will, the French would have been defeated. But the commissioners of the states distrusted the English general, yet new to fame, and the campaign of 1702 passed in Flanders without any remarkable results.

On the Rhine the imperialists had taken divers towns, without being troubled by Catinat, who kept the other side of the river. Villars, a more active general, with the baton of a mareschal in view, spied from his camp on one bank the moment that the enemy quitted their positions on the other. The prince of Baden, who commanded, thought little precaution needed, the French having shown little vigor during the year, and having now a bridge to cross, a tedious operation for an army, ere they could arrive to disturb his retreat. Villars, however, did make this unlooked-for attempt. His infantry were unable to reach that of the imperialists, but the cavalry of both armies met; the French took their enemies at a disadvantage, and defeated them in the plain of Friedlingen. An action of similar magnitude took place in Italy, at Luzara, brought about also by a surprise; but here the prince Eugene had the advantage. The most decisive blow was struck at sea. Sir George Rooke and the duke of Ormond made amends for an unsuccessful attack upon Cadiz, by forcing the port of Vigo, and capturing and destroying the fleet of the enemy, together with the galleons containing the treasures from South America.

The year 1703 passed in Flanders without any action of importance. Marlborough took Bonn and Luxembourg, and manœuvred with a view to capture Antwerp and Ostend, without success. More important movements were taking place on the Rhine, where Villars commanded. The object of the French king's pushing the war into Germany, contrary to his usual practice, was to succor his ally, the elector of Bavaria, who was so sorely pressed by the imperialists, that it was feared he would be obliged to abandon the alliance of France. Villars employed the winter months advantageously in making himself master of Kehl, opposite Strasburg. In the spring he succeeded fully in breaking through the imperialist lines, and joining the elector of Bavaria at Ratisbon; thus transferring the seat of war from the Rhine to the Danube. If we are to credit Villars himself, who united with his abilities a habit of vaunting not always favorable to truth, he conceived the idea of marching by Passau upon Vienna; an enterprise, the conception of which was worthy of a later age. The elector, of a more sober school of tactics, could not share the French general's ardor. A difference of opinion, and subsequently coolness, sprung up betwixt them. Even the more sage advice of Villars, to pass the Danube and attack the imperialists before they could be joined by an approaching army, was but reluctantly followed. The mareschal was obliged to shame his ally by threatening to make the attack alone. It took place near Donawert, between Hochstet and Blenheim, and the French were here victorious on a field which was destined to be so fatal to them in the ensuing year. Unable to bring the elector into his designs, Villars proposed to him to invade the Tyrol, and open a communication through that country with the duc de Vendôme, who commanded in Italy. The scheme was unsuccessful. Vendôme was kept in check, not only by prince Eugene, but by the duke of Savoy himself, who had quitted the alliance of France; and the Tyrolese drove the elector from their valley. He made loud complaints against Villars, and that able general in disgust threw up his command.

The elector of Bavaria, however, remained master of the whole course of the Danube as far as Passau. The small army of 20,000 men brought by Villars, but now commanded by mareschal Marsin, swelled his force, whilst mareschal Tallard, with 40,000 men on the Rhine, was ready to march in the spring of 1704 and join Marsin and the elector. These prospects made the court of Vienna tremble. That government was at the same time pressed by the Hungarian insurgents, so that even the recall of prince Eugene from Italy with all the troops that could be spared from keeping the duke of Vendôme in check, might not prove sufficient for defending the Austrian capital: to such distress was the emperor reduced in the spring of the year 1704.

It was then that Marlborough conceived the bold and generous design of abandoning Flanders, that beaten field, so known and trodden by commanders, so thickly sown with fortresses and cut with lines of defence as to render decisive actions impracticable, and of marching on the Danube, to the relief of the empire. Concealing his intentions, the duke crossed the Rhine at Bonn, the Mein near Frankfort, and marched towards Bavaria. The French had in the mean time mustered another army on the Rhine under Villeroy. Him prince Eugene undertook to observe, whilst Marlborough, seconded by the prince of Baden, undertook to pass the Danube, penetrate into Bavaria, and either force the elector to abandon the French alliance, or punish him for his hostility to the empire. Marlborough lost no time in manœuvring or counter-marches, but advanced straight against the French and Bavarians, who were intrenched at Schellenberg, before Donawert, a town that commands a bridge on the Danube. Marlborough's attack was decisive. The intrenchments were forced, the enemy were defeated and fled, leaving many thousand men and several generals on the field, as well as the passage of the Danube free. The English and imperialists instantly poured over the river, crossed the Lech, and, whilst the elector took refuge in Augsburg, until mareschal Tallard could reinforce him, Marlborough overran Bavaria to the gates of Munich, ravaging and punishing the country for the hostilities of its chief. This wretched and cruel system of warfare, of which Louis XIV. had set the example in twice laying waste the Palatinate, was not productive here of the effect intended; at least it did not bring the elector to terms. It irritated him, however, and drove his temper to seek vengeance in a general engagement.

Unable to subsist south of the Danube in a country which he could not occupy, and which he purposely ravaged, Marlborough withdrew to the north of that river. Hoping to draw the enemy after him, he caused the prince of Baden to lay siege to Ingoldstadt. What he sought, took place. The elector of Bavaria, anxious for revenge, and Tallard, who had joined him, sharing his ardor, they passed the Danube, and posted themselves at Hochstet, on the very spot where Villars and the elector had in the last year been victorious. Prince Eugene at the same time contrived to deceive Villeroy, quitting his position, in front of that general, so as himself to arrive with his army in time to join in the action, whilst Villeroy remained perplexed or engaged in uncertain and tedious pursuit.

On the morning of the 30th of August, the French and Bavarians drew up before their camp. Their armies did not mingle, but remained separate; that of Tallard on the right touching the Danube, that of Marsin and the elector in continuance of the line on the left. Before the front of Tallard was the village of Blenheim, on a rising ground, occupied by his infantry. At some distance in advance of the French and Bavarians ran a rivulet with marshy banks, on the other side of which were drawn up the imperialists, the Dutch and English; Marlborough commanding the latter next the Danube, prince Eugene the former. The elector committed a capital fault in not posting his army near to the rivulet, so as either to dispute its passage or to attack the enemy when they had partially crossed it. But he did not suspect an intention to fight on the part of Marlborough. Eugene began the action by attacking the elector and Marsin, from whom he met with a stubborn resistance. Marlborough in the mean time crossed the rivulet, and formed a strong body of infantry opposite the centre of his antagonists. This centre was composed of cavalry; for Tallard and the elector, remaining separate, had each drawn up his army, according to rule, with its horse upon the wings. But these wings, united, formed the centre of the combined army. And thus a body of cavalry, destined by its nature to act offensively, was posted in the principal, the central, the fixed position of the army. Tallard no doubt reckoned that Marlborough would attack Blenheim, and, as Condé would have done, spend a world of lives and heroic efforts to master the position. Tallard knew this would cost hours; and he accordingly rode off to the left to see how the elector was faring, whilst his antagonists were drawing up, after having crossed the rivulet. Marlborough in the mean time did dispatch troops to attack Blenheim, with the view of distracting Tallard from the principal movement. This was his advance upon the centre, the weak, divided centre of cavalry. In fact it made no resistance. Marlborough rushed in betwixt the elector and Tallard, cutting the French and Bavarian line in two. This manœuvre decided the victory. The elector with Marsin, taken in flank, gave up the advantage they had gained over Eugene, wavered, retreated, fled:

whilst Tallard's army, hemmed betwixt the English and the Danube, ended by laying down their arms and surrendering. As for the marshal himself, he was taken whilst endeavoring to return from the elector's division of the army to his own. The entire glory of this victory was Marlborough's; and he enhanced it by that modesty, and those attentions towards the vanquished, which had so redounded to the fame of the Black Prince after Poitiers. From French writers we learn that Marlborough first set the example of treating prisoners not only with clemency, but with the politeness due to misfortune; a trait that redeems those ravages in Bavaria which the custom of war had unjustly sanctioned. The battle of Blenheim, in which from 60,000 to 80,000 men were engaged on either side, cost to the vanquished 12,000 men killed, besides a greater number made prisoners. The quantity of cannon, colors, and other trophies, was immense. But its effects were greater than all. The French armies were obliged to evacuate Germany altogether, abandon Bavaria, and retire behind the Rhine. Marlborough proved to Vienna another Sobieski. His victory re-established the imperial throne; nor was the house of Austria ungrateful.

War was in the mean time raging in the Spanish peninsula. The archduke Charles had been enabled by England to land with a respectable force in that country, which he continued to dispute against Philip, the grandson of Louis. Portugal had been won over to the side of England and the archduke, and her aid proved of the greatest importance. It was singular to observe in this campaign the armies of France and Spain commanded by an Englishman, the duke of Berwick, while Ruvigny, created earl of Galway, a native of France and a Huguenot émigré, commanded the English forces. Sir George Rooke took Gibraltar in the same year in which the victory of Blenheim was won. Louis XIV. saw his power contested even in the heart of his dominions. The Protestant mountaineers of the Cevennes, the descendants of those Albigenses who had escaped the sword of De Montfort, now defied the edicts of the present monarch. Vexed by the new capitation tax, in addition to the persecution which they suffered for their religion, they flew to arms; met with such success, and inspired such terror, that mareschal Villars himself was sent against them. Admiring their valor, which rendered all hopes of subduing them by force hopeless, the mareschal treated with their chiefs, and was obliged to grant them tolerance.

Marlborough had delivered Germany from the French, and driven them beyond the Rhine: he then turned his attention to the north, and aimed at expelling them from those provinces of Spanish Flanders which they had taken possession of in the beginning of the war. During the entire campaign of 1705, the duke manœuvred in vain to attain this object by bringing the French to action. A signal victory could alone enable him to reduce a host of strong towns by a single blow; long watching for this opportunity, it did not offer till the spring of the year 1706. The mareschal Villeroy, a favorite both of the king and of De Maintenon, took the command in Flanders, and with orders to give battle. Louis was weary of the tedious war, so many enemies besetting him; the mere expense of resisting on every side being sufficient to crush the monarchy. He was no longer in a condition to wait the effect of Louvois's preparations, or Turenne's manœuvres. Experience, sagacity, or skill, no longer presided over either his councils or his armies: Louis cried out for something decisive—for battle; like the gamester, whom prudence has deserted, and who is anxious to stake all in a decisive throw, which may relieve or ruin him. He bade Villeroy, therefore, give battle. He had even selected Villars for the important task! But Villars was an indifferent courtier, being rude, independent, and proud. The "short-geniused and superb Villeroy" was preferred, and dispatched on the difficult errand of giving battle to Marlborough.

The French army, of about 80,000 men, reached the banks of the Mehaigne near Ramillies, about half distance betwixt Namur and Tirlemont, on the 23d of May, 1706. Despite the king's order and his own ardor to fight, it was Marlborough who marched to the attack. Villeroy was waiting to be joined by Marsin; but knowing himself to have a force stronger than the English general, he resolved to await the attack, drawing up his army in the position that chance had placed it, at an acute angle with the Mehaigne. The French right wing was near this river, with the village of Ramillies on a rising ground in front of it, precisely as Blenheim had been with respect to the French army, in the action called by that name. Villeroy's left was here covered by a little marshy river called the Gheete, which rendered it unassailable indeed, but also rendered it useless unless as supporting his right. Marlborough did not arrive with his army till it was already past noon; he reconnoitred, drew up in line corresponding to the French, and the cannonade began. The duke in an instant had perceived that the Gheete covering the enemy's left rendered engagement on that side impossible; he therefore drew all his force from that side, and drafting it in the most concealed manner possible behind the troops about to attack Ramillies and the French right, he concentrated his force on this point. This manœuvre took a long time to execute, and yet Villeroy took no step to defeat it. When Marlborough advanced, the French household cavalry charged him with such impetuosity and valor as to break the attacking battalions, and to endanger the duke himself; but the English, rallying in front, and allowing these rash enemies to pass to the rear, where there was force enough to deal with them, pushed on both upon Ramillies and upon the French line behind it. The English, being in much superior numbers on this point, owing to the inactivity of the French right, formed in one unbroken line, and charged, numbers breaking in between the intervals of the French, who were drawn up in separate battalions, and taking them in flank. Their rear-guard failed to support those in front; the baggage, it was said, impeded them: at all events, the battle, though begun late, proved ere sunset a decisive victory on one side and rout on the other. The pursuit lasted the whole night, the fugitives suffering greatly in their passage through the defile of Judoigne, which was blocked with cannon and wagons. Here the day of Blenheim was renewed, the loss of the French in killed and captive not being, however, so great. The consequences were not less important; being the loss to France of all the Spanish Netherlands, including Antwerp, Ghent, Bruges, Ostend, Brussels, Mechlin, and Louvain. The fortresses of Menin and Dendermonde surrendered also. Namur and Mons remained the only towns unconquered.

The court was struck with consternation on learning this second defeat, of which the details were for a long time unknown. No courier arrived, so that Louis was obliged to dispatch Chamillart himself, his minister, to Flanders. Villeroy was distracted, and had lost all self-possession: every one condemned a general whose imprudence had placed the kingdom "within two fingers of its ruin." Still Louis was generous to his unfortunate general, and wrote him to give in his resignation, in order to avoid the harshness of deprival. The duke of Vendôme was recalled from Italy to take the command in Flanders; and the duke of Orleans, the king's nephew, succeeded Vendôme. This last appointment surprised the court, which was aware of the extreme repugnance felt by Louis to employ any of the princes of the blood; but so unfortunate had proved his choice of late, that the monarch resolved at last to trust the defence of the kingdom to the zeal of his family. What La Fare observed as to the impossibility of talents of any kind being developed in an absolute monarchy, was here at length proved. Condé, Turenne, and

Luxembourg, were formed when generals were independent, and when the power of the monarch was but conditional; Colbert and Louvois were schooled in the license and difficulties of the *Fronde.* Compare with them the products of the reign of Louis, Barbesieux and Chamillart and Desmarest, as ministers; Tallard, Marsin, and Villeroy, as generals; and he difference will be found to correspond to the cause. Even the courtly St. Simon himself admits this truth: he says, the quality sought in a general was not talents for commanding, but a character likely to prove submissive; that officers were no longer advanced by merit, but by routine; and generals were kept in leading-strings, more in fear of the court than the enemy. The absence of equality was productive of worse effects. "The luxury that had inundated the camp prevented the generals from living with the officers, and consequently from knowing or judging of their several merits. There was no longer that general converse respecting war, its adventures, its science, triumphs and defeats, in which the young were wont to glean experience from the mouths of the old. Now, the young could speak but of play and women, the old but of forage and equipments. The general officers lived together or alone; the commander-in-chief saw even them but in the crowd, whilst his privacy was consumed in writing and dispatching couriers, and the details of the war were left to three or four subalterns, who perhaps knew nothing about it." It is singular, that these inconveniences of separating the ranks of an army, and forming its spirit after an exclusively aristocratic model, should be found thus strongly signalized by the duc de St. Simon, whose voluminous memoirs might not inaptly be termed the very breviary of aristocracy.

The year 1706 was disastrous to Louis. Barcelona had surrendered to lord Peterborough, who displayed there a chivalrous courage and conduct worthy of being recorded in Plutarch. The conquest of Catalonia by the archduke drew after it the submission of Madrid, from which Philip was driven. In Italy the same fortune ruled: prince Eugene forced the French lines near Turin, and defeated their troops; the mareschal Marsin was slain, and the duke of Orleans was wounded. Had the counsel of the latter prevailed over that of the mareschal, the disaster might have been avoided.

Louis now made overtures for peace; he was not listened to: the allies hoped to reduce him lower; and certainly the prospects of France were never more gloomy. The finances were in the greatest disorder, every part of the administra tion in equal arrear, yet not one capable person could the monarch procure. Chamillart had the management of both war and finance department: the exertion, united with ill success, was too much; it was killing him. He wrote a piteous letter to this effect, tendering his resignation to the king: Louis read it, and writing on the margin of the letter, "Well, we will perish together," sent it back to the minister One active genius, nevertheless, was employed at this tim in the solitude of his cabinet to provide a remedy for the pov erty of the government, and a reform in the financial system this was Vauban, the once celebrated engineer. The product of his labors was a plan for abolishing the numerous and intricate branches of taxation, and substituting in its place one uniform tax on property. He proposed to take a tenth of its yearly value, which he called a *dîxme royale.* This simple mode would have proved the ruin of the financiers, the farmers of the revenue, and the pensioners, that were paid out of divers intricate receipts ere they reached the treasury. The scheme of Vauban was set aside; and paper money now made its appearance in France for the first time.

The allies had beaten Louis on the east and on the north. They now turned their attention towards the south. The capture of Barcelona, and the retention of it, through the aid of an English fleet, encouraged an attack on some of the French sea-ports. Prince Eugene, therefore, freed of his enemies by the victory of Turin, invaded Provence, and laid siege to Toulon. The attempt was not more successful than the similar one made by Charles V.; and Louis had the satisfaction of seeing this first plan of invasion fail. The same year, 1707, a more signal advantage was gained by the victory of Almanza, won over the archduke's forces by the duke of Berwick. It replaced Philip on his throne.

Despite his distresses, Louis was not inactive. He fitted out an expedition for the pretender to Scotland, which failed. Funds were wanting to supply the armies. Desmarest, who had succeeded Chamillart, told the monarch that it was impossible to obtain money, except from Samuel Bernard the banker, who was deaf to all a minister's solicitations. Louis saw Bernard, asked him to Marly, and showed him the wonders of the place with a condescension that made the courtiers stare. Bernard was so set beside himself by the honor, that he declared he would rather see himself ruined than the empire of so gracious a monarch in want; and the loan was instantly effected.

Villars, commanded with his usual activity and success on the Rhine in 1708, whilst the duke of Burgundy, grandson to

Louis, aided by Vendôme, commanded against Marlborough in Flanders. The allies had not troops sufficient to garrison the numerous towns which they had taken in Flanders, and which were far more inclined to French rule than to the Dutch and English. Ghent and Bruges were, owing to these causes, surprised. Emboldened by success, the French pushed cross the Scheldt towards Brussels with rather uncertain intentions. Hearing that Marlborough was approaching, they etired, and invested Oudenarde, which intercepted the passage on the Scheldt betwixt the French towns and Ghent. They hoped to take it ere Marlborough could arrive. But that general making forced marches, the French at his approach decamped from before Oudenarde to retire to Ghent. The duke reached them on their retreat, and a partial action took place, in which the French were routed, and driven, with great loss, back to Ghent. The dukes of Vendôme and Burgundy had a serious difference and quarrel on the field. Never was the known verse—

"Quicquid delirant reges, plectuntur Achivi,"

more fully exemplified; for whilst the commanders were squabbling, their army was beaten. The prince Eugene then invested Lille, a bulwark not yet reduced. The French of that day, and since, exclaim against the enterprise as contrary to all the rules of war. They cannot conceive it possible that Marlborough and Eugene counted upon the indolence of Vendôme, the inexperience of the young duke of Burgundy, and the little harmony betwixt them. Despite of military critics, Lille surrendered; with it fell Ghent and Bruges; and with the exception of one or two towns, the frontier of France lay completely open.

The year 1709 commenced by one of the most rigorous winters ever known. The strongest elixirs, Hungary water for example, the Eau de Cologne of that day, froze, and broke the bottles in which it was kept, though in the warmest rooms of the palace. From this a judgment may be formed of its effects on vegetation. All fruit trees perished, olives and vines. The sown corn was destroyed. The tokens were certain of a general famine. The populace began to clamor under present sufferings, and with the prospects of still greater. Seeing the disastrous and disturbed state of the population, the parliament thought proper to assemble in the great chamber, to consider of the state of things. It was proposed to appoint deputies to visit the provinces, buy corn, and watch over the public peace. It was a bold attempt under Louis XIV., whose choler was extreme on the occasion. He reprimanded the parliament, and told them that they had as little to do with corn as with taxation. The magistrates obeyed, and were silent.

In such a state of threatened famine, aggravated by the oppression of war, commerce remained at a stand: money was no longer forthcoming. Bernard, the great banker, became a bankrupt. Even the insufficient revenue could not be collected; and an adulteration of the coin was had recourse to as the only expedient. Louis dispatched the president Rouillé to Holland to sue for peace; and soon after the marquis de Torcy, minister, he might be called, of foreign affairs, was sent on the same humiliating errand. The states of Holland, or their agents, here repaid the French king all his past insults and pride. His envoys and his offers were slighted. yet these last were sufficiently ample. Louis consented to abandon his grandson the king of Spain, reserving for him merely Naples. The states refused even Naples. Torcy offered them towns to form a barrier in the Netherlands. In this nothing less than Lille and Tournay would content them. They demanded Strasburg and Landau, tantamount to Alsace, and the demolition of Dunkirk. Louis consented to demolish the port of Dunkirk, as also the fortifications of Strasburg. In short, the demands of the allies went not only to reduce France to what it was at the accession of Louis, but prince Eugene pretended to keep possession of his conquests in Dauphiné. Moreover, the allies insisted not only upon the French king's abandoning his grandson, but upon his aiding to dethrone him. "If I am to continue warring," replied Louis, "I had rather fight my enemies than my children."

The negotiations were thus broken off. The monarch gained much by them. He showed his sincere desire for peace; and now making known, in a printed appeal to his subjects, the terms that he had offered, and that had been rejected, the national feeling was roused to indignation. The rich sent their plate to the mint, the king and royal family not excepted; the poor hurried to the armies; and Louis was in a condition to face his inveterate foes. The obduracy of Marlborough, of prince Eugene, and of the Dutch, was certainly impolitic; for Spain might in one campaign have been reduced, the French remaining neutral. France, herself, offered to make every fair concession; and the commanders, n refusing, might well incur the reproach of being actuated by selfish views, if the state of distress in France had not warranted any hopes or pretensions on their part. A great portion of the court of Versailles itself were for abandoning Philip V., and withdrawing the troops from Spain; a measure which did take place in part, owing, however, to a quarrel betwixt madame de Maintenon and the princess de Ursins. An inundation of the Loire came to complete the havoc that the winter had caused. The hand of Providence seemed to accumulate woes. A scurvy in the crowded hospitals of Paris took the appearance of a plague. "In short," writes De Maintenon, in a melancholy letter to Villars, "God has brought us to that lowest point of ruin, from which it may be hoped he will retrieve us by a sudden turn." The pious hope of the wife of Louis did not go altogether unfulfilled.

Meantime the allies had entered the field, well supplied from the copious magazines of Holland. The French army, in a state of starvation and nudity, opposed them. "Send us bread, for heaven's sake!" wrote their commander to the minister; "send us bread; we will do without waistcoats or shirts." This commander was the mareschal Villars. He was indignant at the arrogance of the confederates, and the despondency of the court: it was he who roused the drooping spirits of Louis and of his ministers, and who alone preserved a confidence in the French soldiery and in the fate of arms. Villars appears to be one of the truest and finest specimens of the French soldier: he was ardent, bold, and valiant; qualities which he enhanced by an air and habit of boasting. Full of resources, he never lost confidence in himself; firmly believing that neither Marlborough nor any general could contend with him. With this he was blunt and rude; could not brook to be commanded; too independent to be a courtier; all ministers hated him; and the butterflies of the court joined them. "I am going to fight your enemies," said he to the monarch, as he was departing for a campaign; "I leave you amongst mine."

The duke of Marlborough and prince Eugene had taken Tournay, and now menaced Mons. Villars advanced by the road from Valenciennes to succor it, and posted himself to the right of the road, in an interval betwixt two woods, near Malplaquet. By advancing he might have routed prince Eugene, who was at first inferior in numbers; but Marlborough coming up, the two generals determined to attack Villars, who, on his side anxious to measure himself with them and secure an advantage, had covered his strong position by intrenchments and *abatis*, or trees felled and thrown with their branches toward the enemy. The envoys of the Dutch states dissuaded Marlborough from fighting; and they were right. Mons was in the rear of the allied army, and Villars was in no condition to disturb its siege, without at least quitting his intrenchments. Marlborough, however, accustomed to conquer, somewhat undervalued his enemies, and resolved on the attack.

The battle of Malplaquet was fought on the 11th of September. Each wing of the French was in a wood, covered, and intrenched, whilst the centre, occupying the interval, had taken scarcely less care to cover itself. Opposite the French centre, however, was a farm and a little wood, which prince Eugene occupied, and filled with troops that did not appear. The action began on the wings, Marlborough charging Villars, and driving him back after a struggle. To support himself, Villars drew reinforcements from the centre, and was making fresh head against the English, when a ball struck his knee, and incapacitated him from commanding. Prince Eugene, watching his opportunity, seized the moment that Villars had weakened his centre, and, leading his infantry from the farm and wood, rushed on the centre, and broke it, carrying their intrenchments. This was victory. In the mean time, the Dutch attack on the other wing, where Boufflers commanded, was defeated. Despite the valor of the young prince of Orange, he could not establish himself in the wood, or within the intrenchment; and he was driven back. But the success of Boufflers was to no purpose. The French left and centre were broken; and all that its victorious right could accomplish was to cover the retreat, and prevent Malplaquet from being converted into the same rout as Ramillies. The allies lost a prodigious number of men in the attack of the woods and intrenchments. The number of French slain was much less. Villars, in consequence, was as proud as if he had gained the battle. "If God should grant us another such defeat, our enemies would be destroyed," wrote he to Louis. He afterwards boasted that but for his wound he would have won the victory: Voltaire, who was present, remarks, that few believed the boast. Mons surrendered immediately. This was the last victory of Marlborough. In the next campaign, indeed, he showed his decided military superiority to Villars, by breaking through lines that the mareschal had declared impregnable, and this without losing a man. But whilst France, with the languor of an exhausted but still valiant combatant, was warding off these blows, which the Dutch, in their anxiety for capturing towns and forming a barrier, prevented from being straightforward and vital, fortune was pleased to prostrate Marlborough, and rescue Louis from ruin by the means of a canting clergyman and an obscure woman, who rose to court favor. Sacheverel and Mrs. Masham effected what all the warriors and statesmen of Versailles despaired to do. Marlborough was overthrown, and with him England's inveteracy and force.

Previous to affairs taking this unexpected turn, the situation of Louis was desperate. Again he sent envoys to sue for peace, and they were treated with the same contempt. Sympathy is here excited for the monarch, struggling bravely not for his conquests, but for his crown and country. Louis on this occasion showed a spirit that more entitled him to the name of Great, than all his early triumphs. What were his intentions, in case of the war's continuing, and of Marlborough's invading France? He has himself recorded them in a letter to Villars: "I reckoned," said he, "on going to Peronne or St. Quentin, gathering there every disposable troop, wherewith to make a last effort with you, that we might perish together: for never could I remain a witness of the enemy's approaching my capital." This, indeed, breathes the pride of Louis XIV., but at the same time his magnanimity and heroism. The battle of Villa-Viçosa, gained by the French over the Austrian party in Spain, revived his hopes; the disgrace of Marlborough, and the blunted hostilities of England, restored him to security and confidence.

Whilst the clouds in the political sky were thus clearing up for Louis, a mass of private misfortune, almost unexampled, fell upon him. His pride had been brought low. He was now stricken in his nearest affections: his only son, the dauphin died of the small-pox. The son of this prince became, in consequence, heir-apparent to the crown. The greatest hopes were entertained of this youth. He had been the pupil of Fénélon. Though most violent and extreme naturally in his passions and temper, a sense of religion had worked a reformation in him, and he became forbearing, pious, just. His reign promised to be a golden one for France. Such was the young duke of Burgundy. His duchess was of a character as rare. With the most buoyant spirits and the aptest wit, she was the delight of her royal grandfather, who could not take a journey without her; and with him she took all kinds of liberties. It was she who remarked, on hearing him speak of the triumphs of queen Anne's reign, that "queens reigned more prosperously than kings; because under a queen men governed, and women under a king." This prince and princess were both carried off suddenly by some unknown disease; possibly by the small-pox, which was then universally prevalent and fatal: but none of the external marks of that malady appeared on them. The title of dauphin fell, within a very short time, upon a third head; and it too was carried to the grave. The second child of the late duke of Burgundy was then at nurse, and about two years old. The same malady seized it: and it was saved, probably, by its superintendent, who would not permit either bleeding or emetic to be employed,—the favorite remedies of the time for every ailment. This infant lived, and became soon after Louis XV.

Popular belief could not assign so many deaths of such important personages to the cause of nature or disease. They were attributed to poison; and the physicians, either through alarm and ignorance, or to excuse their want of skill, corroborated, all save one blunt man, the same opinion. Who could be guilty of such crimes? was the next question. And this unanswered, suggested, Who could profit by them? All eyes turned towards the duke of Orleans, nephew of Louis. His life was profligate, his character reckless, and his pride seemed to be to brave public opinion. The king, with his wonted jealousy, had kept the prince from all high or martial employ, except on one or two occasions. In Italy he had shown courage. In Spain, contemning the dullness of Philip V., who at that time had meditated retiring to the Indies, he had intrigued, it was averred, to take his place. This put him in disgrace at court. Even his studies gave handle to calumny. Chemistry was what he most delighted in, and in this pursuit he was said to be actuated by an unholy curiosity to read and influence his future destinies. Of a sarcastic spirit, that despised and mocked humanity, the duke perhaps encouraged these opinions of him in order to cater to his own amusement. The cry of suspicion was now serious. The court entertained it. The people clamored about the Palais Royal, and were only prevented by the police from breaking in and tearing the *poisoner* in pieces. To such accusers the duke scorned to justify himself. He sought however an interview with the king, who, worn with sorrow and tormented with suspicion, granted it. Orleans demanded to be sent to the Bastile, confronted with witnesses, and tried. Louis for answer could but shrug his shoulders. The monarch's mind was paralyzed with his misfortune. The duke's teacher of chemistry was arrested; and there the matter ended. Posterity seems to have acquitted Orleans of the crime; but his contemporaries, more credulous, were far from resigning themselves to the same opinion. Some indeed accused the house of Austria; and the absurdity of this supposition, upheld by many creditable persons, has the effect of invalidating the other. But none at that time dared to doubt the agency of poison.

Conferences for peace had opened at Utrecht in the commencement of 1712. It was no longer Marlborough, but the duke of Ormond, who now commanded in Flanders. He concluded a suspension of hostilities with the French; and Villars, delivered from the English, undertook to strike a blow against the prince Eugene. That commander besieged Landrecies, communicating with his magazines through the intrenched camp of Denain. Villars, pretending to assault the besieging army round Landrecies, made a side march suddenly, broke into the fortified lines, called arrogantly by the imperialists the road to Paris, and advanced upon Denain. His officers cried for *fascines* to fill up the ditch. "Eugene will not allow you time," cried Villars, "the bodies of the first slain must b our fascines." They advanced, stormed the camp, which wa commanded by lord Albemarle, a Dutch general, and carried it ere the prince could arrive. This gallant action roused the spirits and fortunes of the French, and gave weight to their efforts at Utrecht. By their own writers Denain is almost swelled into comparison with Ramillies; its success is said to have saved the kingdom. The defection of the English, under their tory minister, from the grand alliance, was, however, the true and only cause of their safety. Without it Villars could not have won the day of Denain, nor Louis made peace at Utrecht on any terms less than the abandonment of the crown of Spain by the house of Bourbon.

In April, 1713, the plenipotentiaries of France signed the treaties of Utrecht with England, Holland, and Savoy. The former country was gratified by the demolition of the port of Dunkirk, the cession of Gibraltar and Minorca, together with Newfoundland, Hudson's Bay, and the island of St. Christopher's. Spain remained to Philip V. on his renouncing for ever all right of succession to the crown of France. The English ministry endeavored to render this unwelcome part of the treaty palatable to the parliament by a number of advantages stipulated in favor of British commerce, which, however, as savoring of free trade, and inimical to the connexion with Portugal, failed of being well received. The duke of Savoy, in addition to his paternal dominions already recovered by him, had Sicily thrown into his lot.

The treaty with Holland was but provisional till the following year. The emperor held out and refused to accept the ample concessions secured to him in exchange for the crown of Spain. But the brilliant campaign of marshal Villars on the Rhine soon made Austria recede from its warlike tone and the treaty of Radstadt came in 1714 to complete that of Utrecht. The Rhine was here acknowledged the frontier line on the side of Alsace. The elector of Bavaria was restored to his dominions. The emperor, in lieu of Spain, received Naples, Milan, and Sardinia, together with Spanish Flanders, in which however the Dutch retained the right of garrisoning the principal towns, forming, as it was called, the barrier against France. Namur, Tournay, Menin, and Ypres were amongst these. Lille and French Flanders remained to Louis. He retained this important conquest, as well as Alsace; advantages which the triumphs of Villars materially tended to gain. The title of the king of Prussia was acknowledged, and a certain accession of territory procured to him. The Protestant succession to the throne of England was also uarantied by France. It is remarked as singular that a treaty ontaining this clause, so fatal to the Stuarts, should have been negotiated and signed by the cardinal de Polignac, who had received his *hat* under the nomination of the pretender.

One of the principal difficulties of the treaty was to procure from the kings of France and Spain a valid renunciation of their mutual rights to either crown, so as to obviate the possibility of their being united upon one head. The verbal renunciation, or even the oath of the monarch, was found insufficient, and not without reason, seeing how lightly the declaration of Louis XIV. on his marriage had been set aside. The English required the guarantee of a national assembly corresponding to their parliament, that in short of the states-general. Louis was, however, more indignant and hurt at this suggestion than at the most arrogant demands of the allies. He represented the nullity of the states, and his own omnipotence. "*L'état, c'est moi,*" (the state, 't is I myself,) argued he. Still his sovereign word was not sufficient. Different modes were suggested. St. Simon advised to call an assembly of dukes to affix their signatures. Others proposed the entire peerage: but Louis was as jealous of noble as plebeian, and could not tolerate the aristocracy except in the garb and in the submissive office of a courtier. All the guarantee he would give was the solemn registry of the renunciation in his parliament or assembly of legists; and even to this he took care to invite the peers with less than the ordinary form and solemnity.

This was almost the last act of the reign of Louis, in which his ruling passion, the establishing of absolute power, is manifest. He had been but too successful in this aim. The nobility stood submissive before the throne, the people in silence and suffering, far beneath and beyond its ken. Nevertheless, Louis might have observed, that, as nor virtue nor happiness is without alloy, so neither is despotism. His met resistance, a very slight resistance certainly, and hidden in the minute folds of but a few consciences; still it was resistance, and as such angered and fretted and distressed the monarch almost as much as rebellion. To explain this:—The French king had established the monarchic principle of absolutism. His will was law; and all classes found it impossible to resist *politically*.

In the domain of conscience alone could a demur be made or independence shown. It was so shown; and a sect was formed, of which the fundamental maxim was, that religion and religious truth or belief were independent of either royal or pontifical power. This is the true, though never avowed, principle of Jansenism; which, though it always put forward some other pretext for dispute, nevertheless looked to this as the source and the aim of its arguments. Jansenism was the only *opposition* that the government of Louis XIV. met with, and as such he hated and persecuted it.

The doctrines upheld by Jansenius were chiefly, that man was indebted to *grace*, and grace only, for well-doing, for pardon, for redemption. The Jesuits, or courtly part of the church, disliked this doctrine as independent. They traced the greater portion of divine power as transmitted to the head of the church, and through him to each confessor, whom they endowed with full authority over the conscience of penitents, to cleanse, to direct, to forgive. The Jansenists said no to all this, and drew up a code of morals which they opposed, as fixed, and deduced from reason and the scriptures, to the arbitrary and often absurd as well as impious maxims of the Jesuits. It was here that the former had the advantage; it was on this theme that Pascal triumphed. Jansenism, to which every independent mind rallied, from madame de Longueville the insurrectionist of the *Fronde*, to the pious Fénélon and the aristocratic St. Simon, was still more opposed to ultra-montanism and the pope's universal power than even to that of the king. In the affair of the *regale*, or right of the crown to appoint to inferior benefices during the vacancy of the see, they declared for the king against the pontiff. The privileges of the Gallican church were above all things dear to them; but afterwards, when the Jesuits had got complete hold of the king, and through him of the pope, obtaining from the latter a bull in condemnation of the propositions of Quesnel, the Jansenists withstood pope and monarch, and refused to acknowledge the bull; saving themselves, however, from the accusation of heresy, by arguing that the pope, infallible as to faith, might err as to matters of fact,—an ingenious mode of avoiding the open schism of Protestantism. The archbishop of Paris, Noailles, was the chief opponent to the king and the Jesuits in this matter; and he was ably supported by D'Aguesseau. The details of this quarrel and the history of the famous bull *Unigenitus* would fill an ample chapter. It must suffice here to glance at them, and to mark the exertions of a certain portion of the church represented by the Jesuits to share the monarch's despotic power by extending it over the domain of conscience, and at the same time the counter-efforts of an independent party to resist where resistance was alone possible, and to preserve some particle of at least spiritual independence, since political and civil freedom was no more.

Louis now began to feel his health seriously decay. The hour of his dissolution could not be distant. The future fate of his family and kingdom occupied his thoughts. Of his legitimate descendants but one feeble infant remained, with the exception of the king of Spain, who by his renunciation was set aside from inheriting the crown of France. The duke of Orleans thus filled the place of heir presumptive, and from his station aspired to the regency. Louis dreaded to trust the infant Louis XV. to the keeping of this prince, who bore the worst of characters. Though unconvicted, suspicion still rested upon him of having poisoned his relatives. Louis did him more justice in calling him a *fanfaron de crimes*, a braggard of crimes. But still the objection in the royal breast was not removed. Actuated by these motives, as well as by tenderness for the children born to him of madame de Montespan, Louis issued a decree, giving to the illegitimate princes the full rights of the legitimate blood, calling them in succession to the throne immediately after the young dauphin. Nothing marks the extreme submissiveness of the parliament more than their registry of this decree. But this obsequiousness was evidently owing to the inutility of disturbing the last moments of the monarch. Louis completed this attempt in favor of his illegitimate children by a testament which gave to the duc du Maine, the eldest of these princes, the command of the household troops and the chief power during the minority.

Having thus by his last act endeavored to extend beyond the grave that despotic will which he had raised above all obstacles in life, Louis prepared with piety and firmness for his end. A gangrene in his leg was the immediate cause which threatened the decay of the system. His great-grandson and heir he bade be brought to him to hearken to a few words of counsel. The principal advice of the dying king to his successor was, that he should avoid war, and consult the happiness of his subjects by peace: the disasters occasioned by his wars hung heavy on the conscience of Louis. The monarch lingered long, the crowd of courtiers thronging to the palace of the duke of Orleans in order to worship the rising sun, for the testament of Louis was not known. At intervals the king rallied; and in one of these that seemed like recovery, the crowd flocked back to Versailles from the

Palais Royal; but at the moment of death Louis was utterly deserted: even madame de Maintenon, either unable to bear the sight, or to consult security, had retired to St. Cyr. On the 1st of September, 1715, Louis XIV. breathed his last, after a reign of seventy-seven years.

Montesquieu characterizes Voltaire by observing, that he had in an infinite degree those qualities of mind which all the world had. A similar judgment might be passed of Louis. He had all common virtues and talents in perfection, without any of those striking and salient attributes which constitute the hero, or, in history's eye, the great. There are few mortals to whom a more glorious epitaph might be inscribed: but his career was neither of that astounding or interesting class which claims and wins apotheosis.

Yet the grandeur of superiority of character of Louis XIV. becomes more evident on a close examination. One may mock the facility, contrasted with the pride of his early conquests, and with his latter reverses. But to have ruled over every mind and every class that ever came in contact with him, as Louis did, and coming to power when he did, in troublous times, during which all authority and principle of authority were questioned,—this required a spirit whose claim by nature to rule equalled at least his right by birth. During his reign the historian has little need of descending to detail the lives of minister or mistress, unless indeed, to vary his narrative, or fill up the blank annals of despotic power. None had material influence upon him. We can trace no war, no act of policy or legislation, to favor or intrigue.* Colbert and Louvois were but instruments in the monarch's hand. Desmarest, who was minister in the latter end of the reign, was their equal in talents and in probity; but the difficulties of the time were such as no minister could support, and thus Desmarest passes for a blockhead and Louvois for a genius. It was only in the declining days of Louis that we begin to trace the effects of influence, and this influence that of his confessor. The Jesuits having won the monarch's ear through Père La Chaise, kept it by an audacious threat. That priest gave a dying injunction to Louis to choose another Jesuit for his confessor, else the *order* might be tempted to strike a blow, in other words, poison him. Louis hearkened to this request; perhaps he applauded the audacity of the Jesuit principles, which would dare any crime in order to advance their fortunes. Letellier succeeded La Chaise; and

* The story of the war occasioned by the window of Trianon being found not perpendicular, and Louvois being scolded for it, may be set aside as the mere gossiping of the court.

from the moment this dark *incubus* mastered the conscience of Louis, one can indeed mark the Jesuit speaking and acting in the monarch's garb.

Louis XIV. was the most despotic monarch, in proportion to the civilization of his people, that ever lived. His will effected this; which proves superiority and strength of mind. Is he to be censured? Scarcely. He thought it the best, the only remedy against anarchy; and his people, though not so confidently, partook at first of the same opinion. The reign, in fact, and the despotism of Louis, was an experiment, a great experiment, to try if absolute power was compatible with modern civilization, and whether it was the natural, the durable, the just form of government. It failed: and with our advanced experience we might now declare, that it would and should fail. But it tells strongly in favor of liberty that the experiment was made; and without that full and universal knowledge of its consequences, of the whole phenomena in short, with which history presents us, dreamers might still at this day find a Utopia in unlimited monarchy.

CHAPTER VI.

1715—1723.

MINORITY OF LOUIS XV. AND REGENCY OF THE DUKE OF ORLEANS.

In looking back over the reign of Louis XIV., it is impossible to avoid comparing it to that of an Oriental sovereign. We find the same absolute authority producing similar effects; the absence of prosperity, talent,* and even life amongst the people; and amongst the great, rendering ceremonial distinctions the all-absorbing object of ambition and of thought. Several chapters of St. Simon seem to transport us to China, or to the capital of the Mogul, where the privilege of wearing a cap or sitting on a stool is contested with as much fury, as of old the possession of a fortress or a province. In order, however, to reduce France to a state of Oriental simplicity in government, it would have been necessary to destroy heredi-

* St. Simon thus describes the state of the nation on Louis's death: "There were no true personages," says he, "in any kind or state, so much had this long reign of the vile burgessry," (so he styles the ministers of Louis,) "adroit to govern by itself, and to take the king by his weak side, tended to annihilate every thing, to hinder man from being man, in rooting out all emulation, all capacity, all fruits of instruction, and in banishing and destroying every individual capable of application or of entertaining an opinion."

tary right in the aristocracy, and to check the progress of studies and of intellect in the mass of the nation. Richelieu, had he lived to the commencement of the eighteenth century, might have conceived the former plan: and that minister's unshrinking use of the executioner's ax might have accomplished it, in which case the French monarch, like the Turkish, would have found his authority checked merely by his guards and by the Ulemas, the body of clerks and magistrates depositaries of the legal habits and prejudices of the people.

But Louis XIV. did not dream of depriving the noblesse of their vital principle, hereditary right; and, consequently, they survived. They were, however, in a most oppressed state; authority, they had none in the government; they were employed in the armies, in which they acquired renown perhaps, and grade, but no solid remuneration. From the captain to the general, the officers of Louis XIV., instead of amassing fortunes from their pay, universally spent and wasted their own. A visit paid by Louis to a camp at Compiègne absolutely ruined the mareschal commanding, although the king paid him 10,000 livres towards the expenses. Military service, instead of being a resource to the noblesse, proved a tax upon them. Louis made them pay the capitation, the royal tenth, moreover took their plate; and, all things considered, the nobles, though exempt from the *taille*, contributed amply towards the expenses of the state in this reign. Those who fattened on the revenue were the ignoble class of contractors and financiers. It required the nicest and narrowest management on the part of the aristocracy to keep up their great fortunes; and this they only effected by means of distributing their younger sons in the church, or in the order of Malta, and keeping their daughters "sibyls in the corners of their old châteaux." This expression, as well as the facts, is from St. Simon, who gives in full the history of several noble families, such as that of La Rochefoucault.

No wonder, then, if we find the nobles discontented with the despotism of Louis XIV., and forming a party towards the end of his reign in tacit opposition: in this the magistracy joined, and the more independent portion of the church. Jansenism was the name to which they rallied, and which designated the anti-court party, most of whom in the mean time cared little for predestination or grace, or any of the original and abstract doctrines of Port Royal. They were political Jansenists in fact. Their first hopes were placed in the young duke of Burgundy, who had avowed sympathy for the degraded state of the aristocracy, and who had determined to restore them to influence. When this young prince met with an untimely fate, the duke of Orleans became the sole prop of the party. Some of their chiefs, St. Simon himself, was in his confidence, and the duke accordingly found himself at their head.

The Jesuits on their part, masters of Louis and of madame de Maintenon, exerted themselves to thwart the noblesse, and to continue the absolute rule of the sovereign For this purpose they elevated the duc du Maine, son of madame de Montespan, in opposition to the duke of Orleans, appointed him virtually regent by the last will of Louis, and through him hoped to reign. The good fathers had miscalculated their force. On the day after Louis XIV.'s death, the parliament assembled to hear his testament read: the duke of Orleans addressed them with confidence and art, stated his rights, and his intentions to avail himself, should he be intrusted with the government, of the *sage remonstrances* of the parliament. The will was read, which appointed a council of regency, consisting of the old ministers; and preserved to Orleans the name of president of this council, in which the majority, governed by the duc du Maine, would completely dominate. Moreover, the latter was to have the care of the young king's person. The parliament, without hesitation, declared these provisions null, broke the testament of Louis XIV. ere he was cold in his coffin, and proclaimed the duke of Orleans regent. To obviate all suspicion, however, the care of the young king was left to the duc du Maine, and to his father's friend the mareschal de Villeroy.

The character of the duke of Orleans, given by St. Simon, is, perhaps, the most acutely drawn and speaking portrait that ever the pen of writer delineated. His mother applied to him the old story of a prince, to whom every talent was given by the genii, until one old fairy, unfortunately forgotten in the general invitation, arrived, and added to his other talents the quality of making use of none. Conscious of great abilities, the young duke had borne with impatience that inactivity to which he was condemned by the jealousy of his royal uncle: he turned as a resource to dissipation. Louis then forced him to marry one of his illegitimate daughters by Montespan: the duke of Orleans felt himself disgraced by the match; and hatred to his wife drove him, with the impulse of revenge, into debauch. Then the tutor Dubois, who had been given to him, was a monster of iniquity. Under all these causes, the duke of Orleans became an accomplished profligate. We have seen the horrid crimes of which he was accused; the prince, however, was not capable of murder: he was too indolent, too humane for such crimes. His affectation was to resemble Henry IV., and he unfortunately copied that monarch in his illegitimate descendants, the duke and prior of Vendôme, whose indolence, gallantry, valor, and voluptuousness, were proverbial. Darker and more singular traits are to be added to the character of the duke of Orleans: he disbelieved all religion, was a deist or atheist. This daring denial of all creeds had sprung up in England from the absurdity of the sectarians naturally producing an opposite extreme. Its seeds had blown across the Channel, and were germinating in France, soon to spread and overshadow the entire land. The regent gave an example of it in the highest station. Yet how little such opinions were the product of reason or enlightenment, is evident from the fact, that with them were coupled a belief in sorcery and in the absurdities of divination. The regent, who had become too refined and intellectual to worship God, did not disdain to invoke the devil; and he descended into the stone-quarries near Paris for this purpose. Thus do the extremes of credulity and incredulity meet in the absurd.

As a ruler, however, the duke of Orleans had advantages amongst others, that of not having been born to a throne, which, in the present day, is beginning to be fully appreciated. He had been brought up without an idea of his ever arriving at power; "a courtier beaten by storms, and thrown into the throng; one who had mingled in private life, and known all its habits, and personages, and experience." Obstinacy was not to be expected from such a character; which, however, on the other hand, had been rendered too facile by this buffeting, joined to the reckless habits of dissipation. Thus the regent was totally without those passions which give consistency: he could no more hate than love; and to make a return in either vengeance or gratitude was beyond his power. He had no memory for either benefit or injury; and he was thus detested by those whom he forgot—despised by those whom he forgave.

This latter part of the regent's character was the first that manifested itself on his elevation. Though raised by that union of the magistracy and noblesse, who might be called political Jansenists, he instantly showed that he would not enter into their resentments. Some of them proposed to banish the Jesuits from the kingdom; but this extreme act of retaliation was not for a moment entertained. The duke paid madame de Maintenon, his former political enemy, a visit of condolence at St. Cyr, showed her the most respectful attentions, and secured to her a handsome pension. Even in that great modification of the system of the government, the substitution of councils consisting of many members, in lieu of single ministers, or state secretaries, which took place at the request and for the gratification of the noblesse, the regent preserved men of all parties; even those supposed the most attached to the policy of the late king, such as the chancellor Voisin, Villeroy, and Villars. These seven councils, to which the several departments of policy were committed, were imagined in order to obviate the despotic power exercised by upstart ministers, *gens de plume et de robe*, as they were contemptuously called, as also to allow to the nobles a sphere for acquiring experience and exercising influence. D'Aguesseau sat in these councils, and represented the magistracy. The dukes of St. Simon and of Noailles had as yet the chief influence with the regent.

The first act of the new government was to liberate the prisoners confined for Jansenism. They crowded the prisons of the Bastile and Vincennes. Amongst them was D'Aremberg, who had been immured twelve years for favoring the escape of Quesnel. The sight of these victims was enough to call forth the popular voice against the Jesuits. The regent, though urged to it, would not indulge them by persecution. He visited them with the severest punishment that can fall on a religious sect or party, viz. with toleration and contempt. The Jesuits in consequence abandoned the field, and fled to Spain, where, obtaining the confessorship of Philip V., and the support of the minister Alberoni, they continued their machinations against the regent of France.

The most pressing subject of consideration was finance. The expenditure, which, in the year 1670, amounted to eighty millions of livres, had, in the last years of the war, reached 260 millions. Every means were used to meet this enormous outlay. The royal tenth on all property, planned by Vauban, was laid on in 1710. The capitation was raised. Paper money was issued at an enormous discount; Louis giving thirty-two millions in paper for eight millions of specie. Vanity seemed the national commodity most productive when taxed; and offices of all absurd kinds were created for sale, such as comptrollers-general for piling wood and trying butter, and royal counsellors inspectors of wigs. Despite of all these ways and means, Louis left a debt in bills, demanding immediate payment, that amounted to upwards of 700 millions of livres, besides a funded debt, of which the yearly interest was ninety-six millions.

To get rid of this burden, the duke of St. Simon proposed a bankruptcy. This, he said, would fall chiefly on the commercial and moneyed classes of the capital, who were not to be feared or pitied. The measure would operate, in his view, not only as a momentary relief, but as a salutary and permanent warning to the ignoble classes not to lend money to strengthen the hands of a minister or a king. This was aristocratic policy. But then no statesman could support the odium of such a measure; consequently, he proposed calling the states-general together, and making them decree it. The regent very plainly saw that they would decree no such thing; and that they might, at the same time, set about decreeing a regular representative government, of which an example rose so near on the other side of the Channel. He would not, therefore, hear of the states-general; and the parliament, which affected to represent the commons in their own body, was of the regent's opinion. The hatred of St. Simon and the nobles towards the men of commerce and finance, the wealthy upstarts of the plebeian class, was nevertheless amply gratified. A decree was issued for verifying the bills of the public creditor: he was examined as to the value given for each; and if his account did not satisfy the commission, his bill was cancelled. By this means one half of the 700 millions due on bills was rubbed off. The denial of payment being found so successful, it was resolved to proceed further, and attempt not only to curtail debts due, but to reclaim gains that had been made. The commission changed its nature and functions into an inquisitive court, or *chambre ardente.* It summoned before it all people guilty of having lent money to the state, or of having farmed the revenue. The greater part of these were flung into prison, threatened with capital punishment, and treated precisely as the poor Jews were by the feudal barons of old: in other words, tortured till they redeemed themselves from pain. The regent made merry with their woes, and sold his pardon and protection. His counsellors followed his example. Even women meddled in the traffic. A certain count visited a certain poor financier in prison, and offered to procure his release for 300,000 livres. "I am infinitely flattered and obliged, monsieur le comte," was the reply, "but madame your countess has just procured me my liberty for half that sum. You see you come too late." Never was the spoliation of a pacha by an Oriental sultan more barefaced than this; and yet it was not the act of an absolute monarch, but of those very nobles who were making an outcry against absolutism. But their Saturnalia were now come. They recompensed themselves for long submission by oppressing the classes beneath them; and for the poverty, or rather for the stopping of fresh supplies of riches to them in the last reign, by grasping pension, and place, and gratification, and at the same time throwing every tax upon the ignoble orders.* The most surprising thing is, that the magistracy joined in these acts, or remained silent as to them. They blot the name of D'Aguesseau. Another financial measure of the same epoch, and quite in harmony with the rest, was a recoinage, by which one-fifth was subtracted from the value of each piece. The current money of the kingdom may be estimated from the fact, that this operation brought in seventy-two millions of livres to the government.

In the foreign policy of the kingdom, a still greater change took place than in its internal affairs. We have seen the old rivalry between France and England roused during the latter part of Louis XIV.'s reign. It had almost expired in the fifteenth century; and in the two hundred years which succeeded, the house of Austria, encompassing France, holding Spain and Flanders, as well as the empire, was what people pleased to call the natural enemy of that country. The branch of the family that ruled in Spain was looked on as the most inveterate foe, owing, no doubt, to its interference in the League: and during the reign of Henry IV. and Louis XIII. it was always towards the Pyrenees that the French looked in hostility. The animosity could not even be allayed by mutual intermarriages. The events of Louis XIV.'s reign turned in altogether a different direction the current of national rivalry. When that monarch sought to conquer Spanish Flanders, the English started up on a principle of self-preservation to prevent his aggrandizement; and the victories with which they checked and blighted his career, filled Europe with amazement and France with despite. Spain, at the same time, fell subject to a Bourbon; the emperor, separated from the Rhine and the Alps by those second-rate powers that had sprung up in the sixteenth century, was no longer an imminent neighbor; and thus England became, in the eyes of France, the sole object of those diverse sentiments with which a great nation beholds its rival.

Her assuming of this position was sudden too. Britain had previously acted but as an auxiliary, and not always a successful auxiliary either: the part she played was secondary: but now she took the lead. Her armies were those of a great empire; and Marlborough's glory filled Europe with a splendor more dazzling, because unexpected. England became the mode, the cynosure; and, on a closer examination, showed perfections that equally startled the inhabitant of the con-

* The capitation-tax, levied on all classes, was allowed to expire, whilst he *taille*, levied on plebeians only, continued

tinent. Her constitution, her liberties, her senatorial eloquence, the boldness and independence of the national character, were qualities hitherto vaguely heard of, but now seen and studied. Montesquieu and Voltaire both visited London at this time; and such voyagers were alone sufficient to convert an unknown into a known and admired region. The man of the continent, the Frenchman, hitherto confined to his own classic and elegant models in literature, and not dreaming of finding in this department any rival near his throne, stumbled upon our more original and robust, yet scarcely less refined writers; and his amazement at our literary genius was even still more great. He became familiar with the names of Locke and Newton, and with their discoveries. Such glories as these in intellect, united with the more popular ones of Marlborough in the battle-field, might well command the admiration and captivate the affections of a stranger nation. It did so: France, conscious of her own grandeur and eminence, was above all mean jealousy; her applause was loud and sincere.

Such a feeling was, however, as may be supposed, not unanimous. A considerable portion of the French could not forget the days of Blenheim and of Ramillies. They pointed out England and Austria as the true, the natural enemies of France; and Spain, at the same time, with a king of the Bourbon race, as its natural ally. But the regent was not of this opinion. His sentiments were rather those previously described; which consisted in a generous admiration of England, and esteem for Englishmen, who, at once aristocratic and enlightened, free in opinion and in life, caught peculiarly the predilections of Philip of Orleans. Lord Stair, the British ambassador, was a favorite and friend of the regent. This able diplomatist had warmly embraced the party of the political Jansenists in the life of Louis, to whom he was particularly odious; and the regent was thus grateful to him. He gained Dubois also, a churchman, who, from tutor to the duke, was rising daily in the scale of confidence to reach the place of minister: and thus a perfect understanding and amity was established between the governments of England and France.

The previous jealousies of the duke of Orleans and Philip V. of Spain contributed materially to produce this estrangement between the countries which they governed. The duke had of old aspired to reign in Spain: the king now pretended to have the best right to the French regency, as also to succeed to Louis XV., despite past renunciations, should that infant monarch die. Alberoni it was, who suggested these views to Philip, and kept them alive in his breast. This minister, like

Dubois, was a person of the lowest birth, an Italian, whom the duc de Vendôme had placed as secret agent at the court of Spain. He had been instrumental in marrying Philip to his second wife, the princess of Parma; and she, in gratitude, used her influence in his favor, and he became prime minister and cardinal. His internal administration was sage: he restored order to the finances, and put the kingdom into state of vigor, which he soon thought of employing for its aggrandizement. The queen of Philip pressed the minister to procure establishments for her children, shut out from the crown by the offspring of the king's first wife. Alberoni proposed to conquer those provinces in Italy which had been severed from Spain by the war of the succession and the treaty of Utrecht. He might rationally hope to be seconded by France in such views; as he inevitably would have been, had Louis XIV. or his policy survived. But the amicable inclination of France and England had produced a treaty between them early in 1717, by which the latter country guarantied the regent's succession to the throne, in the case of the young king's decease; France, in return, promising to banish the pretender and his Jacobite followers. Holland, following England, acceded to this hence called Triple Alliance.

Alberoni, whilst his intentions were mainly bent towards regaining some of the lost possessions of Spain in the Mediterranean, kept watch, nevertheless, upon other countries, especially on the maritime powers, who might interfere to thwart him. He had early sought to form a close alliance with England; but she had slighted his advances, and now stood united with France in more than tacit enmity to Spain. Here, then, the far-stretching policy of Alberoni sought out enemies and occupation for England; communicating with the count de Goertz to unite the great rivals, Charles XII. of Sweden and Peter the Great of Russia, in a kind of crusade for the purpose of restoring the pretender to the throne of Britain. The czar took a journey to Paris, with the view of shaking the friendship of the regent for the house of Hanover. Alberoni's project was a vast one; and had it succeeded even in ever so small a part, the north of Europe would have been too seriously embroiled to have leisure to interfere in his plans of conquest. What these were, soon appeared. A fleet wa fitted out in the ports of Spain: its destination, avowedl against the Turks, alarmed more than one power in the Mediterranean. At length, in July, 1717, it sailed, and proceeded to Sardinia, where it landed an army, that met with no obstacle in reducing the island. Notwithstanding this, and his intrigues with Sweden, Alberoni sought to impose on

England and Holland, and endeavored to purchase the neutrality of both countries. England, aware of the meditated league, and afraid of the czar, hesitated to declare against Spain, and continued negotiating to restore peace between that country and the emperor, France imitating her policy. The number of intrigues and counter-intrigues throughout Europe at this moment render its diplomatic history a perfect chaos.

In 1718, Alberoni took another stride, and dispatched a fleet and army against Sicily, which by the treaty of Utrecht had been adjudged to the duke of Savoy. This fresh act of aggression aroused the powers of the triple alliance. The emperor was summoned to join in it, in order to put a check to the ambition of Spain and of Alberoni; and his accession converted the triple into the quadruple alliance. A British fleet under admiral Byng sailed to the Mediterranean. As the Spaniard refused to desist in his attempt on Sicily, Byng attacked his fleet, which was taken and destroyed, whilst an Austrian force passed into Sicily to contest with the Spanish army the possession of that island.

The regent during these events approved of the policy of England, and supported her menaces against Spain. Alberoni's resentment in consequence against both countries was at the highest. England he resolved to punish by affording aid to the pretender; whilst to be avenged of France, and to overthrow its rulers, the cardinal had already, to use his own expression, undermined the regent's seat of power. His plan to effect this was by leaguing with the court-party attached to Louis XIV.'s memory and policy, and to the duc du Maine. This prince, destined by the late king to exercise the office of regent, had been set aside in the first days of the new reign. His enemies had followed up the blow by repealing the edict which called the illegitimate princes to the throne in preference to the collateral blood of Orleans. This was but just. The dukes at the same time reclaimed their ancient precedence over the bastard princes, of which they had been deprived. These indignities naturally exasperated the duc du Maine, but still more his duchess, a daughter of the house of Condé, and endowed with those bright parts and that superior intellect so enhancing to woman's pride. The memoirs of De Staal represent her abed, surrounded by musty volumes, in which she and her attendants were employed in searching out authorities to the honor of illegitimacy. She enlisted men of letters to aid her in a dispute which reason was little likely to decide. The party contained many of the noblesse, amongst whom are found the names of Montmorency, Richeieu, and Chatillon. The parliament were also won over That body was irritated and alarmed by the successful scheme of Law, a Scottish financier, who had established under the regent's protection a royal bank in Paris, connected and supported by other commercial plans, which threatened to render the sovereign completely independent in the important matter of finance. Religious differences, the Jesuits beginning already to stir, came to blend with this medley of interests. and, in fine, a strong party was forming against the regent, in the capital, the court, and the parliament, which Alberoni's emissaries kept alive till the hour had arrived for its breaking forth. Their first plan was to demand the assembling of the states-general, in which they hoped to see the regent stripped of his power. But a public request being made for this purpose, those who signed it were sent to the Bastile. The duke of Orleans asserted his authority boldly. He pronounced in council on the disputes of precedency, as Louis XIV. might have done. The chancellor d'Aguesseau was sent into exile for adhering to the judicial body in their condemnation of Law; and the young king was made to hold a bed of justice in the Louvre, to which the parliament was summoned, and compelled to register not only the degradation of the duc du Maine, but a condemnation of themselves in the affair of Law, declaring that they had no right to discuss affairs of state. The popular voice was at the moment in favor of Law and his scheme, from which every one promised himself immense riches; and the parliament imprudently put itself in opposition to the court on a point which deprived it of the support of the people. Three of its members, who resisted, were imprisoned by order of the regent. Thus the attempt to renew the troubles of the *Fronde* was frustrated, and Dubois and the duke of Orleans succeeded by the very same means and display of authority that had foiled Anne of Austria and Mazarin.

The duchess of Maine and the nobles in her confidence, though mortified by this defeat, did not despair. Alberoni supported them. They stirred the public mind with writings. They counterfeited a demand on the part of the parliament for the states-general, which the parliament, however discontented, was by no means disposed to make. A proclamation appeared, counterfeit also, in the name of the king of Spain, making the same demand. But Law's scheme occupied every mouth and every mind, and it was found impossible to excite popular tumult or discontent. The intrigues, however, continued; when by chance some papers relative to the conspiracy were purloined from the agent of Cellamare, the

Spanish ambassador. The agent was arrested, and further documents found, plainly proving a plot for raising insurrection, especially in the province of Britany, for compelling the assembling of the states, and overturning the regent. On these flagrant proofs, the duke and duchess du Maine were both seized and imprisoned, and with them their principal adherents. Amongst these was the young duke of Richelieu famed afterwards for his gallantry. The regent had now his enemies completely in his power. Louis XIII. or Richelieu would have sent them to the scaffold. The duke of Orleans punished only those Breton conspirators who were taken with arms in their hands: the rest, after publishing the proofs of their treason, he released after a certain term of confinement. The duke and duchess of Maine were restored to their princely mansion at Sçeaux, where the former sunk to insignificance: the duchess soothing her wounded pride by the cultivation and patronage of letters.

The regent, having thus shown a magnanimous clemency that somewhat redeemed his vices, declared war against Spain, and resolved to punish Alberoni. The mareschal de Berwick took the command, crossed the Pyrenees, and reduced Fontarabia and Urgel; whilst the imperialists, aided by the English fleets, pressed the Spanish army in Sicily, and at length compelled it to surrender. Philip V. was thus obliged to submit to the dictation of the quadruple alliance. Peace was concluded in January, 1720, by which Sicily was abandoned to the emperor, Sardinia being given in exchange to the duke of Savoy. Philip was indulged with a promise of Tuscany and Parma for his son by his present queen, in case the reigning duke of that country should leave no heirs. The emperor acknowledged the king of Spain, who in turn recognized the rights of the regent to the crown of France superior to his own. Alberoni's disgrace was at the same time stipulated: he was banished from Spain, and traversed France on his way to retirement in Italy,—a proof that he considered the duke of Orleans above any unworthy act of vengeance.

The regent, victorious over foreign and domestic foes, had every reason to be pleased with fortune. He might have even adduced it as a proof how little the profligacy of his private life marred his public prosperity. The royal bank had taken away the burden of the debt and the difficulty of the finances: the duke might have believed in the promises of the fairies at his birth; and Law might have aptly figured as one of their agents. The bank, which this Scotsman first proposed, was to have a capital of 6,000,000 of livres, to be paid by the acceptors of shares, half in money, and half in government bills: the half in money was sufficient to carry on the bank. A considerable share of government paper was thus absorbed, to the delight and relief of the regent, who immediately urged Law to do the same by it all. Law promised that he would, and he did so; increasing, however, the credit of his bank, by procuring for it the monopoly of commerce to the Mississippi, to China, and to Senegal. The name of these mighty and mystical regions, *El Dorados* in the eyes of the Parisians, gave them promises of gigantic profits; and Law's paper was accordingly sought for with such zeal, that all the efforts of the police were required to prevent the crowd of buyers from suffocating each other in the rue Quincampoix. The bubble was soon blown to bursting: the original 6,000,000 of paper had been extended to 3,000,000,000. The bills began to depreciate, and the downward rush was as precipitate as the uprise. Government did all that madness could suggest to check the fall: first, the common remedy of a premium on paper; then it forbade individuals to keep coin of any description, making domiciliary visits to enforce the order. A decree at length reduced the shares of the bank to half their value. The parliament at length interfered, when the public ruin was completed, and when the government saw its fairy fabric of riches vanish before its eyes. The liquidation, with which the unfortunate scheme closed, increased the national debt by nearly one half. As for Law, its author, he contrived to escape to Venice, poor from the wreck of so much wealth. He had purchased some of the first estates in the kingdom, and had been in treaty for that of Rosny: they were of course confiscated.

What threatened to be most serious in Law's ruin was the manner in which the parliament declared itself, and raised its head after the humiliation of the bed of justice. That adventurer is said to have advised the regent to pay off the parliament, give to each member the price of his place in the bank bills—then an inexhaustible fund—and thus rid the state of a troublesome body. He put this plan in practice with respec to the parliament of Britany. Hence came their opposition to him. But the parliament was no longer in the days of the *Fronde;* even a stranger could crush it. Law, then superintendent of the finances, and minister, procured the exile of the whole body to Pontoise: they obeyed without a murmur, the people showing no sympathy for their distress.

The regent proved ungrateful to all those interests that had raised him to power, and rendered him triumphant over the will of Louis XIV. The noblesse had been at first gratified by the appointment of ministerial councils, but these had been found troublesome and inefficient. Dubois superseded them as secretary of state. The parliament, flattered with the hope of being indulged in the right of remonstrance, was afterwards silenced and exiled. The Jansenists, religious and political, were treated still more scurvily. The regent allied with the Jesuit party, and forced the parliament, as the price of its recall from exile, to register the bull *Unigenitus*, the great object which all the power of Louis XIV. failed in attaining.

Dubois was the cause of these changes. It had been the maxim of the last king never to admit an ecclesiastic to council; "a wise maxim," says St. Simon, as they aim always at a cardinal's hat for themselves, rather than the welfare of the state. Dubois was of a character so infamous, that all ecclesiastical advancement seemed impossible: nevertheless, when the archbishopric of Cambray became vacant, he asked for the appointment, in a tone certainly more jocular than serious. "Ah!" replied the regent, "should I bestow the archbishopric on such a scoundrel as thee, where shall we find a prelate scoundrel enough to consecrate thee?" "I have one here," quoth Dubois. Knowing that the archbishop of Paris, Noailles, would refuse, the minister had sought out Rohan, a prelate of the Jesuit party, to which he promised to bring back the favor of the court, if he would consecrate him. Dubois thus became archbishop of Cambray. St. Simon said that he should blush to be present at the consecration; and yet he offered to undergo that humiliation, provided the regent would not disgrace himself by attending. The regent promised, but, pressed by a mistress who was in Dubois's intimacy, he went notwithstanding. The next object of the minister was to replace his mitre by a cardinal's hat; and this he at length obtained from the pope, on condition that the bull *Unigenitus*, or the *constitution*, as it was called, should become the law of the kingdom. Dubois procured this triumph for the Jesuits, and became cardinal. Another article of the negotiation appeared soon after, when a Jesuit confessor was appointed to direct the conscience of the young king: and at the same time was concluded a double project of marriage between Louis XV. and the infanta of Spain, and between the prince, heir to that crown, and a daughter of the regent.

Dubois did not long enjoy the dignities that his baseness had earned. Cardinal and minister in 1722, he expired in the following year. When on his bed of death, a curate advanced in haste to administer the sacrament to the dying man: Dubois repelled him. "What! administer the *viaticum* with so little ceremony as that to a cardinal; gc, and consult us to the necessary forms." Ere the forms could be ascertained, the cardinal had died, as he had lived, not in the odor of sanctity. In a few months after, the regent was struck with apoplexy in the apartments of madame de Phalain, his mistress, and in the palace of Versailles: she cried for aid, but it did not come till the duke was cold. He expired in December, 1723, leaving three daughters, all notorious for extreme dissoluteness,* and a son, remarked for his piety and narrow intellect.

"The regent," says the duke of St. Simon, whose incomparable memoirs conclude with this epoch, "was far more regretted abroad than at home." The English especially had cause to be grateful to a prince, the first wielding the sovereignty of France, who had sympathized or joined with them in amity. The great majority of the French, however, accused this policy of selfishness and baseness; and were indignant at beholding their country acting, as it seemed, a part subordinate to English views. The duke of Orleans had moreover betrayed all parties in the state. The very Jesuits were dissatisfied at not obtaining complete predominance. The parliament felt itself juggled; although its resentments were not so profound, or did not proceed from views so exaggerated as St. Simon lends to them. "The parliament," says he, "could not console itself for not having changed its simple nature as a court of justice into that of the parliament of England, holding, however, the house of lords under the yoke." The general cause of complaint was the enormous increase of price in every article, first brought about by the depreciation of Law's paper, but which by no means subsided to its ancient level as soon as the crisis was past. The nobles acquired little increase of influence. Pensions certainly were heaped upon them; and not content with their hereditary domains, they shared with the sovereign the contributions levied on the inferior classes. But this indefinite and unearned resource proved but a temptation to extravagance and to an oblivion of all economy. Habits of expense and luxury increased in a tenfold proportion; and the reign of Louis XV., which showered pensions, and aids, and employments, on the noblesse, had the effect of impoverishing that order much more than Louis XIV. had done; who indeed gave them naught, but who asked naught of them save obedience.

This history has been almost silent as to the splendid litera-

* The following satirical epitaph was inscribed upon the tomb of the duchess-dowager of Orleans;—"Here lies Idleness, the mother of all vice"

ture of the last reign. That literature, in fact, was but the gilding, the precious ornament, of the stately edifice. Its tragedies and odes, its satires, sermons, fables, were written for the perusal of the audience of court. They were not born of popular feeling, and neither propagated nor influenced opinions deeper than taste. They are the domain of criticism, not of history. With the regency, however, French literature, though of a lower grade in genius and perfection, begins to assume much more importance. It was then that the great mass of the public, freed of the *prestige*, the moral ascendency, of a court which could excite nothing save contempt, arrived at the hardihood of having ideas and opinions of its own, not only in religious but on political and philosophical subjects. Writers began to sow the seeds of thought, no longer on the narrow inclosure of the court and aristocracy, but in the open field of the public mind. Books, that had hitherto never raised discord, except upon abstruse points of faith, amongst learned doctors, began in the regency to have general influence. A libel became a weapon as common and as poignant as the sword. The duchess du Maine employed men of letters in her husband's cause, and the regent employed others, Fontenelle for example, to draw up his manifestoes. No sooner did men capable of wielding the pen become conscious of their force, than they hastened to employ it. They were chiefly of the lower and degraded class, and felt sensibly the heavy oppression that weighed even less on personal than upon mental freedom. Not daring to affront the immediate instruments of this oppression, writers attacked or sapped the principles on which they were supported. Bayle had already assailed religion with his army of doubts and questions. The meekly froward Fénélon had dared, in his Telemachus, to define and criticise the duties of royalty. Voltaire and Montesquieu now followed in the track. The former, ridiculing intolerance, found wit so powerful and successful in his hands, that he was carried forwards unfortunately to attack religion itself; an attack, however, that must have redounded to its triumph, had the national church not disgraced its creed by corruption, and betrayed it by ignorance. Montesquieu at the same time carried his inquiries into the unexplored regions of political philosophy. He was moderate, sage, shrunk from revealing abuses, and often, when in his researches he has undermined or discovered the weak foundations of monarchic bulwarks, we find him instantly set to work to prop the tottering wall. But to counteract his own exertion was impossible. He excited inquiry; and when the curiosity of man is awake on such points, it must be satisfied by experience or demonstration. The latter is not to be met with in political theory; and the former is most often to be purchased at no less a price than revolution, anarchy, and crime.

CHAP. VII.

1723—1748.

FROM THE MAJORITY OF LOUIS XV. TO THE PEACE OF AIX-LA-CHAPELLE.

WHATEVER were the faults or crimes of the regent, he had at least acted an honorable part by his royal ward. He intrusted young Louis to the care of Villeroy, the attached friend of Louis XIV., and consequently, the regent's personal opponent, if not enemy. For confessor and instructor, Fleury was chosen, "because he was neither Jansenist, nor Molinist, nor Jesuit." Fleury was one of those mild personages to whom extremes are repugnant, and who prefer the middle course in all circumstances. A more fitting tutor could not have been selected to form a monarch's principles; but, unfortunately, he communicated to Louis much of the timidity and meekness of his own character. Diffidence is the great bane of the privately educated, especially when they are afterwards to mingle with persons not on an equality with them. It matters not whether they descend or ascend. Louis XV. could no more set himself at his ease in the company of his courtiers, than an upstart could have done in the same society. Bashfulness becomes irresolution in one born to influence and to act: and this apparently venial quality was the chief cause of all the crimes and follies of his reign.

The young king became sincerely attached to his kind and indulgent tutor, who, on his side, was not blind to the advantages of such influence. He refused an archbishopric, that would have removed him from court. On the occasion of a quarrel between Villeroy and cardinal Dubois, the mareschal was arrested; Fleury took fright, and retired also. The young king no sooner missed his tutor, than he gave way to the most noisy grief; wept, lamented, and was not to be pacified. Fleury was sought out, brought back, and the joy of Louis was extreme. The future influence of the instructor might be augured from this: but his meekness, and also his extreme age, disarmed all envy. When the death of the duke of Orleans was known, the duc de Bourbon, lineal heir of the house of Condé, and first prince of the blood, aspired to be minister. The name of the regent was extinct, Louis being now of age. The duke got the patent of prime minister drawn up, went with it to the king, and asked him boldly for the place. The young monarch looked at Fleury, who made a sign of assent, and the duc de Bourbon had the appointment.

Monsieur le duc, as the prime minister was universally called, had hitherto distinguished himself by meddling in the affair of Law, and by his inveteracy against the duc du Maine. He was thus a political Jansenist. In the conspiracy stirred up by Alberoni against the regent, the Huguenots had partially joined. The few that still remained in France had thought this an opportunity favorable for rebelling. On the failure of the conspiracy, they had remained quiet; and the regent would not break through his principles of toleration to punish them. One of the first acts of the duc de Bourbon was to display his zeal for orthodoxy; and, at the same time, be avenged on the partisans of the duc du Maine, by a fulminating edict against the Protestants, renewing all the barbarities of the year 1685. England and Holland interfered, however, in behalf of their persecuted brethren, and the edict was modified.

In abandoning the ministry to a competitor, whose rank as prince of the blood awed and dazzled him, Fleury had reserved himself two privileges: one was the management of ecclesiastical affairs; the other, the right of being present whenever the duke consulted the king. Bourbon was obliged to be contented with his share, which was indeed considerable. He himself was governed by a mistress, the marquise du Prie, daughter of a financier, and an adept in the mystery of jobbing in the public funds. She introduced to the duke four brothers of the name of Paris, who had been in favor with the regent, and afterwards exiled by him. These were his finance ministers and counsellors. The marriage of the king was the most important point to be considered. He was betrothed to the infanta then educating at the French court: but the duc de Bourbon had his old political dislike to Spain; and he also proposed, by forming a new marriage, and making a queen of his choice, to gain full ascendency over the mind of Louis. A menacing illness of the king hastened this resolution. The duke turned his views first towards his sister. Madame du Prie dispatched one of her confidants to make a trial of the sentiments and temper of the princess; but the latter, disgusted with the meanness and vulgarity of the messenger, showed all the pride of a Condé, and refused to enter into either terms or promises. Madame du Prie would therefore no longer hear of this lady, mademoiselle de Vermandois. A daughter of Russia was proposed and rejected. At length it was recollected that Stanislaus, the exiled king of Poland, had a daughter, who now shared his wanderings and misfortunes. A creature, thus raised from distress to the throne of France, could not but be grateful to those who elevated her. Thus reasoned madame du Prie. Moreover, Maria Leczinski was lovely, mild, humble, pious. Fleury, when he heard the choice, could not disapprove of it. Stanislaus and his daughter could not credit their good fortune. It was confirmed, however; and the daughter of the fugitive king of Poland became queen of France.

Relying on the attachment of the young queen, the duc de Bourbon became less scrupulous in his plans of administration. An edict was prepared for a new tax, called a fiftieth, but which, from its arbitrary valuation, was likely to prove a tenth. It was to last twelve years. The noblesse, who were not exempt from this tax, protested. The parliaments of the kingdom poured in remonstrances; and a scarcity of corn happening at the same time, raised the popular voice, in unison with that of the court and judicial body, against the minister. At such an unpropitious moment did the duc de Bourbon think proper to affront Fleury; wishing to bar him of his privilege of being present during the minister's consultations with the king. The duke arranged with the queen to entice Louis to receive his minister, and consult about public affairs, in her apartment. The monarch, who did not suspect any affront to Fleury, consented; and the latter, finding himself excluded, took the resolution of leaving Paris, and retiring to Issy: he, at the same time, wrote a pathetic and meek letter of resignation and farewell. Louis, on reading it, burst into tears, as of old. He dared not at first demand the recall of his preceptor; but the courtiers insinuating that he was now the master, he at length spoke the word, and Fleury was recalled. The old ecclesiastic was as timid as the monarch; and neither at first dared to break with the duc de Bourbon. An opportunity was, however, sought. The court, upon inquiry, found the duke extremely unpopular; and hence took courage to get rid of him. As Louis was departing on a journey to Rambouillet, he begged the duke to follow, and to "be sure not to keep supper waiting." The royal carriage drove off; the duke was preparing to follow, when an order, written by the monarch, was put into his hand, commanding him to retire to Chantilly. Madame du Prie, who was with the queen when she heard of the duke's arrest, exhorted that princess to interfere. But it was too late: a letter from Louis desired even her to obey Fleury, who assumed the functions of prime minister, although, with characteristic humility, he declined the honors and the name.

Never was statesman apparently more unfit, from character, to rule over a quick and high-spirited nation than Fleury. He was timidity—benignity's self. His policy towards foreign nations was peace; at home, economy and quiet. Fortunately for his success, he reached power at a time of domestic calm, when every flame of dissension had burned out. The government he continued in the same despotic path in which he found it; but this without violence or effort. There was no resistance. Fleury did not allow a pretext. His rigid economy made him independent of parliament and people. Then, it was an age of utter mediocrity. There was not a personage amongst the princes of the blood, or the noblesse, who could head a party, were there pretexts of discontent to form one. The duke of Bourbon, it has been seen, was without capacity; the duke of Orleans, son of the regent, was a monk in habits and in mind. The long cessation from war, and consequently from all counsels and negotiations, had left the nobles no avenue to lead to eminence. Singularity and expenditure were their only means of shining. The French aristocracy declined, in fact, from the day in which it ceased to struggle with absolute power. With that motive it lost all principle of life. When the noble sunk into the mere courtier, he forfeited not only his independence, but the continuance of his caste.*

Thus the administration of Fleury presents, in the interior of the kingdom, an almost unbroken calm. The minister recalled to court those who were in disgrace during the regency, the duc du Maine, mareschal Tallard, Villeroy. Yet these spirits, once so turbulent, were now known but as the bearers of titles, or as the owners of saloons in which good society was received. The first years of Fleury's administration present, in short, a perfect blank in history. Let us fill it up by a glance at European politics.

Philip V., who gained the crown of Spain as much by con-

* There is no more important political truth than that the continuance of an aristocracy is incompatible with despotism. Physical existence or prosperity is not sufficient to uphold a privileged caste. It must have, moreover, a spring of intellectual activity, that is, interests to defend, and the means of defending them. When those, or when the latter fail, then commences their decline; such was the case of the Roman nobles after Augustus, of the French after the *Fronde*. An elective, or constitutional, or a feudal monarchy, are the only forms compatible with an aristocracy. Hence, the absurdity of the French noblesse, in seeking to restore the *ancien régime*; they but struggled to die over again.

quest and good fortune as by right, becoming, in his declining days, scrupulously devout, proposed to resign in favor of his son. His confessor had reasons to strengthen this resolve; and Philip abdicated. He had scarcely done so, when he perceived the selfish reasons of those who promoted his resignation. His successor, Louis, was completely in the hands of a junta of nobles, who wielded, for their own purposes, the sovereign power. This successor, however, died. Philip, anxious to resume the crown, was prevented by scruples respecting his oath of abdication. The papal nuncio removed this objection; the monarch's nurse, by her reproaches, roused once more his spirit and ambition, and Philip remounted the throne. It was immediately subsequent to this that the duc de Bourbon sent back to Spain the infanta, who had been betrothed to Louis XV., and to whom Maria Leczinski had been preferred.

Philip V. was mortally offended at this insult offered to his daughter. It precipitated him into a measure that had been for some time meditated by the court of Spain. This was not only a reconciliation but a treaty of alliance with Austria, the ancient rival and enemy of Philip. The latter was, above all things, anxious for the succession of his son Don Carlos to the duchies of Tuscany and Parma, after the death of the last of the Medicis. This, to be sure, was stipulated in the last negotiations; but might easily be eluded, especially at a moment when France and England seemed so little inclined to respect Spain. An alliance with the emperor would at once secure this; whilst it alarmed and retaliated upon France. Ripperda, a native of Holland, Philip's envoy, made advances accordingly to the imperial court. No offer could have come more opportune to Austria. In order to rival the maritime powers, and thence their influence and wealth, she had established an East India company at Ostend, that had excited lively jealousies on the part of both English and Dutch. They menaced the emperor; and he, to strengthen himself, concluded the treaty with Spain. The articles of it are not of so much importance as the fact of the union.

France and England naturally took alarm at a reconciliation so little to be expected. The monarch of the latter country, tremblingly alive to the safety of his German dominions, called on his ally to prevent or counteract the effects of the treaty. The duke of Bourbon, then minister, continued in the same amicable sentiments towards England that had actuated the policy of the regent. The pension said to have been paid by that country to cardinal Dubois was continued to the marchioness du Prie. Horace Walpole, ambassador at

Paris, had imitated the sagacity of his predecessor, lord Stair, by attaching himself and paying court to Fleury. Walpole was amongst the few who paid their respects at Issay during the minister's last retirement there. The friendship that sprung up betwixt Fleury and the Walpoles, ministers of congenial feeling and pacific inclinations, contributed strongly to preserve the bonds of amity unbroken betwixt the two nations: these were now drawn closer by a treaty concluded at Hanover, in opposition to that betwixt Spain and Austria. At the same time the duc de Richelieu, a brilliant young noble, was dispatched to Vienna to endeavor to accommodate differences, and to counteract Ripperda. He succeeded in outshining this adventurer, who returned to Spain to enjoy a shortlived triumph and reward as prime minister.

In the mean time the jealousies between Spain and England produced open war. The fleets of the latter scoured the West Indian seas and the Mediterranean: the Spaniards laid siege to Gibraltar. But the belligerents had scarcely more than time to put themselves in the attitude of war, when cardinal Fleury interposed as mediator and restored peace. Each country had its point to gain; and, fortunately, each could be gained by mutual sacrifices. England and Holland required the suspension of the Ostend India company: Austria granted this, on condition that the imperial crown was to descend in the female line to Maria Theresa, daughter of the emperor. England guarantied this, and Spain also, on being secured in the succession of Don Carlos to Tuscany and Parma. It was in fulfilment of this that, on the death of the reigning duke of Parma, an English fleet transported a Spanish force to Leghorn, and thus gave to the Bourbon prince his first firm footing in Italy.

The pacific policy of the French minister thus imposed tranquillity upon Europe, until the death of the king of Poland in 1733, and his disputed succession, raised a flame that no efforts of mere negotiation could smother. But it is requisite to recur to the internal affairs of the kingdom previous to that time. Jansenism was almost the only point to which discontent could rally, the only pretext for opposition. Fleury abolished the impost that had made his predecessor so unpopular: he diminished the *taille*, and made up the deficiency by new farming the fixed revenue; he brought the coinage to its just standard: and, in short, on subjects of finance the parliament had no cause of complaint. The policy of Fleury with respect to ecclesiastical affairs was not so unexceptionable. Though not extravagantly ambitious, the cardinal's hat was still the necessary complement of his dignity and power: to procure it, it was necessary to oblige the pope, which could only be done by persisting in the measure that the regent and Dubois had carried: this was, the condemnation of Jansenism, and the support of the bull *Unigênitus*.

The book of Quesnel, and the verbal dispute about grace, seemed little worthy of being dragged from the polemical into the political field. But the principle of Jansenism lay deeper; its doctrines went to render the national church in many respects independent of Rome, and, moreover, to free the consciences of men from the arbitrary will of their spiritual confessors, by establishing a code of morals, founded indeed on scripture, but superior to the glosses of its teachers. The Reformation was the first great attempt to shake off the authority of Rome: although successful, it was not without its blunders, its inconveniences, nay, its crimes; and, its first fervor over, there was little hope of its gaining proselytes, at least in France, where Calvinism, connected with rebellion, and spurning a hierarchy, excited disgust in the well-born, distrust in the ignoble. Still there was a tacit protest in the French mind against Rome and its usurpations. Jansenism was the expression of this protest; but so feeble was it, so timid and involved its aim, hidden in obscurity of words, that, when greater questions arose, it was swept away, and so erased, that unless closely examined it appears to be a mere logical dispute. Such, indeed, it might have been, and might have remained, had not the Jesuits set themselves in opposition to its doctrines, and moreover brought the royal authority into the quarrel. By a decree procured from Louis XIV., the abbaye of Port Royal des Champs, the retreat of Pascal and of Arnaud and of the Jansenists, was razed to the ground,—an empty piece of vengeance, that still excited a universal cry of indignation. Although Louis XIV. levelled their dwelling, he could not compel the parliament to register the papal bull pronouncing their condemnation. The gay regent and the unprincipled Dubois succeeded in this task, having exiled the parliament, and making this the price of their return.

Fleury, in return for his cardinal's hat, promised to support the anti-Jansenist decree. A certain bishop thought proper to publish a charge that savored of these independent doctrines: a kind of provincial council was summoned, under the presidency of Tencin, a noted high churchman; and the bishop was condemned and exiled. The parliament took up his quarrel, not as religionists, but as guardians of the laws. Another pretext for interference was given them by the pope, who, with misplaced zeal, chose this epoch for canonizing the famous Hildebrand, Gregory VII., the proud asserter of papal over royal supremacy. Fleury was obliged to have recourse to the presence of the king in a bed of justice to enforce the registry of these ecclesiastical decrees and bulls. The parliament, obeying at the instant, thought proper to protest on the morrow, drawing up resolutions which declared the temporal independent of the ecclesiastical authority, and asserted all external jurisdiction to be the exclusive province and right of the former. Irritated by the haste and distance of the king, and suspecting that the minister kept him perhaps in ignorance of what was passing, the members of the parliament proceeded to Marly to lay their remonstrances before the monarch. Never, perhaps, was court so shocked, not with the remonstrance, but with the breach of etiquette: "The parliament at Marly! the parliament at Marly!" was the astonished cry of the courtiers and of Fleury. They were too much astounded to be angry: the king, nevertheless, refused to see the judges, and they returned as they came.

In spite of their boldness, of the right on their side, seeing that they were in array for freedom of thought and of creed, the parliament felt that they stood alone, that the Parisian populace were no longer those of the *Fronde*, and that without some support they would succumb. An endeavor was therefore made to stir up the religious enthusiasm of the people. A certain Jansenist priest, named Paris, happening to die, the events of his exemplary life were written and printed. He was the curate of a populous parish, St. Medard. Crowds flocked to his tomb. As his biography enumerated many of his miracles whilst living, his relics could not have less power; and miracles were accordingly worked at his grave. The sick were cured too in the midst of convulsive fits, into which either fanaticism or hypocrisy cast them. This was a great triumph for the Jansenists. The sage Fleury took care not to meddle with the saint until his miracles had swelled to a number, and been degraded by abuse, so as to verge towards the ridiculous. He then attacked them with raillery, and at last ventured to shut up the cemetery. A wit wrote on the gates the well-known lines, in imitation of the royal edicts of prohibition,—

"De par le roi, défense à Dieu
De faire miracle en ce lieu."

There was no end to epigrams and *jeux d'esprit* upon the poor Jansenists and their miracle-worker. This appears to have been the commencement and the signal of those epigrammatic attacks upon religion, which became so much the mode, and which proved so effectual to destroy in the nation all reverence even for Christianity. It is singular that the

Jesuit party, aided by the pious Fleury, should have been the first to let loose the impious wit of the court and its lettered dependants. The comte de Maurepas, afterwards minister, and then an underling in office, distinguished himself on this occasion by the aptness and wit of his verses. The bishop of Arles published a pastoral charge, in which was a *chanson* or song against the parliament. When the church made use of such profane arms, it was no marvel to see the profane adopt them against the church. Voltaire conceived and wrote his poem of the "*Pucelle*" at this epoch.

A country must be very weak indeed that does not contain a numerous party ever anxious for war, for the sake of its chances and its glories. France above all countries abounds in such spirits: their ardor gave the pacific Fleury much trouble. He succeeded in quieting them for a time, until an event occurred which rendered the national voice too strong to be resisted. Stanislaus, father of Louis XV.'s queen, had been elected king of Poland through the influence of the celebrated Charles XII. of Sweden, then a conqueror and the arbiter of kingdoms. His fortune fell at Pultowa, and Russia in turn took advantage of her ascendency, dethroned Stanislaus, and caused Augustus of Saxony to be elected in his stead. Augustus died in 1733, and France instantly turned her views to reinstate Stanislaus. Even Fleury dared not be indifferent to the father-in-law of his monarch. The cardinal forgot at the call not only his indolence but his economy, and transmitted large sums to influence the Polish diet. They were scarcely needed. Stanislaus, who had penetrated into Poland and showed himself in its diet, was elected king.

Russia and Austria declared against him, in favor of the son of the late king Augustus, who was allied by marriage to the emperor. They supported the rights of their candidate by numerous armies, which overran and devastated Poland. Warsaw could make no resistance; and Stanislaus shut himself up in Dantzic. Fleury, in the mean time, dragged into a war for a quarrel, which he imagined ample bribes and negotiations would decide, began operations on a pitiful scale. He sent 1500 men by the Baltic to the relief of Dantzic, a mockery of support. In vain the Polish followers of Stanislaus displayed the utmost heroism in behalf of their sovereign. Dantzic, invested by an army, could not long hold out; nor could the generous citizens think of purchasing their own safety by the surrender of Stanislaus. The monarch resolved to rid them of this embarrassment by leaving the town, and making his escape through the army of besiegers. This he effected, after perils and sufferings that alone might arm a host of warriors in his cause.

Poland was too distant from France to receive effectual aid. Armies however were raised. One under mareschal Berwick, destined to act on the Rhine; the other, commanded by the veteran Villars, crossed the Alps, and in conjunction with the duke of Savoy, invaded Milan. These old generals of Louis XIV.'s wars, won merely the honor of dying in rms. Villars overran the duchy of Milan, the conquest of which satisfied his ally of Savoy, and the Austrians, unmoested, were enabled to rally and return to the offensive. Villars, struck with mortification as well as with years and fatigue, was confined to his couch, when tidings reached him that the duke of Berwick, having formed the siege of Philipsburg, was cut in two by a cannon-ball: "Ah!" said the dying Villars, "that man was always more fortunate than I." The capture of Philipsburg was the limit of French conquest on the Rhine. Prince Eugene was their antagonist, and, though weak in numbers, Austria having Spain and Turkey as well as France to contend with, he succeeded in checking all their attempts to advance.

The most important achievement of the war was effected with least forces and in an unexpected region. Don Carlos, that son of Philip V. by his second queen who had already succeeded to Parma, marched with a small army of Spaniards against Naples. The Austrians were little liked in this country, and a conspiracy in the capital opened the way for invasion. Visconti, the imperial viceroy, in vain endeavored to make a stand, at the head of the militia of the kingdom, which refused to second him. In a short time both Naples and Sicily passed from the power of the emperor into that of Don Carlos. In the north of Italy the struggle was more obstinate and less decisive. A battle took place near Parma, in June, 1734, betwixt the French, under the mareschals de Coigny and de Broglie, and the Austrians under Merci. The latter was slain leading his troops to the charge; his army was worsted but not routed. The prince of Wirtemberg took the command, and was able to give battle again in September at Guastalla. It was contested with equal fierceness and similar fortune. Wirtemberg was slain in the action. The French had the honor of the victory, but none of the fruits. The resistance f the vanquished paralyzed the success of the victors.

Cardinal Fleury now seized the first opportunity to treat. Austria found herself overmatched. In order to give Poland a king, she had exposed herself to the attacks of France and Spain, and had lost Naples and Milan, with little hope of recovering either. Still Russia promised effectual aid in the ensuing campaign, and England, despite of Walpole's pacific views, was shaken by the solicitation of her old ally, the emperor, by seeing Naples fallen as well as Spain to a Bourbon prince. The mutual jealousies of France and England were rising; but they were for the moment quelled. The acquisition of Naples by Don Carlos seemed compensation to Fleury for the ejection of Stanislaus from Poland. Negotiations began, and in 1735 a treaty or rather the preliminaries of a treaty were signed at Vienna. By this Naples and Sicily were transferred, as the fate of arms had already decided, from Austria to Don Carlos. He gave Parma in lieu to the emperor. Stanislaus gave up his claim to the crown of Poland, receiving Lorraine in its stead as an appanage during his life. The duke of Lorraine, heir of its ancient house, made an exchange of this his patrimony for the duchy of Tuscany, which he was to inherit after the last duke of the family of Medicis, whose death was imminent. The good fortune of the duke of Lorraine, hereafter grand duke of Tuscany, was owing to his projected marriage with Maria Theresa, daughter of the emperor. France, by this treaty, acquired the important province of Lorraine, which was to be incorporated with the kingdom after the death of Stanislaus; yet this acquisition, that does so much honor to Fleury's administration, was well-nigh lost by his diplomatic backwardness and modesty. It was Chauvelin, the chancellor, who insisted, against the cardinal's wish, for this cession.

Five years of peace now ensued for France. Her ardent abettors of war were satisfied. Not so those of similar temper in England, where national animosity was excited against the Spaniards on account of their commercial restrictions on the trade with South America, and of the cruelties with which they supported them. The same cry was raised against Walpole in one country as against Fleury in the other; and the English minister was driven into a war with Spain, as the latter had been compelled to hostilities against the emperor. The court of France became occupied in this interval with baser intrigues. Louis XV. hitherto had led a regular and domestic life, attached to his queen, to religious observances, to trifling and innocent amusements. His society was confined to a small knot of young courtiers, empty as himself, whom he admitted to partake of his *petits soupers* in the *petits appartemens.* The monarch, in affecting the pettiness and privacy of humbler life, sought variety and escape from the dullness of grandeur. Even here, however, Louis was tenacious of his dignity; nor did he allow any political influence to those who partook of his convivial pleasures. One or two boy nobles had once indeed endeavored to indispose the king against Fleury. The monarch betrayed them to his minister, as Louis XIII. might have done; but Fleury did not imitate Richelieu in his revenge. He merely sent the young conspirators away from court, stigmatizing the plot sufficiently by calling it that of the *marmousets* or monkeys.

The queen had borne many children to Louis. Her coldness, increased by overstrained religious feeling, alienated the monarch. The courtiers perceived it, and took advantage of this to thrust Louis into licentiousness. His natural timidity and regularity would have preserved him from those failings, into which lively passions had impelled Louis XIV. His successor received a mistress at the hands of the duc de Richelieu and his friends. This was madame du Mailly. To her succeeded more than one sister. But as these amours had little influence upon politics, a veil may be drawn over their scandal.

With the year 1740 opens a new scene for Europe: fresh personages start up; fresh interests absorb. The pacific humor of the last quarter of a century is universally scouted, and the appeal to arms heard and echoed on every side.• Walpole is shaken from his seat; his congenial friend Fleury sinks into the grave. A hero appears on the throne of Prussia; and a princess, no less heroic and intrepid, supports and wins her right to succeed to Austria's wide dominion. One effect of this quarrel was to interrupt the amity that had now existed since the peace of Utrecht betwixt France and England; the former eagerly grasping so favorable an opportunity for weakening the power of the empire, and England, already at war with Spain, flinging her support into the scale of Austria against the house of Bourbon.

Such is a summary view of the interests and jealousies in collision. The efforts of the emperor Charles VI. to secure the Austrian succession to his daughter, Maria Theresa, have been mentioned. Her rights he established by a law, called the *Pragmatic*, which Spain, France, and England had severally stipulated to support. France, however, entered into this solemn engagement with the same bad faith that had characterized her acquiescence in the treaties of partition respecting the Spanish succession. The emperor Charles died in October, 1740; and poor Maria Theresa, instead of finding the sovereigns of Europe true to their oaths and to her, found all, save England, rising in claims and hostilities against her.

Prussia first put forth menaces. Frederick II., afterwards the Great, was but a few months on the throne. His father, severe and economical, had prepared the grandeur of his successor, not only by filling his treasury and disciplining his armies, but by putting the prince's character to the rudest trials. Frederick's spirit received its heroic temper from misfortune. He now claimed Silesia, or a "good part of it," as the price of his neutrality. Maria Theresa treated with contempt the menace of a prince whose parent was raised out a few years since to his sovereign rank by her ancestor. Frederick, without further parley, marched into Silesia in the month of December. The Austrian army, under Neuperg, opposed him; and Frederick fought his first battle at Molwitz, in April, 1741. He was well-nigh routed. It was the first time that his army had been engaged, whilst the Austrian had never ceased to combat either on the side of Turkey or of France. Towards the close of the day, however, the Prussians recovered confidence, and Schwerin, Frederick's lieutenant, won the battle, whilst the king was already far gone in retreat from the field.

France had waited to see the result of Frederick's invasion. Fleury's prudence reined in the ardor of the court; but, after the victory of Molwitz, it was no longer possible to oppose the general wish to crush the house of Austria, and divide her possessions. The mareschal Belleisle, who shared with the duc de Richelieu the personal favor of Louis XV., was the promoter of these councils. France instantly declared for the elector of Bavaria, who aspired to the imperial crown. This prince was the son of him who had suffered for his alliance with France, having been driven from his dominions after the battle of Blenheim. This new emperor—for the gold and the influence of France procured his election—was, however, to yield Silesia to Prussia; another share of the imperial territory to the elector of Saxony; while France was to preserve whatever she might conquer on the frontier of Flanders. With these aims the armies of France and Bavaria advanced without opposition along the Danube, occupying Passau and menacing Vienna: whilst Maria Theresa, crushed in all save spirit by so many foes, made that touching appeal, which is so well known, to her Hungarian subjects. Presenting herself with her infant son in their assembled diet, she first swore to respect their independence, and then demanded their aid, in tones that her beauty and her tears rendered more persuasive. The swords of the Hungarian nobles flashed in air as their acclamations replied, "We will die for our sovereign Maria Theresa!"

The blunders of the French contributed even more than the zeal of her friends to raise the hopes of the Austrian princess. In the beginning of the century, Villars, with the old elector of Bavaria, had possessed the course of the Danube; the French mareschal proposed to march on Vienna, an advice not followed. The present elector of Bavaria was now precisely in the same position; and the young count de Saxe renewed the counsel of Villars. But the elector, or the emperor, for such he now was, was fearful lest he should be anticipated by some of his rivals in the conquest of Bohemia, and he accordingly marched with the French into that country. They met at first with success. Prague, the capital, was carried by surprise and assault, planned and executed by the count (afterwards mareschal) de Saxe. Egra was also taken. The French established themselves in Bohemia; but at the same time left Bavaria open to the Hungarians, by whom it was mercilessly ravaged.

A near view and acquaintance with his allies had somewhat disgusted Frederick of Prussia. He, who was despotic in his armies, could augur little effective co-operation from such men as De Broglie, Belleisle, and the Bavarian emperor, each of whom had his plans and his views, one despising the talents of the other. Frederick, therefore, availing himself of a favorable opportunity, engaged in a general action with the Austrians at Czaslau; and having defeated them, made peace with Maria Theresa, who was then glad to cede Silesia. The French were thus left to their own resources in Bohemia; where prince Charles, commanding the Austrians, and relieved from the hostilities of Prussia, soon shut them in Prague. Mareschal Maillebois was ordered to proceed to their succor with an army, but he not arriving, Belleisle was obliged to make his escape from Prague, and retreat with great celerity, though not without difficulty and loss; abandoning Bohemia and all his advantages. The emperor Charles, driven even from his electorate of Bavaria, and now without an army, took refuge in Frankfort.

In the midst of these reverses, produced by a war that he had opposed, died cardinal Fleury. He left no wealth, the noblest epitaph for the minister of a despotic government; for one who had succeeded Mazarin and Dubois; for one, too, who knew the value of economy, and who practised it for the good of the state. His political views, if not grand, were just. He was averse from breaking faith as to the Austrian succession; and was, perhaps, the only minister of his country whose aim was peace and internal prosperity, not external aggrandizement: but this his countrymen can never forgive him. They espy naught save want of spirit in his counsels; his friendship with England they construed into subserviency; and they principally censure him for allowing the French marine to fall into decay, as if peace was for ever to continue with the maritime powers. There may be some truth in these reproaches. Fleury left the yearly revenue producing 180,000,000, and this without capitation, tenth, or onerous *taille*. The interest of the debt absorbed but thirty of that sum. The noblesse hated his parsimony as much as his pacific measures: war was the harvest in which they gleaned honors and employ.

Great Britain at length stepped forth to succor Austria, in 1743. Her monarch proposed to imitate the famous march of Marlborough, to cross the Rhine, and, uniting with the imperialists, to force the French frontier of Lorraine and Alsace. The army, commanded by lord Stair, and encouraged by the presence of its king, George II. and the duke of Cumberland, advanced to join the prince of Lorraine. The French, under the mareschal de Noailles, were posted behind the Maine, the passages of which they preserved to prevent this junction. The river, before it reaches Frankfort, turns almost at right angles: the English imprudently marched along its right bank as far as Aschaffenburg, when they found that their enemies, in possession of the left, had it in their power to cross the river and cut off their supplies and reinforcements. It was necessary, therefore, to retrograde. They did so, and found their suspicions verified. The French had passed and occupied the village of Dettingen: the British were now under the necessity of attacking, a manifest disadvantage, as the foe in this case can make preparations for a formidable reception. Such were the tactics of the mareschal de Noailles. He drew up his troops with a ravine in front, across which the English must advance, and in passing which they must necessarily be disordered, and become, on issuing from it, an easy conquest to their enemies ready for the attack. To make this sure, Noailles had disposed his cannon to play upon the ravine.

All was ordered, when the mareschal de Noailles resolved to make use of the interval, ere the English arrived, and proceed in person to the other side of the river to hasten the passage of the rest of the army: no sooner, however, had the general departed on this quest, than his nephew, the duc de Grammont, anxious to win without delay the honor of the victory, broke through the order of Noailles, and gave the word to pass the ravine. His troops obeyed, and thus the French found themselves in the very position in which Noailles had thought to place the English. Their cannon was useless, whilst that of the British opened with effect. "They march, nevertheless," say the Memoirs of Noailles, referring to his soldiers; "they endure a furious discharge of shot, which disorders their ranks. Three times they rally: the household troops charge with more valor than constancy or order; the English present strong immovable masses, which send forth a continued murderous fire. In vain the duc de Chartres, now duc d'Orleans, the comte of Clermont, and the rest of the nobility, make the most prodigious efforts; there is no breaking the masses of the enemy: naught is left but retreat." Thus was lost the battle of Dettingen by the French. They fled across the Maine; and more activity on the part of their victors might have destroyed the army. George II. thought but of continuing his retreat. The French guards behaved very ill in this action, according to the dispatch of their general; but their fault was more than redeemed by the valor of other regiments.

Since the death of cardinal Fleury, Louis XV. resided chiefly at Choisy. He affected to imitate his great predecessor, in being his own minister; but the business of state was carried on by Chavigny, Maurepas, the D'Argensons, and cardinal Tencin. The greatest influence, however, was with the reigning mistress, the duchesse de Chateauroux, sister of madame de Mailly. She now emulated the conduct of Agnes Sorel, in inflaming the king's warlike ardor, and urging him to stimulate the French armies by his presence. Louis accordingly proceeded to Flanders to join the mareschal de Noailles, whilst Voltaire was sent to Berlin in order to induce the king of Prussia to resume hostilities. That monarch still hesitated; whilst prince Charles of Lorraine, taking advantage of the French retreat from Prague, and their defeat at Dettingen, penetrated into Alsace and punished France in her turn with invasion. Louis, on learning this, flew from Flanders towards the Rhine: he had reached Metz when a fever seized him, the consequence of fatigue and of intemperance. The monarch's illness speedily became alarming; and some of the more pious courtiers penetrating to his bedside, in despite of the gay duc de Richelieu, reminded Louis of the evil of his ways. The duchess of Chateauroux had attended him in his journey, and was now at Metz. Remorse and repentance seized on the monarch: the unfortunate mistress was discarded, insulted, and, but for the pity of Richelieu, could scarcely have found the means of escape. The queen repaired to Metz, and Louis asked her to forgive him. The whole kingdom was, meanwhile, in emotion and anxiety for the monarch's safety: the story of his repentance touched his people; and never was a more fervent or pathetic display of loyalty; the nation seemed but to have one thought, one prayer,—it was for the recovery of their sovereign. "What have I done to be so beloved?" asked Louis. His restoration to health was welcomed with more joy than would have been the most splendid victory.

Frederick of Prussia seemed to participate in this general admiration for the French king. He now came to his aid, invaded Bohemia, and, by his successes, recalled the imperialists from their invasion of Alsace. Frederick was in truth alarmed at the union of England, Holland, Sardinia, and Saxony, with Maria Theresa; and he chose the present moment to fling himself into the opposite scale, knowing how it would entitle him to the gratitude of France. "I am rejoiced," wrote Frederick at this time, "to replace Sweden, who used to be the favorite ally of France. Now, Sweden is a body without a soul; whilst I have a soul, and can show it." Frederick at the same time addressed Louis in a tone of frankness and superiority that must have startled the latter, recommending him to send a body of troops into Hanover, whilst another army pushed along the Danube, acting boldly on the offensive. The declaration of hostilities by Frederick was chivalric, but unfortunate. Mareschal Traun drove him from Bohemia with disgrace.

Louis in the mean time had returned to his capital. His first act was to recall his mistress, the duchess of Chateauroux, and to exile her enemies. But her triumph was short; death seized her ere she was well re-established in royal favor. In the commencement of 1745, the marriage of the dauphin with a princess of Spain was celebrated. It was at the fête given on this occasion that Louis first saw madame d'Etéoles, wife of a revenue contractor. She was of low origin, her family name being Poisson. She it was who, created duchesse de Pompadour, had the address to retain for such a length of time her influence over the French king, and through him over the fate of Europe.

Charles VII., emperor, and elector of Bavaria, died about this time. France transferred her support to his son; but the young elector, warned by his father's misfortunes, concluded a separate peace with Maria Theresa, and abandoned his pretension to the empire, on condition of being restored to the tranquil possession of Bavaria. Maria Theresa, by this submission, was enabled to obtain the imperial crown for her husband, formerly duke of Lorraine, now grand duke of Tuscany and emperor.

France, by this defection, being rendered unable to carry the war beyond the Rhine, turned her efforts towards the Netherlands. A large army, commanded by mareschal Saxe, and honored by the presence of both king and dauphin, laid siege to Tournay. The duke of Cumberland, who commanded an inferior force of English, Dutch, and Hanoverians, mustering little more than 50,000 men, whilst the French numbered 90,000, marched, nevertheless, to raise the siege. The remembrance of Dettingen, and a wish to rival Marlborough's victories, inspired him with this presumption. Mareschal Saxe advanced, leaving about 15,000 men to observe the siege, and took post at Fontenoy, his right wing resting on that village, his left in the wood of Barri, and his army drawn up in several lines across the interval. Not content with his superior force, the French mareschal covered the wood and Fontenoy with intrenchments and batteries, imitating the position and conduct of Villars at Malplaquet. The duke of Cumberland advanced to give battle on the 11th of May, the prince of Waldeck commanding the Dutch, on his left. The cannonade began, and its first victim was the duke of Grammont, the cause of the loss at Dettingen. The first attack was against Fontenoy, but the batteries repulsed the assailants three times. The duke then dispatched an officer to carry the wood of Barri; but there was no mastering either position. The English were thus exposed to the cross-fire from the right and left of the French. The duke of Cumberland resolved on the daring attempt to push on betwixt them towards the French centre. This he did, the entire force of the English infantry forming, as much from instinct and necessity as from order, into one solid mass or column. Unfortunately, neither the cavalry nor the Dutch could keep up with this attack; the interval between Fontenoy and the wood of Barri being so narrow that they must have fallen upon either of those two formidable positions. The columns of English therefore advanced alone, dragging their artillery: whole files were carried away as they passed between the French batteries; but, these passed, nothing could resist them. A pause of politeness took place as the guards of the rival nations approached each other. Salutations were made and returned. "Fire first, gentlemen of the French guards," cried the English officers. Nay, fire you first, Messieurs," replied their enemies. It came at last, and fatally. The French officers fell thick. Their lines were broken. Despite of the reputation of mareschal Saxe, and although he acted the part of an able general in his preparations for the battle, he was altogether wanting in its heat. His dying state—he was carried in a litter—might excuse this, but could not remedy it. The formidable column still advanced, the French charging it without effect in companies and squadrons. Saxe began to give orders for retreat. The king was already warned of his danger. The smallest aid of cavalry would at this moment have routed the panic-struck French, and secured the victory to the English; but the duke was without that indispensable instrument of victory, whilst the cumbrous columns, for want of it, saw victory before them, but dared not break up their mass to snatch it. Seeing the immobility of the English, Lally, who commanded the Irish brigade, exclaimed, "Why not bring the cannon of the reserve to bear upon them?" The duc de Richelieu caught up the thought, repeated and insisted on it to the king. Saxe approved. The few cannon, by enfilading the column, sufficed to scatter and make fearful breaches in it. The Irish brigade, composed of Catholic exiles, rushed upon their English enemies. The French rallied and returned to the attack, and the almost victorious column, defeated in its turn, was obliged to trace back its perilous path in disorder, leaving the battle-field, dearly purchased, in the possession of the French.

The capture of Ghent, Bruges, Ostend, and Oudenarde, followed the victory of Fontenoy. But it by no means relieved the king of Prussia, who, pressed by superior numbers, wrote to Louis, that the French conquests in Flanders were as useless to him as if they had been won in China. Frederick was piqued to see the armies of his ally strong and triumphant in Flanders and in Italy, where the king of Sardinia was beaten, and Milan taken by mareschal Maillebois, while the army on the Rhine was compelled, from its weakness, to act ingloriously on the defensive. The Prussian monarch expostulated against this kind of abandonment. Louis was affronted by the hero's frankness; and the friendship between France and Prussia subsided into coolness. Whilst the French ministry, therefore, turned their efforts to fit out the expedition which conveyed the pretender to Scotland, Frederick concluded a treaty with England, and prepared to force Austria to grant him peace anew. He won a victory at Friedland. It was not sufficiently decisive. But the conquest of Saxony, and the entry of the Prussian monarch into Dresden, despite the menaces of Russia, humbled the proud tone of Maria Theresa. She made peace, ceding Silesia to Frederick, who acknowledged her husband as emperor.

The early part of the campaign of 1746 was favorable to the French. The British were engaged at home against the pretender; both Brussels and Antwerp surrendered to mareschal Saxe. The empress, now, however, secure on the side of Prussia, made ample preparations, and dispatched two armies, one under prince Charles of Lorraine into Flanders, the other commanded by the prince of Lichtenstein to Italy. The latter, a young and talented commander, brought the united force of French and Spanish to action, under the walls of Placentia. The battle, which was fought in the month of June, was long and hotly contested, and terminated in so total a defeat, that the French were not only driven from the field, but obliged to evacuate the entire of Italy. The Austrians in Flanders were far from turning the scale of victory so speedily. Prince Charles of Lorraine was attacked near Liege, between that town and Maestricht, by mareschal Saxe. He was defeated, and obliged to retire behind the Meuse. This battle of Raucour was said not to have been decisive: but mareschal Saxe was satisfied to have repulsed the fresh army of Austrians, and retained his ample conquests of Flanders and Brabant. He had now advanced almost as far as Louis XIV., in his first memorable war. Holland was menaced in its vital territories. The isle of Zealand was threatened with invasion. The Dutch had recourse to the same measures which they had adopted in the preceding century. The prince of Orange was raised to sovereign power, and created hereditary stadtholder. In the mean time the duke of Cumberland arrived from the field of Culloden, to defend the ally of England against the mareschal de Saxe. Immense armies on either side seemed to promise a decisive campaign. Maestricht and Bergen-op-Zoom were the only two fortresses that held out against the French. In manœuvring to besiege the former town, the French came in front of their enemies advantageously posted at Lawfelt. It was now the turn of the duke of Cumberland to be intrenched and defended by cannon, whilst the mareschal Saxe attacked in close column. It was the day of Fontenoy reversed. The French, in their attacks upon Lawfelt, were thrice repulsed. The English cavalry, under Ligonier, advanced to the charge, drove through and routed them; when the French mareschal, anxious for the fate of the day, and forgetful of his infirmities, brought up his squadrons, and the English, too far advanced to retreat, and unsupported by their allies, were obliged to surrender. This decided the day. The village of Lawfelt was won. The duke of Cumberland retreated; he was worsted, but remained still strong enough to cover Maestricht. Mareschal Saxe, unable to besiege this town, sent Lowendahl to invest Bergen-op-Zoom, considered as impregnable. It was nevertheless taken by assault, after a month's siege.

These successes in Flanders were compensated by reverses in Italy. Genoa, it is true, had risen in insurrection against the Austrians, and driven them out. Boufflers, and after him the duc de Richelieu, aided by the populace, were enabled to preserve the town. But to Genoa was limited their footing on Italian soil. The imperialists even penetrated into Provence. And when the chevalier de Belleisle attempted to force the passes of the Alps, he was defeated at Exilles, and slain, with the greater part of his soldiers. By sea, the French lost almost their last ship of war. Their very coasts were insulted: and Port l'Orient, the seat of their East India trade, had almost capitulated to the English.

There was lassitude in the movements of each belligerent. France made frequent overtures for peace. Philip V. of Spain was dead; Ferdinand VI., his successor, was not inclined to spend the resources of his kingdom in order to procure his step-brother, Don Philip, a principality in Italy. To establish this prince, the brother of Don Carlos, in Parma, was the original pretext for Spain's joining in the war against the emperor. England was, perhaps, the country least pacifically inclined. Holland, however, in terror at the successes of the French in Flanders, used every influence and entreaty to ward off their danger by a peace. The allies were obstinate, seeing France now stand alone, whilst Russia was marching to their aid. In the spring of 1748, however, mareschal Saxe invested Maestricht: the prospect of this last fortress falling, rendered the enemies of France more inclined to listen to her overtures. Negotiations commenced; and when they did, it appeared as if no cause of difference had existed to produce so prolonged and calamitous a war. Hostilities ceased in May; and in October was signed the peace of Aix-la-Chapelle.

France made no demand. Her ambassador declared that his orders were to make peace not for a merchant but a king. Louis not only yielded all his conquests in Flanders, but allowed that stipulation, so disgraceful to the country, of rendering the port of Dunkirk useless, to be inserted. Savoy was given up to the king of Sardinia. In exchange for these, Don Philip of Spain was established in the duchy of Parma; Maria Theresa recovered Austrian Flanders; England, giving up Louisburg in North America, kept Acadia. Such was the peace of Aix-la-Chapelle; which, recompensing neither France nor England for their enormous expenditure of blood and treasure, at least achieved one aim of the latter, in preserving the unity of the Austrian dominion, establishing the heroic Maria Theresa on her throne, and thus preserving the due balance of power in the east of Europe.

CHAP. VIII.

1748—1774.

FROM THE PEACE OF AIX-LA-CHAPELLE TO THE DEATH OF LOUIS XV.

We have hitherto sailed down the stream of French history, from the obscure wilderness of its rise, through the rugged and picturesque gorges, the breaks and rapids of its middle course, to the wide majestic flow of the monarchy in its latter days. Embarked upon its tide, with calm around and before, we now begin to perceive that the current grows suddenly more rapid, and that, without any apparent or external cause, we are hurried along with a swiftness at once menacing and unaccountable. Although not within hearing, we are yet within the influence of the distant cataract.

The very men who lived in those days began to perceive the movement; not only the philosopher and reflecting man, but Louis XV. himself. "The monarchy is very old," said he, "but it will last my time:" a selfish remark, no doubt. But could he have stopped the current of its decline? And was not his conscious powerlessness, more than his selfishness, the prompter of his thought? His subjects, his compatriots, took precisely the same view: nor class nor individual knew whither they tended; but all were dissatisfied and ill at ease. A change was necessary, it was inevitable: the acts of every one—of king, of priest, of minister, of noble, of parliament, of writer—all henceforth worked to bring about and hasten this change. The king degraded royalty by his dissoluteness, and weakened it by his profusion. The minister, turning away from the task of internal administration in disgust, directed his views abroad, and sought to gild his day of triumph by the trophies of a war, undertaken under some idle pretext of supporting the balance of power. The noble. like the monarch, degraded his order, and showed himself pressing on the lower classes, not for any public end, but for his own private gratification. The legists defended the cause of religious liberty and their own independence, indeed, but did so selfishly and blindly. The writer flattered royalty and aristocracy, and, at this price, was allowed to attack religion, the court finding itself in opposition to the priesthood. The priesthood itself increased its odium as a privileged class, by its intemperance, its ignorance, its absurdity and its scandal.

In such a general abandonment of the ancient system, such a despair of supporting it, it is absurd to ascribe to any particular class the catastrophe in which the epoch ended. None set about revolutionizing *intentionally;* but each stirred when it found its place irksome; each, where and how it had the power. As the noblesse had proved malcontent at one time the magistracy at another, so now a new combination of so ciety, the lettered class, rebelled with better success, for universal sympathy supported them; and step the first was taken in revolution.

It has already been stated, that when all hostility against royal power ceased, the frowardness of opposition took refuge in Jansenism. This was in fact the second position taken up in France against sacerdotal tyranny: the first was Calvinism; its defeat has been recorded. And after it to resuscitate reform became impossible, because it must savor of Calvinism, which was hated as ignoble, as fanatical, as disloyal, and, above all, as past: for though zeal may innovate, it scorns mere imitation. Jansenism had not much more success: the base of its religious creed, at least, was narrow and sophistical; it suited legal heads, but was incomprehensible to the people. The third and last stand against papal supremacy was taken on the broad ground of infidelity; and the philosophers of the eighteenth century might plead that they were driven to this, as the last and only resource against the intolerance and tyranny of the priesthood.

The ecclesiastical power was, at the present epoch, the most prominent, the most felt; it was the vanguard of oppression. Not only was it guilty of those gross instances of injustice and crime, the breaking of Calas on the wheel, the execution of La Barre for pretended sacrilege,—enormities equal to those which sully the dark ages,—but it also wreaked its petty despotism in being the torment, the spy, and the bugbear of domestic and social life. This chapter will contain an account of its arrogant pretensions, and of that absurd and fatuous conduct which disgusted the whole kingdom with the very name and institution of religion. It united the most odious attributes of the police and the censorship, and it peculiarly galled that rising and active intellect which characterized the society of the capital, That society combined the aristocracies of talent and of birth; it had now become the *public;*—at least its representative. Voltaire, Rousseau, Diderot, D'Alembert, were far more the organs than the teachers of this society. In attacking the church they acted in self-defence, for that church was determined to allow them neither liberty of speech nor of writing; it presented itself as a wall against the advance of knowledge and of enlightenment. The heads of the church began the war, and put the creed, which they professed and represented, to the same risk that their usurped tyranny incurred. To separate the cause of religion from that of Catholicism had been tried by Huguenot and Jansenist, and they had both failed: the sole and unfortunate alternative that remained was to attack religion itself, to confound creed and hierarchy. That alternative was embraced. Infidelity reared its standard: Voltaire poured forth his volumes; the Encyclopédie appeared; Diderot, D'Alembert, Condillac, formed new principles of mental science and moral conduct independent of religion. Vain these were, indeed, and baseless, but novelty and the exigence of the moment gave them force. The philosophers conquered. We have to regret that triumph; inasmuch as the impiety that blend edwith the principles of freedom was one great cause of their bearing such bitter fruit, and being blighted by so sudden a decay. But, in the guilt of having caused that lamentable state of impiety and demoralization, the Catholic church and priesthood of France must share, at least in an equal degree with her philosophers and men of learning.

France was now governed by madame de Pompadour. She was certainly a woman of talent. The empire which she held over Louis XV., long after her charms had ceased to fascinate him, proves this. She bound him, as she says herself, "in the chains of habit." Her boudoir became the council-chamber, the ministers her creatures. The king was present at each determination, but was spared the trouble of either thinking or speaking. It was Pompadour who appointed generals and bishops, proposed laws and plans of campaigns. After a glorious victory, it is a complimentary letter from the mistress that we find coming to reward the triumph of the hero. This paramount influence the duchess of Pompadour had the art to wield, taking from the monarch merely that power which was irksome, and leaving him all the liberty that he could desire. Thus she had no womanish jealousy, and cared little to monopolize his heart. She permitted him even to form the disgraceful *parc-aux-cerfs*, as an establishment containing a royal seraglio was called. From the base and ineffable debauch of such a haunt, Louis would recur to the chamber of La Pompadour, for the more refined entertainments of conversation. The mistress was not a stranger to the intellectual movement, the new ideas, of the day. Voltaire was amongst those who paid court to her. His muse was oft invoked to celebrate her wit as well as beauty: and even a paragraph of grave history is devoted by him to her adulation. Montesquieu presented her with his "Esprit des Lois;" and Diderot begged her interference when the printing of the "Encyclopédie" was stopped. It is well known that she protected Quesnay, the founder of the sect of Political Economists. She introduced him even to the monarch, and contributed not a little to bring into notice these at once abstruse and practical studies. To the last she protected Quesnel, and was to him a faster friend than madame de Maintenon had proved to poor Racine.

La Pompadour, thus in connexion with the philosophers, naturally adopted their prominent ideas. These, as we have seen, were directed against the church. Accordingly, in 1749 appeared the edict of *mainmorte*, forbidding any new conventual establishments without royal permission; also incapacitating them from inheriting or acquiring any increase of territory. This law, taken by the learned from the English statute-book, was indeed called for at a time that the church possessed more than one third of the entire landed property of the kingdom. The royal tenth, called afterwards a twentieth, had begun to be levied during the war, and was now continued upon the privileged classes. The clergy made a stubborn resistance to the tax. Unfortunately, at this critical period, a prelate, of tenacious character and narrow intellect, was promoted to the important post of archbishop of Paris. In Christophe de Beaumont the Jesuits immediately found a stay and a firm support; and under the shadow of his power, and the instrumentality of his arm, they soon began to harass their enemies. A letter was written in this year (1749) from madame de Pompadour to the French ambassador at Rome, to the effect that he might procure the relics of some saint for the chapel of St. Cyr, but take care that the said dead saint should not have *two left legs*, as was the case with the last importation of the kind. The letter continues, "The clergy of France grow daily more turbulent. If they were masters, we should see the *dragonnades* of Louis XIV. renewed; but, thanks to heaven, our most Christian king is neither devotee nor persecutor: he has no authority over consciences, he says, and wants none—the good prince! As for me, I hate intolerant priests; and, were I a sovereign, would never persecute any save the persecutors."

Such were the sentiments of those in power, when the archbishop of Paris began his crusade against conscience. One should have thought that at such a time all believers should have united their efforts to ward off impiety. But no. it was against the latent and almost extinct sect of Jansenism that Christophe de Beaumont directed his blows. He invented billets of confession, which each person was obliged to take out from an orthodox ecclesiastic, swearing, at the same time, belief and submission to the bull *Unigenitus*. The archbishop ordered that no person unprovided with one of those billets of confession, should receive the sacraments or consolations of religion, or should be entitled to Christian burial. The consequence was, that some of the most pious inhabitants of the capital died without communicating, and were refused burial. Amongst them was the duke of Orleans, the devout son of the regent. His rank procured him burial, and previous absolution; but the almoner who was thus guilty of disobedience was excommunicated. These facts, that one might imagine to be taken from an ironical tale of Swift, are actual events of the eighteenth century. The parliament intervened in behalf of common-sense and justice, and decreed that the bull *Unigenitus* was no article of faith. The archbishop was obstinate. The priests resisted; and the altar, with the Lord's supper, awaiting communicants, was become universally the scene of scandal, of quarrel, of anathema, opposition, and abuse. These scenes were repeated through the whole kingdom; the dead remaining unburied, the mysteries of religion profaned; whilst the Jesuits, in addition to these acts of violence, recurred also to the weapons of the impious, and represented the Jansenists in farces and in caricatures.

At length the quarrel between the ecclesiastical and judicial powers reached a point at which one or other must succumb. The trick of a minister, D'Argenson, turned the court against the parliaments. A sick nun was refused the sacraments by a curate. The parliament condemned the latter. The archbishop interfered, and was condemned too. D'Argenson then came, and carried off the Jansenist nun, who was still alive, by a *lettre de cachet*. The parliament was incensed at this, turned its resentment from the clergy to the ministry, and made remonstrances against illegal imprisonment and *lettres de cachet*. This threw the royal power instantly into the scale of the Jesuits. Hitherto the court was inclined against the clergy. "The king is *ennuied* like every one else," wrote madame de Pompadour; "the quarrels of parliament and clergy torment him. The administration does every thing to bring them to an agreement, but the clergy refuse to retreat a single step. Yet I cannot think their billets of confession so necessary, or that the soul of an honest man would be driven from the divine presence for want of one. On the contrary, I think this priesthood for the most part to be composed of vain, ambitious men, bad subjects of the king, and worse servants of God. But their credit is unfortunately so great, tha we must respect them. The king feels that the parliament is supporting the rights of his crown against the clergy; nevertheless he is compelled to punish his friends and caress his enemies." According to this policy, the chiefs of the parliament were taken and sent to different prisons. This, however, was not decided without a struggle in the ministry. Machault, the finance-minister, was for the parliament, as D'Argenson was for the clergy. The opinions of the latter prevailed, through means of the manœuvre mentioned; but he was unable to complete his plan. This was, to substitute a new court for that consisting of the imprisoned members; but no suitor nor advocate would plead. The remaining courts would not admit of such a menacing usurpation. The *châtelet*, or police-court, intrusted with the execution of condemnation, refused to act, or even to execute a criminal. An accommodation became indispensable. The imprisoned members were allowed to return; silence was imposed upon the clergy as to these disputed matters of faith; and the only point which they gained was the transferring of their enemy, Machault, from the department of finance, in which they had most dread of him, to that of marine affairs. This kind of treaty took place in 1754, on the occasion of the dauphiness being confined of her second son. This child was afterwards Louis XVI.

Such were the public events that filled up the interval of peace betwixt 1748 and 1755. Feats still more important than these took place in the publication of the first volumes of the "Encyclopédie," and of the "Esprit des Lois." The intellect of the middle classes began to flourish, and to cover, like the ivy, with its verdant honors, the walls and buttresses of the social edifice, whilst the high towers and battlements were falling to decay. The finances were in a state of disorder of which no description can convey an adequate notion. Louis XV., in drawing on the treasury for those infamous pleasures, supposed to have cost a hundred millions of livres, blushed to specify the name or the deed; and he established the pernicious custom of drawing for sums without any mention of the purpose to which they were to be applied. This suited but too well the prodigal greediness of the mistress and the courtiers. The treasury was drained in peace more recklessly than even in war; and the finance-minister could only discover the amount of expenditure, without any knowledge of its items and subdivisions. Madame Pompadour in vain thought to compensate for her profusion, by what she considered useful establishments, such as manufactories and public buildings to encourage art. Some laudable efforts, too, were made to correct flagrant abuses. The edict of *mainmorte* was one; another, allowing a free trade in grain, shows the influence already acquired by the economists.

War now came to distract attention from the internal state and administration of the kingdom. It may be said, that the governments of Europe were of pacific inclinations, whilst the people of each nation showed on the contrary a warlike spirit. The French especially betrayed an impatience of what they esteemed the pusillanimity of their government. The peace of Aix-la-Chapelle was universally stigmatized as inglorious, because it did not add new territories to France. Those in power, however, had ample materials for judging how dearly Louis XIV. had paid for his conquests, and they were prepared to make great sacrifices to preserve peace. In England the court party entertained the same peaceful sentiments, so wise in their principle. But the opposition, headed by Pitt, and supported by popular clamor, demanded the excitement of war, the glories of triumphs and trophies. The great and ignominious sacrifice which France had made to English friendship, the arresting and expelling the pretender from her dominions, was forgotten. The instances of national collision now taking place abroad, were exaggerated with premeditated hostility. Each country accuses its antagonist as the aggressor.

In the East Indies, the rivalry of France and England dated from the preceding war. Dupleix, governor of Pondicherry, an ambitious, turbulent, ostentatious man, never ceased to intrigue with the native powers, and with the court of the Mogul, to extend his country's territories and influence. The English naturally intrigued and armed against him; and war was carried on betwixt him and Clive, whilst the respective nations remained at peace at home. In this instance the French government displayed a spirit of fairness and even backwardness. They disowned and recalled Dupleix, to the indignation of their countrymen, and even of their historians, who flatter themselves that, despite their naval inferiority, they might yet have disputed the empire of the East.

In North America arose a more serious cause of quarrel. The French possessed Canada and Louisiana, one commanding the mouth of the St. Lawrence, the other that of the Mississippi. The intervening territory was occupied by the English colonists. The French aimed at possessing themselves of the whole course of those rivers and of the Ohio, which almost joins them; thus inclosing British America within a long frontier line of posts, and, consequently, excluding her from the rest of the continent. Such pretensions were untenable from the nature of things, even if treaties favored them, which they did not. To draw thus a narrow line across the whole extent of a continent, that line itself unoccupied except by stray forts, and these too, for the most part, in embryo, not in being; to draw this around a vast and peopled region, can only be compared in arrogance to the act of the Roman ambassador, marking around the foreign potentate a line in the sand, and daring him to step beyond its magic circle. The only surprise is, to see the French ministry, so forbearing in Europe, risking war upon such unsupportable claims in America. But the science of political geography was not well understood in these days.

The limits betwixt Canada and Nova Scotia, the latter having been ceded to England by the last treaty, were not accurately defined. The officers of each nation, participating little in the moderation of their governments, proceeded to extremities. A French captain was slain. Reprisals followed. Braddock attacked Fort Du Quesne on the Ohio, but was defeated by the French and the Indians,* whose alliance they had hired. England, on her side, declared war by capturing all the merchant vessels of her rival. Whilst hostilities thus commenced in 1755 betwixt France and England, Europe was astounded by the dreadful earthquake at Lisbon. Twenty thousand inhabitants of that town are said to have fallen victims to the catastrophe.

Such were now the bonds of interest and alliance of the different states, that the quarrel betwixt any led inevitably to a general war. Maria Theresa was still dissatisfied with the loss of Silesia. Naught could reconcile her to the king of Prussia. In this hatred she not only forgot the ancient enmity of the house of Austria against France, but also the deep obligations of that house to England, which had more than once saved it from destruction. England esteemed the empress fortunate to have inherited her wide dominions at the price of a single province. This province, Silesia, she could never hope to recover by the aid of England. She therefore turned towards France, and, both by her own letter and the exertions of her ambassador Kaunitz, endeavored to knit the bonds of friendship and alliance betwixt France and Austria. She urged, that the great states of Europe ought to unite to keep down the lesser ones. Shall an elector of Hanover, of Brandenburg, or a duke of Savoy, thwart and despoil us, the rulers

* Madame de Pompadour expresses herself with delight at the alliance with the Indians. "Quoique je n'approuve pas qu'on mange les morts cependant il ne faut pas se quereller avec ces honnêtes gens pour des bagatelles."

of the most ancient monarchies? Maria Theresa even stooped to address madame de Pompadour as a dear friend and cousin. Louis XV. was not ill inclined to Austria. He had a jealous feeling towards Frederick, personal as well as political. The rhymes and sarcasms of the royal wit of Sans Souci galled the French monarch and his mistress; whilst his abandonment of France twice during the war gave them more legitimate cause of dissatisfaction. Frederick, in the mean time, alarmed, and well aware of the storm which menaced, concluded a defensive alliance with England. England sought in this alliance the security of Hanover: Frederick aimed at neutralizing the power of Russia, then linked to England. Austria and France, learning this, hesitated no longer, and the treaty was signed betwixt them in May, 1756.

The French commenced the war by an expedition against the island of Minorca, then in possession of the English. The duc de Richelieu was the commander. He effected a landing, and soon inclosed the English, whose force was very insufficient for defence, in Fort St. Philip. The British fleet soon arrived under admiral Byng. La Galissonière, the French admiral, had a squadron somewhat superior. In a partial action that took place betwixt them, the hesitation or incapacity of Byng would not allow him to conquer. He retreated, or was driven from those seas; an abandonment which the unfortunate admiral paid with his life. Richelieu, unmolested, pressed the siege of fort St. Philip with increased vigor Given to intemperance himself, he found it difficult to preserve his soldiers from the same excess, until he ordered that none should have the honor of mounting the breach that transgressed the rules of sobriety. This delicate appeal to the soldier's honor had effect. None were found for the future guilty of excess. The fort surrendered; and the French were in raptures at their conquest of the important island, and their advantage over a British fleet.

The king of Prussia, however, was the most menaced. He had appeased the enmity of Russia by an alliance with England. That power was preparing an army on his eastern frontier, whilst Austria, from the south, had gathered all her strength on the borders of Silesia and Bohemia. Saxony, too, was secretly in the league against him. Frederick, resolving to anticipate rather than await his enemies, entered Saxony in the autumn. The army of the elector, who was also king of Poland, unable to maintain the open field, kept in a strongly intrenched camp at Pirna, on the Elbe. The king of Prussia after having taken possession of Dresden, invested this camp defeated the Austrians under Brown who marched to its relief·

and obliged the entire Saxon army to surrender to him as prisoners of war. Thus gallantly opened, on the part of Frederick, the celebrated Seven Years' War.

Early in January, 1757, as Louis XV. was proceeding to enter his carriage from the palace of Versailles, a man advanced and stabbed him in the side with a penknife. "There is the man who struck me," said Louis: "take him, and do him no harm." The wound was slight; but as the knife might be poisoned, the whole court was in alarm, and Louis himself not least. The madman, who had made this foolish attempt, was named Damiens. The keeper of the seals seized him, conveyed him to a chamber of the palace, and there causing a pair of pincers to be heated, the chief officer of justice began by torturing the criminal. What was to be supposed the death-bed of the monarch, was immediately surrounded by intrigue. Machault and D'Argenson, though mutual enemies, united in working on the king's conscience, with a view to exile madame de Pompadour. An order was sent her to retire from court. But the wound was no sooner found to be insignificant, than the mistress was recalled, and the two ministers sacrificed to her. Both were exiled. As to Damiens, his crime seems to have proceeded from no deeper cause than that itch for action and notoriety, the extreme of which the sane find it so difficult to comprehend. In the choice of a victim he was, however, guided by the popular odium against the monarch, which was great. The Parisian populace, who had offered up prayers for his recovery at Metz, were not long since persuaded that children were stolen and slain to afford baths of blood, calculated to renovate the exhausted frame of the royal debauchee. Louis never showed himself in his capital. Damiens muttered and scribbled several names; and, with a glimmering instinct, sought to give reason and respectability to his crime by associating it with the cause of the parliament and Jansenism. The incoherent ravings and confessions of this crazy being, extracted from him partly by torture, filled the court and kingdom with suspicions, and greatly increased the animosities on both sides.

The accommodation brought about between parliament and clergy did not produce peace. The archbishop De Beaumont took the first opportunity to renew his refusal of the sacraments. The king sent the duc de Richelieu to him to remonstrate upon his absurd zeal. "My conscience," replied the bishop, "can allow of no accommodation." "Your conscience. retorted the witty duke, "is a dark lantern, that enlightens no one save yourself." The archbishop was exiled to his country seat by the king's order. The parliament condemned and fined the bishop of Orleans for refusing the sacraments, and even sold his furniture to pay the fine. The old scandal was renewed throughout the kingdom. The clergy were, however, obliged to find some less extreme mode of acting against the Jansenists. They did away with the necessity of billets of confession, but demanded preliminaries tantamount, such as the name of each person's confessor, and the right of each curate to make domiciliary visits to learn this. The court consented to the plan. The parliament was inexorable as ever: and the Jesuits again succeeded in kindling a quarrel between king and parliament, during which the clergy were forgotten, or left in possession of their prerogatives. Louis, in order to subdue the magistracy, had recourse to a scheme which Francis I. had before attempted without success. This was to attribute to the great council of state the same privilege and authority as that wielded by the parliament. The latter summoned the peers to join them in an assembly. The king forbade them to attend. In the midst of those differences arose the necessity of new taxes to support the war. The monarch came to register them in a bed of justice. The morrow brought remonstrances from the parliament against the clergy and against the taxes. Louis in anger imprisoned the refractory members. The struggle between the legists and the Jesuits seemed to be, which should first wear out the patience of the monarch. The legists vanquished, through the support of madame de Pompadour, and of one of her counsellors, the count de Stainville, afterwards duc de Choiseul.

Notwithstanding her conquest of Minorca, France was aware that her colonies must fall before the maritime superiority of England: it therefore behoved her to occupy the continental dominions of the king of that country. An army was sent against Hanover, commanded by the mareschal D'Etrées. The duke of Cumberland levied a German force to oppose it; but being far inferior in numbers, he retired step by step before the French, allowing them to cross the Rhine, and even the Weser, which river forms the natural defence of Hanover. The king of Prussia, England's ally, had begun the campaign with the invasion of Bohemia, where he at first established himself by winning the celebrated and sanguinary battle of Prague over the Austrians under prince Charles of Lorraine; but seeking to follow up his advantage, Frederick experienced in the following month a severe check, being defeated by mareschal Daun at Kolin. At the same time D'Etrées was pressing the duke of Cumberland, who at length made a stand, strongly posted, however, and intrenched between Hameln and Hastenbach, near the Weser. It was the lieutenants rather than the generals of both armies that were destined to distinguish themselves. Chevert attacked the duke's left, drove it from its intrenchments and cannon, and pushed on; Maillebois, who was to support him, hesitated: prince Ferdinand of Brunswick seized the opportunity, marched his division between Chevert and the French, and charged the latter, so as to put them in disorder. Chevert, however, had precisely the same success against the duke, who was the first to sound a retreat. D'Etrées was about to issue the same order to his troops, when he observed the enemy retiring, and became thus informed of Chevert's success. The duke of Cumberland, after this affair, was obliged to abandon Hanover. The mareschal de Richelieu arrived on the following day to supersede D'Etrées, and under him the French continued their pursuit of the Hanoverian army, plundering and levying merciless contributions on the unfortunate electorate. Richelieu was called *father Maraude* by his soldiers. The duke sought to retire to Stade: he hoped, late in the season as it then was, to be able to hold out in that marshy country near the mouth of the Elbe, which is impracticable for military operations: but Richelieu's activity deprived him of this resource. The duke of Cumberland was obliged to sign the capitulation of Kloster-Seven, called from a convent of that name, which was the head-quarters of the French.

This disgraceful capitulation, which abandoned Hanover to the French, and left the Prussian dominions exposed to their inroad, would have reduced any prince except the great Frederick, to despair. Deserted by his only ally, all Europe was in arms against him. Russia advanced from the east, Austria, Poland, Saxony, united their forces; whilst a German army, called that of the Circles, headed by Soubise and strengthened by 30,000 French, menaced him from the south-west. The enemy occupied his capital, Berlin, from which the royal family had escaped to Magdeburg. In this extremity Frederick endeavored to negotiate with Richelieu: he flattered the duke; upbraided him for counteracting the policy of his great-uncle, the celebrated cardinal, by raising up the power of Austria; and besought him, in covert terms, to oppose La Pompadour in her fatal obsequiousness to the empress. These attempts had the good effect of amusing Richelieu and paralyzing his activity. Frederick was not blind to the critical state of his affairs: full of classic studies, and recurring, unfortunately, to those rather than to religion for consolation, he contemplated the necessity of perishing by his own hand, if not in the battle-field. To die with dignity was his thought, his Roman thought—

> "Pour moi, menacé du naufrage
> Je dois, en affrontant l'orage,
> Penser, vivre, et mourir en roi—"

"to think, to live, and die like a king," was his noble determination. Twenty thousand men were all that he could muster: with these Frederick resolved to fight the united army of French and Germans commanded by the prince of Soubise and the prince of Hilburghausen: they numbered upwards of 50,000 men. Despite of this inferiority they dreaded Frederick, and retreated from Leipzig at his approach, crossing the Saale: he passed it after them, and, coming in sight, hesitated: the opportunity was not favorable. The Prussian monarch kept his army hidden, as it were, in the low village of Rosbach, the heights around which, covered with batteries, served at once to defend his position and conceal his movements. The Germans and French, gathering audacity from the king's inaction, hovered round him, marching along his flank, and menacing an attack. It was the morning of the 5th of November: Frederick spent it in reconnoitring the enemy. It was not till the afternoon that he gave his orders; gathering the greater part of his troops on one point, on his left, and concealing the movement by the inequality of the ground, as well as by his tents, which he left pitched. Ere Soubise or Hilburghausen could make a corresponding movement, the Prussians broke through all before them on the point of attack; and the rest of the confederate army, seeing its flank laid bare, turned and fled. So simple was the decisive battle of Rosbach,* that retrieved the fortunes of Prussia. On the same day, the 5th of the following month, Frederick, who had marched into Silesia, defeated the Austrians at Lissa, and recovered his ancient superiority in despite of his numerous enemies.

In the mean time the duke of Richelieu, having broken so far through the terms of capitulation at Kloster-Seven as to seek to disarm the Hanoverian troops, which by that agreement were to remain quiet, indeed, but not to lose their arms, found those vanquished enemies start up afresh. Their new leader, prince Ferdinand of Brunswick, far surpassing the duke of Cumberland in military talent, was now able to hold Richelieu in check. The English ministry, roused by the spirit of the elder Pitt, made every effort to second her gal

* The field of Rosbach is near those of Jena, of Lutzen, and of Leipzig. The banks of the Saale are fully immortalized by carnage.

lant ally: a body of English troops reinforced the Hanoverian army, and the next campaign seemed to promise revenge for the duke of Cumberland's defeat.

In the beginning of the year 1758, Richelieu was superseded in his command by the prince de Clermont, who being at the same time abbot of St. Germain des Près, was called the general of the Benedictines. Under him the French commenced their retreat from Hanover. Prince Ferdinand precipitated this retrograde movement by anticipating their arrival on the Weser: he attacked and took Minden. In May, the French were already behind the Rhine, shamefully routed without even the honor of fighting, and leaving upwards of 10,000 prisoners in the hands of the enemy. Prince Ferdinand soon passed that river. The French general purposed to continue his retreat towards France, when the indignation and wounded pride of his officers obliged him to await the attack of the prince at Crevelt in the duchy of Cleves. There the count of St. Germain offered a gallant resistance to the enemy; it might have been a successful one, when the comte de Clermont gave abrupt orders to retreat, and abandoned his lieutenant. The French left 7000 dead on the field, and with them all hopes of retrieving the disasters of the campaign.

It was at this time that the dauphin, touched by the reverses of the French armies, demanded to put himself at the head of one of them. This being refused, he recommended peace, as a fitting measure. He was a pious prince, and of an exemplary life, but priest-ridden. The Jesuits placed great hopes in him, and considered him as the head of their party. Louis XV. was not a little jealous of the dauphin; and madame de Pompadour shared in this sentiment. Both felt themselves tacitly censured by the almost puritanic strictness of the prince's court. The dauphin being now for peace, and opposed to the Austrian alliance, La Pompadour held firm in her friendship to the empress and in hatred to the king of Prussia. Yet at this juncture, the very diplomatist who had counselled and concluded the treaty with Maria Theresa; the cardinal de Bernis, a creature too of the mistress, thought fit to oppose his conviction to her obstinacy, and speak in opposition to the war. La Pompadour was positive. Bernis was disgraced; and Choiseul became secretary of state in his stead. The new minister, though too sage not to perceive the folly of persisting in a war from whence so little was to be gained, paid, nevertheless, the price of his elevation by renewing the treaty with Austria, and making fresh preparations for carrying on the war.

Whilst the king of Prussia, with unchanged courage and

talent, but with most uncertain fortune, was making head against his enemies, the French army was mustered near Frankfort in the spring of 1759. Prince Ferdinand of Brunswick began the campaign by attacking it at Bergham, but was repulsed by the mareschal de Broglie. The slightest success then filled the French with audacity, and impelled them to advance boldly on the offensive, whilst the least check was apt to precipitate them into a contrary extreme. They now drove the prince of Brunswick before them, and reached once more the banks of the Weser. Minden was taken; and the inhabitants of Hanover began to look forward to fall again into the power of the French. Prince Ferdinand rallied his forces, however, and took post near Minden, putting an isolated column in advance to entice and deceive his enemies. The mareschal de Contades marched, on the 1st of August, to attack this body, placing his cavalry in the centre, and his foot upon the wings. The French attribute to this disposition the loss of the day, their horse being swept away and routed by the batteries which prince Ferdinand had prepared, whilst the infantry, disordered by its defeat, were unable to act with effect, and were driven from the field. The right wing of prince Ferdinand did not advance to complete the victory, as he had ordered. The general blamed lord George Sackville, who commanded it, obliquely censuring him in his dispatches, by observing, that, had the marquess of Granby been in the place of lord George, the battle could not have failed to be much more decisive. The loss of the French was severe; amongst their colonels slain at the affair of Minden was the marquis de la Fayette, a noble of an ancient family. He left his marchioness, a lady of the house of Lusignan, pregnant. This posthumous child is the La Fayette of the revolution, and of the present day.

This year proved most unfortunate to the French. Hitherto the English fleets had more insulted than harmed them. They had made frequent descents, at Rochefort, at Saint Maloes and at Cherbourg, causing damage, indeed, and bearing away trophies, but reaping no advantage, whilst it deepened the generous rivalry of the hostile nations into bitter and inveterate hatred. Pitt brought vigor and largeness of purpose to the British war-councils; and France now saw her fleets destroyed, and her colonies fall one by one. Admiral Boscawen fought La Clue near the Straits of Gibraltar, took two men-of-war, and burnt several others. In the same season, Hawke engaged, or rather pursued, the Brest fleet under Conflans, who took perilous shelter from his enemy amongst the shoals and rocks of the coast; he run his own vessel aground and burned it: few of the French ships escaped the gallant Hawke, who in this day annihilated the remains of the French maritime power. The fate of Canada was about the same time decided in that action when Wolfe fell in the achievement of victory, bequeathing Quebec, and the wide provinces of which it is the capital, to the possession of his country.

Notwithstanding the defeat of Minden, the duke de Broglie was enabled to keep his positions in the countries of Hesse and Cleves. Prince Ferdinand of Brunswick endeavored generously to put forward his nephew, the young hereditary prince. But neither birth nor favor can make a general. The French defeated him near Cassel. The young commander was then sent against the town of Wesel, but here too he was repulsed by the marquis de Castries. It was in this campaign that the chevalier d'Assas, whilst in advance of his regiment, fell alone in an ambuscade. "If you speak a word, you die," cried the enemy, whose success depended upon being yet undiscovered. "To aid! here is the enemy, Auvergne," cried the gallant young officer, calling and warning his regiment, whilst he received his death-shot on the instant for his heroism.

The struggle of the rival nations for superiority in the East Indies was this year decided. Count Lally, the Irish officer to whom the victory of Fontenoy was chiefly owing, had succeeded to the command as well as to the activity and talents of Dupleix. He had worsted and harassed the English, and had even laid siege to Madras. In Coote, who now commanded the British, he found a countryman and a triumphant rival. Lally was worsted in turn, and besieged in Pondicherry, which was taken in the early part of 1761. Lally was a zealous soldier, but an overbearing and despotic governor. His conduct excited powerful enmity. He cared not on whom his censure fell; whether on the ministry, the court, or the very country for which he fought. Accused of causing the loss of Pondicherry, he repaired to Paris and faced his accusers. Committed to the Bastile, pursued by the calumnies of the French India Company, and the populace who joined them, the unfortunate Lally was condemned to lose his head. So much was his ferocious temper dreaded, that a gag was placed in his mouth as he was led to execution. So iniquitous a judgment proves how unfit the parliament was to exercise even judicial functions, much less the legislative authority which it claimed.

The duc de Choiseul in the mean time sought fresh support, and was happy enough to secure it by an alliance with

Spain. The present king of that country was Charles III., formerly known to us as that Don Carlos, to whom Naples was adjudged. Betwixt him and France was concluded the family compact, by which the houses of Bourbon promised mutual aid. It was an unfortunate act for Spain, whose colonies of Cuba and Manilla, with her ships of war and commerce, fell at once into the hands of England. In short, had France or her government been bribed to enrich and afford triumphs to Great Britain, she could scarcely have adopted other measures, or persisted in policy more pernicious. She now lost Guadaloupe and Martinique, every colony almost and foot of earth beyond her continental realm. Even Belleisle on her own coast was captured. When one country had naught left to lose, and the other little to win, the overthrow of Pitt, and the rise of lord Bute's influence, consequent upon the death of George II. and the accession of his grandson, opened the way for peace. It was signed at Paris in February, 1763. France ceded Canada and Cape Breton. The Mississippi was declared to be the boundary betwixt the colonies of the respective nations; New-Orleans, however, on its left bank, adhering to Louisiana. In India, property and territories were restored to their ancient limits; but the French were to send thither no more troops. Guadaloupe and Martinique were restored; Grenada kept by the British, who at the same time appropriated St. Vincent's, Dominica, and Tobago. Senegal was also ceded to them, and Minorca restored. The demolition of the port of Dunkirk was to be completed, and an English commissioner to oversee the execution of this article. Peace could scarcely have been rendered more disgraceful to France, and yet she signed it, so pusillanimous was her government, so exhausted her finances, so spiritless and disorganized were her armies. The nation, proudly susceptible, deeply felt the humiliation. They attributed it not to their own want of courage or talent, or resources, but to the imbecility of their government, and fundamentally to the vice of its constitution. Whatever of loyalty, or of ancient attachment to despotic rule, still lingered in the country, evaporated with the national honor on witnessing this disgraceful treaty. As religion had lost its hold over French minds by the absurd conduct and misrule of its chief, so did royalty. Both fell as much from mismanagement as from the arguments or attacks of enemies. Facts and not words produce ultimate effects, and decide the opinions of the many; and governments, like individuals, gain solidity and general esteem, much more by their achievements and fortunes, than by the pleas of birth right or good intentions.

Almost simultaneously with this treaty of Pa is, that betwixt Austria and Prussia was signed at Hubertburg. Frederick still held the much-contested Silesia. Far more than a million of men had been sacrificed in vain. The frontier betwixt Austria and Prussia remained the same. Maria Theresa had reaped less advantage from the alliance of France than she formerly found in the friendship of England. The glory of the war chiefly remained with Frederick, who, through an unexampled course of victories and reverses, still preserved the character of great. Perhaps the most astonishing reflection is, that the Prussian monarch ruled over not more than four millions of subjects, a population that constitutes but a very secondary state. Yet out of this he raised armies and funds to combat at once France, Germany, Poland, and Russia. Bonaparte effected wonders with ample means; but when reduced to play the forlorn game of Frederick against united Europe, the great French captain fell, the Prussian lived and died a king.

Although lost in the noise and events of foreign war, the under-plot of domestic politics, the struggle betwixt the Jesuits and high-churchmen on the one side, and the parliament, the men of letters and the public voice on the other, was continued with unabated inveteracy. The sovereign interfered from time to time in these disputes, through the influence of La Pompadour, who from her life and station, as well as from her liberality, was opposed to the church party and the dauphin. The clergy were censured, and the prelates exiled. The opposition of the parliament, however, against papal and sacerdotal usurpation, was confounded with that which it offered to taxes and fiscal edicts; and when this latter species of frowardness became troublesome, the court was compelled to punish the magistrates, and give an apparent triumph to the high church. Historians have not sufficiently explained and dwelt upon the general resistance of the magistracy to Louis XV., and which, not confined to the capital, but spread all over France, amounted almost to rebellion. This resistance was most considerable in the *pas d'états*, or those provinces which had preserved the privilege of holding provincial assemblies or states, for there the parliament could with greater plausibility uphold their principle of representing in their own body the commons, or *tiers état*. A letter of De Sévigné fully describes what a mere ceremony the assembly of the states of Britany was in the reign of Louis XIV. Yet now we find them affecting all the rights of a representative body; the Breton parliament claiming the same rights during the recess of the state. Languedoc was equally bold, equally froward. In short, there was a near approach made to a federal system in France during the latter years of Louis XV.

This menaced encroachment of the parliaments upon the sovereign power was interrupted, in the first place, by the minister Choiseul, who took the part of the legists, and who adroitly made them desist from such pretensions by allowing them a complete triumph over their immediate enemics, the clergy. The duc de Choiseul was an exception to the long succession of ministerial mediocrity. Extremely ugly, his conversation and address soon removed the disagreeable impression made by his appearance. Though bred in diplomacy, he was vivacious, quick-spirited, strong-willed, and impetuous; captivating by a frank straight-forward manner. He had the boldness, the nationality, the independence, of the first Pitt. In the open struggles and on the public stage of a representative government, he would have still more resembled that great statesman; but at a despotic court, supremely governed by the monarch's mistress, talents for intrigue necessarily filled the place of eloquence, and suppleness that of honesty. Such was the minister.

The Jesuits, instituted to support sacerdotal authority, proved the principal cause of its overthrow. Their ambition, their corporate spirit, excited fear and envy; their corruption of morality's plainest principles made them unpopular; and, finally, their efforts to master the throne excited a league of sovereign princes against them, which now produced their complete destruction. In their peril they clung around the church; any blow directed against them, especially those which ridicule aimed, fell upon it. Religion was at once sullied by their alliance, and weakened by their fall.

Their attempt was, in fact, to recover the ascendency which general ignorance had allowed to the priesthood of the middle ages. Some of the nobility entertained from time to time similar projects in favor of their order: the Jesuits not only conceived but realized their project. Masters of education and of the confessional, their plan was profoundly laid for universal sway over opinion. In this resuscitated attempt to gain ascendency, the priesthood found the same enemies and opponents which had overthrown them in the fourteenth century. The legists, who then stood forth as champions of the royal authority, now battled for it as well as for popular rights. In Portugal, where the reign of the Jesuits seemed most assured, it was a lawyer, the marquis de Pombal, who, arrived at the ministry, undermined and destroyed the order. Divers circumstances reinforcing the hatred of the judicial body towards the Jesuits and their power over them, produced the same catastrophe in France. Not content with ruling Europe as tutors and confessors, and using largely that exemption not only from monkish but ecclesiastical rules, which forbid lucrative professions to the priesthood, father La Valette, a Jesuit, set up a mercantile establishment in the West Indies, supporting it by the funds of a mission for propagating Christianity. This commercial house of the Jesuits flourished for some time, until the capture of vessels by the English, and other effects of the war, ruined it, and left it bankrupt. The brothers Lionci of Marseilles, being creditors to a large amount, and becoming themselves almost bankrupt by the loss, sued not only father La Valette, but the order itself of the Jesuits. The society denied that they were liable for the debts of their mercantile brother. The judges of the French tribunals decreed that they were, and condemned them to pay the debt. The parliament having in this affair found their arch-enemies in the grasp of the law, and on grounds that could not be disputed, resolved to make the most of the opportunity. They forced from the plaintiffs a copy of the secret rules of their order, it being on those secret rules that they pleaded exemption from the debts of La Valette. These rules formed a subject of new inculpation. The most eminent of the rising legists drew up reports on the tendency and illegality of such societies. La Chaletais, especially, attorney-general of the province of Britany, distinguished himself by the talent and virulence of his report. A judgment of the parliament of Paris deprived the Jesuits first of the liberty of teaching, or of receiving new proselytes. Great efforts were made to shake Louis XV., and deprive the ministry of his support. The dauphin, the pope, the cardinal of Lorraine, exerted themselves to this effect. But the duc de Choiseul, supported by madame de Pompadour, succeeded in carrying his point. The order of the Jesuits was abolished in 1764, and its members banished the kingdom.

There was a sad and unfortunate similarity in the positions of Louis XV. and of Louis XIV. in the latter part of their respective reigns. Both, unsuccessful in their wars, had been reduced to a disgraceful peace: both to this great cause of unpopularity joined a secluded and dissolute life; for madame de Maintenon, in the eyes of the people, could never be other than a royal mistress. The same splendor, the same misery, profusion in expense, poverty in finances, marked the conclusion of either reign. Both monarchs were doomed to see their children perish by an unaccountable decay, and to have the prospect of their crowns falling on the head of an infant

The dauphin now died; and the dauphiness did not survive. The people murmured to behold the pious and the young carried off, whilst the aged and licentious monarch survived. Suspicions of poison and foul play circulated. That horrid credulity, which loads royalty with every crime, then became prevalent in France: it soon swelled into a fatal prejudice, far from being eradicated at this day. The queen followed her son to the grave. Madame de Pompadour expired in the royal palace, preserving her influence, like Richelieu, even on the bed of death. Louis XV. was thus bereft: yet he bore each successive blow with apathy, except, indeed, the loss of his queen, whose pious, affectionate, and unrepining nature touched him. Some of his courtiers hoped to see a reformation in the monarch's life brought about by this event; but his remorse was shortlived. His old habits of dissipation were resumed.

The Jesuits being now swept from the scene, the legists turned their frowardness against the court. They seemed, indeed, to have lost, in the ebriety of triumph, that ancient sense of justice and of prudence that had never till now altogether forsaken the magistracy. Three famous processes of this epoch occurred, to show how essentially illiberal and pernicious is the spirit of any corporate body. They destroyed the parliament in the public opinion; set men of letters, and every friend of toleration, in array against them; and fully proved the unfitness of a judicial body for political functions, which, implicating it in the opinions of party, necessarily trouble the source of justice. In the first of these trials, Calas, an unfortunate Protestant, was condemned by the parliament of Toulouse to be put to the rack for the supposed murder of his son. The youth had been insane, and committed suicide. His Catholic neighbors whispered that the unfortunate boy had meditated recantation, and that his father, to prevent his forsaking Protestantism, had strangled him. The bigot mob greedily received and propagated the report; the not less bigoted magistrates hearkened to it; and although Calas could have proved that he made an ample allowance to another son, who had embraced Catholicism, the parliament of Toulouse set aside his proofs, and condemned the parent to perish on the rack. The goods of his family were forfeited, and they themselves exiled. They took refuge in Geneva. Voltaire, then at Ferney, heard their story, and it kindled all his indignation. The poet called forth all his activity, his genius, and his hatred against the priesthood, to avenge the murder of Calas, and to reinstate his memory. In this he succeeded. The parliament of Toulouse was overwhelmed with shame, and with the public indignation; the magistrate who had most influenced the sentence was driven into madness.

The execution of La Barre, some time after, came to corroborate the assertions of the lettered, who exclaimed that the legists had succeeded to all the bigotry of the Jesuits. A wooden cross on the bridge of Abbeville was broken down in the night. A very vague suspicion rested upon La Barre and another youth. Their gay and dissipated lives seemed the only proof. It was sufficient, however. The magistrates were irritated against the growing impiety of the age; and, in their not illaudable desire to strike an example, were criminally precipitate. La Barre was condemned and executed; but as no sufficient proof sanctioned the verdict, all the odium, not only of sacrilege, but of murder, fell on the tribunals.

In completion of these two flagrant instances of injustice, came the condemnation and death of Lally; who was sacrificed not indeed to bigotry, but to ministerial influence. His innocence of the principal charges of treason and corruption was so clear, that shame, in a very short space, reversed the verdict of condemnation; but Lally had, meanwhile, suffered a disgraceful death.

The duc de Choiseul, in the mean time, though unequal to the task of restoring the declining monarchy to health, kept up, nevertheless, its pride, and made it wear an appearance of vigor. He had the boldness to conquer Corsica, and, by so doing, provoke a war with England. He was fortunate, too, in finding the vulnerable part of that great rival of his country. The American colonies began at that time to raise the voice of discontent. Choiseul, by fair words and emissaries, did his utmost to foment a spirit so menacing to Great Britain. No triumph could be so grateful to France as to see the power which had despoiled her of all her colonies, lose in turn the most important of her own. At the same time that the French minister, with a policy of which the patriotism covered the bad faith, was preparing to support the Anglo-Americans in opposition to their mother-country, his diplomatic agents were using exertions in the east of Europe to uphold the independence of Poland against the domination of Russia. When the indignant Poles rose in arms against the ambition of the latter country, a body of French troops, under the afterwards celebrated Dumourier, marched to the aid of the confederates of Cracow. The number of these auxiliaries was indeed inconsiderable; but Choiseul, from old and personal connexions, being assured of the alliance of

Austria, Poland was for the moment, sufficiently protected. Nor, if Choiseul had remained in power, could the partition of that kingdom, so disgraceful to France and to Europe, have taken place.

The confidence of Louis XV. in his minister, was first shaken by the accession of a new mistress: this was mademoiselle Lange, a creature found by the king's valet in one of the low haunts of Parisian debauchery. Introduced to the voluptuous monarch, her vile perfections fascinated him; and straight the nobles hostile to Choiseul paid the most assiduous court to her, and sought, by the sacrifice of all decorum and dignity in her favor, to raise for themselves a partisan against the minister. The duc de Richelieu, and the duc d'Aiguillon his relative, were at the head of this intrigue, in which the old Jesuit or high-church party joined. Choiseul might still have held his ascendency, could he have stooped to flatter the new favorite, who, by a mock marriage with some ruined rake of noble birth, had become countess du Barry. The duke, however, was the first of French ministers who relied on popularity for support: he enjoyed the esteem of the parliaments, and the approbation of men of letters, whilst the public voice hailed the spirit of patriotism that defied England and sheltered unhappy Poland. Choiseul would not degrade his character by stooping to such a creature as madame du Barry: he sought, in the sageness of policy, a counterpoise to her influence. He knit closer the bonds of alliance with Austria by the espousals of the young dauphin, afterwards Louis XVI., with Marie Antoinette, daughter of the empress. Yet even here the favor of the mistress showed itself predominant. The first society in which the innocent and lovely dauphiness found herself at the court of France, contained, among other guests, the infamous du Barry. This wedding, attended by some melancholy events, that seem to us prophetic of disaster, such as the dreadful crowd in the Rue Royale to witness the fire-works, in which upwards of fifty people were crushed to death, took place in May, 1770. In a few months after, Choiseul ceased to be minister.

His rival and successor was the duc d'Aiguillon, who boasted that cardinal Richelieu had been his grand-uncle. The duke had all the harshness, the imperious temper and tendencies, of his great relative. In his government of Britany, to which his political career had hitherto been limited, he had distinguished himself as the foe of parliament and parliamentary rights, as well of all that favored the popular cause. He had been engaged in fierce quarrels with the states of that province, where he found a powerful enemy in La Chalotais, the famous accuser of the Jesuits. La Chalotais was exiled by the duke's influence. In short, D'Aiguillon presented himself as the leader of the high-church, anti-parliament, anti-popular, and, moreover, anti-Austrian party: in his wake followed Maupeon the chancellor, and the abbé Terray, minister of finance. These declaimed against the bold, or, as hey called it, the mad policy of Choiseul, who was meditating the resuscitation of the maritime power of France and Spain and a war with England, on the one hand, whilst on the other Dumourier was, by his orders, organizing the means of resisting Russian influence in Poland. Maupeon presented madame du Barry with a celebrated picture of Charles I. by Vandyke: she suspended it in her boudoir, in order to strike the eye of Louis XV.: it caught his attention. "Ha, *La France*," exclaimed she, (such was the familiar name she gave to the monarch,) "look at that picture: if you continue to support Choiseul and the parliament that is in his interests, they will cut off your head, as the parliament of England did that of Charles." Importunity, it may be supposed, and the influence of a woman over her weak admirer, had more effect than such absurd arguments as these in convincing Louis, and in wringing from him the disgrace of his minister. The duc de Choiseul was at length exiled to his country-seat at Chauteloupe. His retreat was a triumph: the public acclamation, the verses of poets, and the visits of seven-eighths of the noblesse, accompanied the minister as he retired; whilst Versailles remained a desert, abandoned to Louis, his vile favorite, and her mean adulators.

The time was past when a monarch could disgrace his minister with impunity. The parliaments stood up, as might the majority of a representative assembly, against the court. The imprudence of the latter offered to it ample means. The quarrel, or process, as it had now become, between the duc d'Aiguillon and the parliament of Britany, had been brought before the parliament of Paris: the king sought to clear the duke of all stain ere he elevated him to the post of prime minister; whilst D'Aiguillon himself, and Maupeon, in their hatred of the judicial body and of Choiseul, then but on the eve of dismissal, were anxious that the parliament should proceed to extremities, and give the monarch a specimen of their intemperance. For this purpose Louis was made to assist at their debates. True to Choiseul and to their political creed, the parliament declared the duc d'Aiguillon not exculpated, but on the contrary, stained by the accusation brought against him. The fall of his rival and his own advancement followed, as if to brave this decree; and a bed of justice soon after reprimanded the parliament for its frowardness, and for endeavoring to form a political union, under the name of *classes*, with the seventeen provincial parliaments throughout the kingdom. The policy of Choiseul in these matters is not to be mistaken. The object of his emulation was Pitt: him the French minister rivalled and imitated, not only in his bold nd patriotic schemes for advancing the glory and dominion of the kingdom, but also in his supporting himself on popuarity, and on the majority of a representative assembly. Choiseul's house of commons was the French parliament: he endeavored to make use of it as a counterpoise to the capricious whims of the king, the high-church party, and the mistress. Such policy was, however, in the duke not profound, it proceeded from no deep and meditated plan of altering the constitution of the country. If he renewed the scheme and revived the ideas of the legists of the *Fronde*, it was unwittingly: he leaned on the parliament as a temporary support; and, in common with the statesmen of his time, he little understood the machinery of a limited government.

A decree of the king's counsel, in the mean time, reversed the judicial verdict of the parliament condemning D'Aiguillon. The sentence was even erased and torn from the registers of the palace. The inculpated minister kept his place, and sat as a peer in the body of parliament, which, though it had suspended its functions as a court of justice, pretending itself dishonored by the royal edict of reprobation, still assembled to discuss the public interests, the new corn-law, and other affairs of state. This interruption of all law pleadings, this kind of civil interdict, wielded by the legists in imitation of their ancient rivals, the ecclesiastical power, was seriously felt throughout the kingdom. It was the signal of discontent; a measure so extreme, that hitherto no minister since Richelieu had been bold enough to resist it. But the magistracy, however supported by the popular voice on the present occasion, had lost much of their ancient influence; and despite of all the importance attributed to them by the late minister, and despite their being made a screen and a bulwark by his party, the parliament had nevertheless fallen considerably into the same disrepute with all privileged classes and constituted uthorities. Hence Maupeau and D'Aiguillon were able to rush the body with impunity. Choiseul had been dismissed n the 24th of December, 1770. On the 20th of the following month, and in the night, each member of the parliament was surprised in his bed by two *mousquetaires*, who presented a written promise to resume their functions. To this a signature of *yes* or *no* was compelled. *No* was the general reply

Some in their surprise signed in the affirmative; but no sooner had the parliament assembled in the morning after this act of authority, than the whole body unanimously declared their determination not to obey. The following night, in consequence, brought another visit from the *mousquetaires*, who now signified to each member, that he was degraded from his office, and the parliament broken and cancelled. A decree of exile was at the same time put in force against the entire body, which was dispersed in different remote parts of the kingdom.

To appoint new courts of justice, and to find chiefs, was now the task of Maupeon. He declared that such offices should be no longer venal; he destroyed the overgrown jurisdiction of the capital, by the establishment of inferior and provincial courts; promised a new code of law, more in harmony than feudal traditions and imperial canons, with the intellectual civilization of the day. In short, the chancellor made every effort to bring round the public voice, and that of men of letters, to the new ministry. His endeavors, aided by threats and force, succeeded in weaning attachment from the exiled parliament, but could procure none for himself. The hopes of the French began to turn in another direction, and to look for amelioration in a change more radical, and in an assembly that would be truly national. The states-general became already the silent wish of all men possessed of thought or of political ideas.*

The noblesse alone seemed on this occasion to make common cause with the parliament, with whom they were united in the court of peers, abrogated by the late act of authority. All refused to attend the bed of justice held by Louis XV. to open and sanction his new judicial court. The prince of Condé, his son of Bourbon, and the prince Conti were exiled in consequence, as well as the duke of Orleans, and his son, the duc de Chartres. This last personage was afterwards the famous Philip Egalité. He was now the zealous opponent of the court, and partisan of parliaments.

Royalty was thus triumphant over both these bodies, the Jesuits and the legists, whose quarrel had occupied public attention, and by balancing which the court had hitherto kept itself shielded from the weight or the serious attacks of unpopularity. Louis XV., under madame du Barry and D'Aiguillon, destroyed these outworks, which stood before the fortress

* "It was at this time," says Dumourier in his Memoirs, "that I undertook an Essay on the States-General, of which every one, endowed with foresight, began to perceive the urgent necessity"

of his power; and henceforth we shall find all classes confounded, advancing together, and making common cause against the monarchy.

Had a successful, a glorious, or patriotic ministry broken the parliaments, they most probably would never have recovered their power; but the incapacity of the duc d'Aiguillon, and the blunders of the abbé Terray, soon nullified all their acts. The latter had however a difficult task. He was finance minister, and obliged to meet an annual expense of 400 millions of livres with a revenue far inferior. This deficit was increased by an undertaking to repay the price of their places to such members of the exiled parliament as would submit. To meet this, and to cover the profusion of madame du Barry, Terray increased the *taille*, or tax upon the peasantry, and this at a time of such general distress, that politicians exclaimed against the surplus of the population. In addition to this, the abbé ventured on the simple expedient of a partial bankruptcy. By a stroke of his pen, he reduced the interest of the public debt by one half.

The partition of Poland, however, was what principally set the seal of imbecility and disgrace on the ministry of the duc d'Aiguillon. Russia, with overwhelming power, still pressed on that unfortunate country, usurping the rights of a king whom she had placed on its throne: her armies occupied the country, merely opposed by a patriotic but weak confederation of Poles. Dumourier had supported these. Viomenil succeeded to him, and kept up the character of French generosity and valor. But Austria no longer maintained her friendship and connexions with Choiseul, and was no longer opposed to the views of Russia. Prussia joined in the schemes; and whilst Louis XV. was slumbering in the arms of du Barry, and his minister d'Aiguillon employed in imprisoning the adherents of the parliament, the ancient kingdom of Poland was dismembered and almost blotted from the map of Europe.

In the midst of this decay and disgrace of his kingdom, Louis XV. was stricken with a mortal malady: it was the small-pox. Considering his age and free life, there were few hopes, from the first, of his recovery. The bedside of the dying monarch from thence became the scene of the most disgraceful quarrels and intrigues. The Choiseul party urged the necessity of chasing madame du Barry from court with disgrace; and loudly argued, that Beaumont, archbishop of Paris, should refuse the sacraments to the dying monarch, if this sacrifice was not made to decorum and piety; but the archbishop, who had so oft refused the consolations of the church and the ceremony of burial to a refractory Jansenist, would not be severe with madame du Barry, who, however base, had humbled Choiseul and the parliament, the great enemies of the high church. The mistress, therefore, was allowed to retire without scandal or public disgrace. Louis, attended with the most exemplary affection by his daughters, expired on the 10th of May, 1774.

Etiquette required that the body should be embalmed. But already in a state of putrefaction, no surgeon could be found to undertake the office; nor could a courtier be induced to oversee the last duties paid to the monarch. His remains were huddled into their last abode by the workmen of the château: spirits of wine were poured on them; and in this state they were abandoned, till conveyed to St. Denis. The dauphin was with Marie Antoinette, awaiting tidings of his royal grandsire's fate. A noise, like thunder, was heard suddenly in their antechamber. "It was that of the courtiers," says madame Campan, "who had deserted the apartments of the deceased monarch, to do homage to the new power of Louis XVI." The first act of this prince and of his queen, was to fling themselves upon their knees, and exclaim, "My God! guide us, protect us: we are too young to reign."

CHAP. IX.

1774—1789.

FROM THE ACCESSION OF LOUIS XVI. TO THE ASSEMBLING OF THE STATES-GENERAL.

From the commencement of this history, care has been taken to bring into view, at intervals, those natural and marked divisions of society which share and dispute political influence. Of these, for several centuries, three alone have preserved ascendency; and each of the three may be said to have obtained this, as representing one of the great elements of power: royalty represented birth or hereditary right; the noblesse, property or wealth; the priesthood, intellect. Movable or commercial property, as possessors of which the democracy pretended to municipal and political rights, was too insignificant in feudal times to be allowed as a fit plea or basis for such. Democracy was humble and enslaved. The king and superior classes, founding their claims on tradition, came to consider them as irrefragable, and increased each in the pride and tenacity with which they held to power, at the very time when the original source and principle of that power was departing from them. The noblesse in fact were losing fast the preponderance of wealth: the clergy had lost the monopoly of intellect: and yet, in right of these privileges, they offended the natural dignity of man in the ignoble, by the marked and invidious distinction that reigned between the castes; whilst the high clergy denied that intellectual freedom which is dearer than even personal liberty to an enlightened nation. It was hence against the two privileged orders, more than against the crown, that the popular odium was really turned.

To this description of the upper and enlightened classes must be added that of the lower orders: they had been brought to a state of extreme indigence and suffering. A country like France, so richly endowed as to suffice for its own luxurious as well as necessary wants, is but late and feebly driven to seek the advantages of foreign commerce, to which poorer countries are forcibly impelled. A despotic government proved a still greater obstacle: in the interior of the country it perpetuated the commercial barrier between province and province, whilst the grasping hand of the financier seized wealth wherever it became manifest, and thus checked all spirit and improvement. Hence trade and manufactures existed but in an infant and undeveloped state. The peasant population had now reached the limits that the national agriculture could employ or could feed, and distress was the consequence. Although not twenty millions covered in indigence the soil which now supports thirty millions in prosperity, the population was declared to be too great. A generation of the poor sprung up, which, homeless and unemployed, felt itself released from that feudal tie which hitherto bound the peasant to the proprietor: these crowded into towns, or remained listlessly and idly vegetating in their native place, until the sounds of commotion and the hopes of plunder came to call them, as ready volunteers, into the ranks and the cause of sedition.

Such is the true nature of that denuded and wretched state of the lower orders of the French, which afterwards added the ferocity of famine to the horrors of a revolution, which promised, if ever revolution promised, to be fair, moderate, and even gay. In the last years of Louis XV.'s reign, scandalous as was the court, disgraceful as was its policy, and cruel and unjust its administration, the public of the capital showed its censures more by epigram and *jeu d'esprit* than by indignation. When the abbé Terray defrauded the public creditor by a partial bankruptcy, what would have raised a rebellion in any capital of Europe, Constantinople scarcely excepted, excited but witticisms in Paris. "Terray is a spoiled child," said the cheated Parisians; "he puts his fingers into every one's pocket."

Louis XVI. was twenty years of age at his accession to the throne. His father, the devout dauphin, had intrusted his education to the duc de la Vauguyon, a noble of rigid and ascetic piety. This man bred up the future heir to the throne of France as if he were destined to be a monk; and took care to render him not only scrupulously ignorant of all polite learning, but even of history and the science of government. The very external appearance of Louis betrayed this tutelage: he was slovenly, melancholy, ungraceful, bashful, and so diffident, that his eyes often shrunk from the regard of his meanest subject; with all this, he had been inspired with such a religious horror of carnal affections, that he remained for many years on no closer terms than those of mere politeness with his young and lovely queen. Such was the character of the new sovereign, called to administer the realm at the most critical period of its history.

The first important step was the choice of a minister. The duc d'Aiguillon, as the ally of the prostitute Du Barry, was of course set aside. Choiseul had hopes, which were supported by the favor of Austria, and, consequently, of the young queen; but there remained too strong a prejudice in the mind of Louis against the minister who had humbled the high church. The dauphin, father to the monarch, had left a note containing his opinion of political characters: in this, the comte de Maurepas was characterized as strongly attached to those true political principles that La Pompadour had forsaken and opposed; in other words, he was the enemy of Choiseul and of the Austrian alliance. This suited the church party, and Maurepas, who was, moreover, the uncle of D'Aiguillon, was sent for to assume the place of minister.

The comte de Maurepas was an aged, experienced, cunning man of the world, somewhat resembling the prince Talleyrand of later days, unrivalled in address, in epigram, and *persiflage*. He had been exiled to his country-seat at Bourges, where four-and-twenty years' retirement had not weaned him from public interests. He had learned much in that time, and was too enlightened not to have progressed with his age. Hence the high church found Maurepas not what he had been or what they expected: he had corresponded with men of letters, was a friend of the Encyclopedists, and, in short, approached in principle much more near to Choiseul than to D'Aiguillon. This became manifest in filling up the places of the ministry: the count de Vergennes, the ambassador who at Constantinople had seconded the views of Choiseul against Russia, was recalled to preside over the foreign department. The hated Maupeon and Terray were both discarded. Turgot, the friend of the economists, the statesman vaunted by the philosophers, replaced the latter; his name was a pledge of reform and amelioration. The first act of the new government was to dismiss the parliament of Maupeon, and re-establish the ancient judges and courts which had been dissolved by Louis XV.

The whole policy of the new government seemed to be that of conciliating public opinion; but, unfortunately, this opinion was not sufficiently general, enlightened, or united, to lead the monarch into the path of his own and the nation's safety. Turgot announced his financial plans and projects of reform. The principal of these were to do away with *corvées* and such taxes as weighed exclusively on the people, establishing a territorial impost, that would be borne equally by all classes of society, nobility and clergy not excluded. But these privileged orders, instead of deeming themselves called on to make sacrifices to the state, thought, on the contrary, that they were unjustly oppressed. Unfortunately the traditions of royalty, of aristocracy, and of the church, showed each possessed of paramount and almost sovereign authority. Each cherished the past, and looked there for its right and rule of conduct rather than in reason and in the present nature and condition of things. Neither could thus be induced to make sacrifices. Noblesse and clergy, the parties of Choiseul and d'Aiguillon, united against the audacious innovator Turgot, who pretended, that the privileged classes should support, according to their means, the burdens of the state. What is more astonishing, the parliament or legists united with these orders; they, too, saw danger in innovation: and thus the monarch's ministry, in its attempt to relieve the people and middling class, and in its attempt to introduce a necessary reform in government, was marred and checked and flung aback into the ancient and pernicious courses of absolute monarchy. Who were to blame in this? The aristocracy, the clergy, the parliament. Never did blindness and selfishness combine more grossly, or more deservedly merit the ruin and the punishment which they afterwards incurred. They were culpable. The crown was unwise. Accustomed to hold the balance betwixt these three parties, it knew of no other in the nation, of which the great body could then have saved it, as the commons centuries back had preserved royalty from the predominance of the feudal lords. Had Louis now summoned the states-general, they would have been grateful for their existence and for the influence which they afterwards wrested from the monarch. At this time, not only was the monarch beloved, but his queen was still uncalumniated, and had not yet been made to lose the affections of the people by the base slander of envious courtiers. But neither Maurepas, nor Louis, had the courage to rely on the popular mass. The tates-general were still the bugbear that they had been for enturies; and the sovereign, rather than recur to this his only support, the only body that could give him funds, and confidence, and stability, remained leaning alternately on the frail prop of mere court parties, sharing and bringing upon himself all the odium and contempt which the ignorance, the selfishness, and the empty pride of such counsellors earned from the public voice.

Turgot fell before this opposition of the privileged orders. Malesherbes, his friend and brother minister, who, as a legist of high character, and as a statesman not stained with the accusation of being a philosopher and a theorist, might be expected to have more influence in mastering the resistance of the parliament at least, fell also: both were successively dismissed. The unfortunate Marie Antoinette is accused of having influenced the king to get rid of them. Some of the courtiers might indeed have incited her to this act; but the blame rests not with her. Turgot and Malesherbes fell by the opposition of the noblesse and parliament, the latter then allowed to possess a legislative *veto.* They were sacrificed not to the queen but to circumstances; for of what use was their remaining in place, when neither their plans could be effected nor their counsels adopted?

Had, indeed, the monarch the good fortune to have met with a practical statesman, a hand and head like those of Richelieu, devoted to the principles of Turgot, then the parliament might have been again broken or reduced to its judicial functions, and the states might have been summoned to support the patriotic intentions of the crown. But Turgot was not fit for such a task, and Maurepas soon shrunk from the prospect back into the party of the aristocracy. The ideas of the finance minister embraced a vast scheme of amelioration. They were not limited to an equable and territorial tax, but contained a free municipal system, and an assembly of the deputies of the provinces to supersede the parliament in their functions of consenting to new imposts. An edict, issued to establish one of his principles, the free commerce of grain, unfortunately did not produce favorable results. The year being one of general scarcity, the want of corn was attributed to the edict, and Turgot's theories lost a great part of their influence. A sedition broke out in Paris, occasioned by famine. Similar scenes took place throughout the kingdom, occasioned by the indigence, the unfixed and suffering state, of the peasant population, which has been described. The police, it seems, were not active to repress the tumult. Turgot declared that it was excited, not by the effects of his edict, but by his enemies. Maurepas represented this to the king as false and presumptuous. That minister already began to be disgusted with the popular ally that overshadowed him. This took place in 1775. In the following year, Turgot, who still held his ground, caused six edicts to be presented to the parliament. The chief ones ordered the abolition of the *corvée* as well as of certain monopolies and corporations. The parliament refused to register: the king overcame the opposition in a bed of justice; but the clamors of the noblesse at court were too great for Louis to resist. "It is only monsieur Turgot and I who love the people," said the monarch; but the minister was nevertheless dismissed, and was followed in his retreat by Malesherbes.

Turgot is reproached with having been stiff, cold, and uncourteous, as wanting that tact which all offices require, in which men are to be dealt with. It required, certainly, great powers of address to reconcile the courtiers to innovation. An imitator of his, one who had caught up the mania for reform, was the count de St. Germain. He was created minister at war, and his first act was to reorganize the army. He introduced the Prussian discipline; and in his love of change broke up all the old regiments of household troops and *mousquetaires*, and much diminished the body-guard. Such reductions, however called for by economy, had the effect of disgusting the noblesse, which exclusively composed those corps, with the very name of reform; and was one of the great causes that accelerated the revolution, by disorganizing the army, and leaving no force to resist or awe the insurrectionary movements of the populace.

To Turgot succeeded Clugny in the department of finance. He re-established the *corvée*, to gratify those under whose auspices he was elevated. He died in a few months, and was succeeded by Taboureau. Maurepas held still the place of prime minister, or rather that of favorite. Without principles or party, his sole object was to reign; and thus the true administrators of the government had to please not only a royal but a ministerial master. Those were stormy days, however, in which incapacity could not long hold the helm. Louis XVI. was himself impatient at the difficulties of the government, and the feeble attempts of his ministry to surmount them. Necker was recommended as a financier capable of effecting wonders; and he was accordingly appointed director of the treasury, subordinate to the comptroller-general Taboureau. He was a Swiss; a man of commercial wealth; and of social eminence, from the intellectual society that he gathered round him as envoy from Geneva. He had claims, too, as a writer: he had defended the establishment or resuscitation of the East India company against the sweeping condemnation of the economists. He had, with the same views, written against Turgot's doctrine of the free commerce of grain. His opinions formed a medium between the extremes of the old and the new systems: and he, who can thus occupy middle ground between contending parties, bids a fair chance to bear away the palm of wisdom for a time. Necker was honest, and skilled in business; these qualities formed his merits as a financier. His political knowledge was, however, as yet but narrow; and he entered into the ministry, as his daughter informs us, without the least idea of the necessity of a political change in the form of government. From Necker, in consequence, less was to be expected than from Turgot; and yet such is the confidence ever placed by the public in practical men, that the man of commerce in the ministerial seat rallied around him infinitely more confidence and popularity than the profound and systematic politician had acquired. Necker's high commercial character was his recommendation and support. Through it he procured loans on no exorbitant terms, and by this means relieved the distresses of the treasury. These, however, were only temporary expedients, such as Turgot had disdained, and to which that statesman declared that he would not stoop. What that bolder minister failed in procuring, viz. the diminution of expense and increase of the revenue, Necker could not and did not succeed in. Necker simply borrowed, and added yearly to the public burdens (a state of war certainly proving his ex cuse); making fair promises of an excess of revenue, yet to accrue from an economy that the minister had not the power to enforce.

Whilst the monarchy was thus scrambling on from expedient to expedient, a fresh quarrel broke out with England. The French public had always looked with satisfaction on the resistance of the North American colonies of that country. Choiseul had entertained the project of declaring for them, and aiding them in the commencement of the struggle. D'Aiguillon, and after him Maurepas, had not the boldness requisite for such a stroke. Under the administration of the atter, arms had been dispatched from France to the insur gents. La Fayette and other officers had joined the cause of independence in America; and latterly privateers, manned by natives of that country, had been allowed to be fitted out in French ports. Still Maurepas hesitated to brave England and embrace the American cause, until tidings of the surrender of Burgoyne came to assure him that the colonies had ample means of resistance. Then, in the eleventh hour, the French ministry stepped forth from its hesitation, and concluded a treaty in February, 1778, acknowledging the independence of the United States. War between France and England was the necessary consequence.

There is little variety or interest in the minor details of a naval war; and the contest between the two countries was chiefly confined to the ocean. The first year somewhat dashed the high hopes of the British. The French had the advantage in several petty encounters; and in an action near Ushant, between the fleets under Keppel and D'Orvilliers, the victory remained undecided. The young duc de Chartres, soon after the duke of Orleans of the revolution, fought, but did not distinguish himself, in this battle. In the year 1789, the comte de Vergennes succeeded in realizing the old scheme of Choiseul, to excite Spain to unite her maritime force with that of France, in order to crush the naval superiority of England. The fleets of the two royal houses of Bourbon rode triumphant in the Channel, insulted Plymouth, and menaced an invasion; but soon abandoning such audacious projects, they resolved to strike an important blow by laying siege to Gibraltar, which Rodney, however, was able to revictual, after defeating and capturing several sail of the Spanish line.

The events of the war, in the mean time, occupied the unquiet minds of the French people. The loans of Necker supported the war; and the government—for Necker, with the weight of affairs upon him, personally still held but a subordinate place—seemed inclined to repay him with little gratitude. Maurepas treated him with the proud airs of a superior, and was not the less jealous of the finance minister's talents and influence. Necker had dared to complain to the king of the insufficiency and profusion of M. de Sartinis, minister of marine, and even ventured to propose the mareschal de Castries for his successor. To this offensive act of independence he added an unpardonable breach of ministerial etiquette, in publishing the *Compte Rendu*, or statement of revenue and expenditure. Publicity was the requisite, the indispensable, support of that credit, which was Necker's only resource for carrying on the government. The necessity was not taken into consideration, but the novelty was regarded as dangerous and treasonable. The noblesse, the courtiers, joined in the clamor against the rigid minister, who checked the wonted liberalities of the king, and who threatened the reform of pension and private gratuity. The usual mode of court vengeance, calumny, was employed to blacken Necker. Envy and spleen, however, no longer vented itself in the mirthful shape of epigram. Tempers had grown more serious; and the low libel, as a weapon, had succeeded the song and the witticism. Necker, who should have despised such attacks, was, on the contrary, most sensible to them. Popularity was his idol. He, therefore, demanded that his libellers, whom he had discovered to be in the service of the count d'Artois, should be dismissed. Maurepas, of whom he made the demand, declared this impossible. "Then," said Necker, "if I am not to have this satisfaction, at least let there be given me some mark of the royal favor, in order to confound my enemies. Grant me entrance to the council." Maurepas objected, that Necker was a Protestant. "Sully was one," urged the unorthodox minister; "and if my demand be not conceded, I must resign." It was not granted; and Necker, having at first sacrificed his pride by accepting the labor and responsibility of finance minister without its rank or rights, sacrificed this place to his vanity, at the very moment when his remaining in power would have been most beneficial.* Maurepas died in a few months after. Had Necker remained in the ministry, he might have succeeded to the first place: at least he would no longer have found it occupied by a man whose age and address gave him paramount influence, whilst his selfishness, and courtliness, and petty jealousies, rendered all plans of real amelioration impracticable.

Necker during his ministry operated one important change, in realizing the project imagined by Turgot of creating provincial assemblies in those parts of the kingdom that had not states of their own. As these assemblies were merely to be intrusted with the task of partitioning the imposts, thus exercising administrative rather than legislative power, Necker ordered that the number of the members chosen from the commons should be equal to those of the two privileged orders united. Thus the noblesse composed a fourth, the clergy a fourth, the burgesses and unennobled proprietors of land one half. This was a precedent that afterwards decided the great question how the states-general should be organized

* 1781.

By it was at once secured the predominance of the middle orders, who soon transferred to great legislative rights and questions the same share of influence that had been granted them merely in the office of regulating the levy of the taxes. Necker, who had few political ideas, did not see the tendency of his scheme. It equally escaped the jealous eyes of the court. The parliament had perspicacity enough to espy the importance of the measure, and it formed one great cause of their discontent against Necker. It will soon be seen how decisive the arrangement proved in giving a republican form to the representative assembly of the nation.

The year of Necker's dismissal was nevertheless a glorious one for France and America. The minister of marine, De Castries, chosen by him, proved his talents by the successes which his combination and activity procured. A French army, wafted over the Atlantic, united with that of Washington, and far outnumbered the British, whilst the French naval force, concentrated in the Chesapeake, was superior in those seas, and materially aided the operations of the land army. Sir Henry Clinton commanded in New-York, Cornwallis in Virginia. Threatening both points, and thus preventing them from mutual aid, Washington and the French suddenly turned their combined force against the Virginian army. Cornwallis fortified himself in York-Town; and he was soon attacked by the French on one side, whose force alone equalled that of the British, and by the Americans on the other. The two gallant nations, rivalling each other in zeal, could not fail to be victorious; the English were beaten from their works, and lord Cornwallis was reduced to the disgrace of capitulation. Many noble names, soon to be famed in French annals, here first distinguished themselves. In addition to La Fayette and Rochambeau, were the duc de Lauzun, afterwards de Biron, who perished in the revolution, Alexander Berthier, Mathieu Dumas, the vicomte de Noailles. Charles de Lameth, whose voice with that of La Fayette is still heard in the French chamber of deputies, was wounded in the action. At sea, too, the count de Grasse had the advantage over Hood. Spain wrested Minorca from England. In short, the last year of a mere courtier's administration, that of Maurepas, might have contented the thirst for glory and humbling of Britain that inspired Choiseul. The triumph was short, however. America, indeed, kept her advantages, and won honorable peace by victory; whilst France and Spain met with reverses to counterbalance her success. In April, 1782, the French and British fleets under count de Grasse and Admiral Rodney, the former consisting of thirty-four, the latter of thirty-six sail, encountered each other in the West Indian seas. The action commenced on the morning of the 12th of April, the lines closing, and the French supporting the attack with intrepid valor. De Grasse had his ships full of troops, destined for the conquest of Jamaica. One should have thought that in a close engagement these might have proved an aid. They proved to the French admiral a source of embarrassment, the cannonade making dreadful havoc amongst their numbers, and communicating terror and confusion to the crews. Still, for many hours Rodney in vain endeavored to break through their line. This he effected in the afternoon, scattering and mastering the hostile squadron, the ships of which were overpowered one after the other. The count de Grasse, in the Ville de Paris, made a valiant resistance, combating, though surrounded by numbers, until night and the discomfiture of his crew, only three of the survivors of which remained without a wound, compelled him to surrender.

The united forces of France and Spain met with as marked a discomfiture in their attack upon Gibraltar, towards the close of the same year. Floating batteries of a new construction were employed, whilst an immense army awaited their effect to take the formidable fortress by assault. After a day spent in the hottest cannonade from both sides that ever had, perhaps, been witnessed, the failure of the enterprise became evident during the night, by the floating batteries taking fire. The French historians record with gratitude and admiration the generous conduct of Curtis, who, at the risk of his life, saved from perishing several hundreds of the enemy, whom he had contributed to vanquish.

In the commencement of 1783, a treaty was concluded between Great Britain and the United States of America, whose independence was thus accomplished. Peace was at the same time restored between England and France. The latter, in these negotiations, recovered the dignity that she had been obliged to waive, when, under madame de Pompadour, the treaty of Paris was signed; the advantage and honor seemed on her side. England, besides the restitution of conquests, ceded Senegal and Tobago to France, and Minorca to Spain. The French soldiers in America had shown valor and reaped success. If De Grasse had yielded after a well-fought struggle, De Suffrein in the East supported and redeemed the honor of the French navy. The war, and the treaty which concluded it, would, in either of the former reigns, have been celebrated with popular acclamations, with medals, and panegyric verse; but now the nation was too dissatisfied with its internal state to abate of its censures, or be bribed by even partial victory into quiet and content.

The death of Maurepas, and the retreat of Necker, had left the king at once without a favorite and without a minister. Louis was of that weak mind which requires not only a statesman to suggest plans, but also an intimate and friend to exercise for him, as it were, the functions of his private will: the latter place demanded the address and habits of a courtier such as neither Turgot nor Necker possessed; Maurepas filled the office perfectly to his own and the monarch's satisfaction To him, in influence over the royal mind, succeeded Marie Antoinette. The long estrangement of Louis from his queen had passed away: Maurepas had, from jealousy, contributed to it. The birth of their first child, the present duchess d'Angoulême, in 1778, was at once a sign and a bond of conjugal affection. The dauphin's birth took place in 1781. In the commencement of her reign Marie Antoinette was little courted by the swarm of the selfish and intriguing: her beauty and simplicity could not but charm, indeed, and procure for her a circle of private friends; but her want of influence over her husband, shown by her inability to promote Choiseul, averted from her the ambitious and designing. Hence in those days her political leanings were unbiassed and independent: she supported and showed herself benignant to Necker in his first administration. If she influenced the dismissal of Turgot, it was more as the organ of the noblesse than from her own influence or act. Now, however, that her power over Louis XVI. became confirmed and evident, the princes and the noblesse crowded to pay court to her, as they would have done to a du Barry: they besieged her, possessed her ear, and poured into it all their aristocratic prejudices, their party hates and interested ambition. The effect upon the monarch, and through him upon the ministry and nation, was pernicious, and, indeed, fatal. The unfortunate Marie Antoinette, by taking this position, worked her ruin: she was young, gay, spirited, light-hearted; bred up in the simple, domestic circle of Maria Theresa, she detested etiquette; she could repress neither her smiles nor her impatience at its absurdities and restraints. This made enemies of the dowagers and precisians of the court. Then she was considered Austrian and inclined to Choiseul, and so excited the hostilities of the high-church party. These secret foes first originated the libels upon her character, which the vain and profligate race of courtiers gave consistency to by a tone of converse and of thought, that affected to discredit aught like chastity in woman. The envious rabble greedily swallowed reports that justified their hatred of the great. vulgar imagination and credulity came to complete, with touches of the disgusting and the atrocious, the picture that malignant satire had first drawn. And the queen herself, in the inconsiderate gaiety of youth, of innocence, and high place, gave those handles to calumny that dissolute hypocrisy would have avoided. Her influence over her husband was not less pernicious because of her innocence; whilst the popular rumors that denied this, had the terrible effect of blackening the discontent against royalty into personal odium towards the sovereign and his consort. Another unfortunate circumstance attending Marie Antoinette's influence over Louis was, that being without any well-founded political knowledge or principle herself, without system or ideas to impose, she abandoned the monarch half to his own sagacious and patriotic purposes, breaking in upon them by whims and intervals, diverting him from any one or consistent line of conduct, and giving a color of weakness and irresolution to his acts, that took away all confidence in him alike from friends and from opponents, making him long the sport and at length the victim of both.

To the place of Maurepas in the administration, though not to his influence, succeeded Vergennes: he tried if men of mediocre talents might not manage the routine of finance; moreover, he chose them from the benches of the parliament, in hopes of conciliating that body. Joly de Fleury, and after him D'Ormesson, was placed at the head of the treasury. The government came to a complete stand for want of funds during the ministry of the latter; and talent, or a character for talent, was again sought: it was difficult to find; Turgots and Neckers were rare: in default of such, a man of showy parts and high pretensions was chosen; a clerk, who aped the courtier and the man of fashion, self-sufficient, prodigal, superficial, possessed of address, indeed, but presuming that address alone sufficed to form a statesman. Such was Calonne. Without thought or conviction, totally unprovided with principle or system, he improvised a theory by contradicting his predecessors; an obvious mode of being original. As economy had been cried up by Necker and by Turgot, the new minister declared that profusion formed the wealth of a state. The paradox was not only applauded by the courtiers, but practised by them. Calonne, to support such flattering doctrines, had recourse to Necker's mode of raising loans; although, to do that statesman justice, he deprecated the use of such expedients in time of peace. But this resource, like every other, had its limits. The minister, a vain and confident man, had inspired high hopes; it was incumbent on him to support this character: he resolved, therefore, to follow Turgot's plan, the only obvious one, indeed, of equalizing the taxes, and levying them alike on noblesse and clergy as well as on the commons. In order to effect this, which Turgot had failed in, and Necker had not attempted, Calonne proposed to call an assembly of notables, the chiefs, in fact, of the privileged orders. He hoped to move them, or shame them, or cajole them, to consent to his proposals: and the notables were accordingly summoned to meet in the commencement of the year 1787.

In February, the assembly of notables was opened at Versailles. Calonne, in a solemn discourse, disclosed his plans; and, to prove the necessity of reform, confessed a deficit of 112 millions. His plans alone for taxing the privileged orders were sufficiently distasteful to his hearers, especially to the clergy, who claimed and exercised the right of taxing themselves in their own synods. The deficit gave a handle for discontent; and Calonne, in unjustly throwing part of it upon Necker, called forth a triumphant exculpation from that financier, whom he exiled in answer. Hence Necker's party, including the writers of the day, the ecclesiastics, and the greater portion of the noblesse, were in instant opposition to Calonne, whom they accused of seeking to despoil and humble the higher classes. They called for an account of the revenue and expenditure. After much struggle and reluctance, it was granted. The receipt amounted to 400 millions of francs, whilst the annual expenditure exceeded that by 150 millions. Such a contrast with the confidence and profusion of the minister afforded ample ground of censure against him. He was pressed on all hands, more especially by the cleric notables, headed by Brienne, archbishop of Toulouse. The legists were not backward in supporting their old enemies against the minister. Calonne was exasperated, and gave hints of recurring to popular support. The voice of La Fayette exclaimed against the arbitrary imprisonments, and other abuses of power, and already demanded the convocation of a representative assembly. This, however, was but in the secret sittings of the notables. Calonne, though he durst not betray such ideas at court, made use and utterance of them in his anger against the proud chiefs who proved so little obsequious to his will. They, in return, resolved upon his ruin; and Calonne, whose only support lay in the count d'Artois,* whose debts he had paid, and in the Polignacs, was obliged tc succumb. Although raised by the courtiers, and despite the

* Afterwards Charles X

pains taken by the minister to flatter and to bribe them, he was still driven by the necessities of his situation to despoil the noblesse and clergy of their privileges; and he fell a sacrifice to these orders.

A new minister was now chosen from the triumphant notables. This was the archbishop of Toulouse; "as weak a head," says De Staël, "as ever was covered by the peruque of a counsellor of state." He had fought in behalf of *privilege*, although, in common with the assembly which he led, he affected to be merely actuated by indignation against the profligate Calonne. The notables now left him to the task of still preserving the claims of church and aristocracy untouched. They shook off from themselves, and threw upon him, all the odium of such policy; for they themselves professed to give full assent to the plans proposed by Calonne. Having thus played in their assembly as false a part as if they had been agents in a court intrigue, the notables dispersed, and left Brienne to enjoy the vanity and the difficulties of his pre-eminent station.

The archbishop of Toulouse had now to keep his tacit promise of respecting the exemption of the privileged orders from general taxation; and yet, in order to gain the popular voice, he was obliged to affect the contrary policy. His vanity and love of place made him stoop to play so base a part. The assent of the notables to Calonne's plans of taxation and reform had no legislative force; but still its moral influence was so great, that had Brienne immediately drawn up an edict for a territorial impost, and presented it to the parliament, the legists durst not have refused to sanction it. But Brienne hesitated, and manœuvred to gain time, sending to the parliament edicts establishing stamp duties and abolishing *corvées*, and bringing forward the vital question of the land tax but in their wake. By this means the parliament were allowed both leisure and pretext for resistance. In that body there existed much diversity of opinion. The presidents and elders were attached to their own privileges, which they felt were allied to those of the noblesse and clergy. The provincial assemblies proposed by Turgot, Necker, and Calonne were odious to them; and the great question of the territorial impost did not please them, since it was evident that its effect would be to raise the crown above all want to its ancient height of superiority. This last result was indeed dreaded on all hands, though avowed by none, and was the principal motive of that discontented and seditious spirit that opposed all reform, as saving the country from anarchy to plunge it into despotism. The parliament was embarrassed by these conflicting views and circumstances. One thing, however, was evident, that both notables and minister had cast off the *onus* of decreeing the territorial impost, or the odium of rejecting it, upon the parliament: and the parliament now sought to follow their example, in doing neither one nor the other. But how to escape? There was no way except down a precipice; and they took it. They declared that they had no more right than the notables to sanction law or taxes; thus contradicting their past pretensions for centuries, and abdicating at once their right to stand in the place of a national assembly. The king being unable to decree new laws or taxes, and the notables and parliament successively avowing their incompetence to aid him, the states-general became the only resource. This fearful name, that men dreaded to utter, was nevertheless uppermost in the thoughts of all. Necessity must have suggested it to the dullest. But it was unheard of, until a pert member, gathering audacity from the impulse of his wit, gave utterance to it in the shape of a pun. "It is not states of expenditure and income that we want," said he, "but states-general." When one thus had the audacity to speak the word, thousands found courage to re-echo it.

This sounded as a thunder-clap to the court and to Brienne, who was prepared for the refusal or acquiescence of the parliament, but not for this detested alternative. He was enraged. The refractory body was summoned to a bed of justice at Versailles; and the two edicts of the stamp duty and land tax were forcibly registered, the minister losing sight of his deference towards the higher orders. The parliament returned to its sitting, protested, and declared the registry of the edicts null. Brienne exiled the body to Troyes. Justice was thus suspended; and the government yielded. The parliament was recalled; it gratified Brienne by registering a new loan to meet urgent necessities, and in return the archbishop promised that the states-general should be convoked within five years.

Thus were the cause and high pretensions of the court and higher orders betrayed (if submitting to necessity can be called treason) by the very ministers whom they raised to defend them. They discarded Turgot, and drove away Necker; yet Calonne, their minion, was obliged to adopt the liberal plans of his predecessors, and was in consequence superseded by a chief notable and high-churchman. Vain precaution! this champion of the high orders was himself not only driven reluctantly to propose the hated laws and to compel their registry, but he was obliged in addition to capitulate and yield up every thing in the important promise of calling an assembly of the nation. The chief maxim of an administration had hitherto been to sail between the two shoals of bankruptcy on one hand and the states-general on the other. Brienne struck the vessel of the state on the latter sand-bank. In more favorable circumstances, with more skilful pilots, it might have righted, and floated into port; but, the wind now menacing, the popular tempest soon broke loose, and the monarchy went to pieces.

Such were the events of the year 1787, in which the revolution advanced with an awful stride. The high orders retreated before it. Louis XVI. reformed his court, and dismissed a crowd of high officers; but the minister, despite his concessions, was still at war with the parliament. In the resistance offered to the bed of justice, the duke of Orleans had shown himself most forward. That prince had placed himself at the head of the violent and liberal, or what Weber calls the *American* party. He was exiled in consequence. His friends now stirred in his behalf, and raised discussion as to the legality of *lettres de cachet*. Brienne perceived his blunder in first castigating the parliament and then yielding to them. The thought of important concessions made in vain, galled him. He therefore resolved to imitate Maupeon, and proceed to extremities against a body, that declared itself powerless in reform, whilst it showed itself active in remonstrance and political agitation. A plan was secretly matured and prepared for dismissing the parliament, and establishing other courts, provincial and metropolitan, in lieu, with a *cour plenière*, or body of peers, magistrates, and notables; in fact, to constitute a high court of appeal. The project was not kept sufficiently close. D'Espréménil, a counsellor, obtained a copy of it from the printer; and, hurrying to the palais de justice, assembled his brethren, and communicated it to them. The time passed. On the morrow, the parliament was to be broken. They imitated the conduct of Charles I.'s parliament, when the usher was at the door, in voting a declaration. This set forth, that the states-general had alone the right of granting taxes; that magistrates were irremovable; that no one should be arrested without immediate trial before his natural judge. On a par with these fundamental laws, they place the hereditary right of succession in the crown. The minister replied to this manifesto by issuing a warrant to arrest D'Espréménil. He took refuge in the parliament. The huissier employed, knowing not his person, asked which was he; and the counsellors exclaimed that "they were all Espréménils." Nevertheless he surrendered. The king, in a bed of justice, compelled the registry of his edict, dissolving the parliament. The bailiwicks and plenary court were instituted in its stead. The resistance was now general. Collisions took place universally in the provinces betwixt the troops and the people, who supported their ancient magistracy.

The treasury in the mean time grew empty. A loan was impossible. Brienne had recourse to his own order. He summoned a convocation of the clergy, and asked of them a subsidy. Even here he was destined to meet with opposition; the deputies of the curates and lower clergy were as hostile to the bishops as the commons were to the noblesse, and, as usual, there were not wanting men of the higher ranks to seek influence on the popular side. The clergy were deaf to the archbishop of Toulouse. To his demands for supply, they gave in answer the universal echo, the states-general; and, as if impatient of ruin, requested the immediate convocation of the assembly. Overcome by this last blow, the minister yielded, and dared to hope from the commons that support to the throne that the noblesse, the parliament, and the clergy, had successively and factiously denied. In August, 1788, appeared in consequence an *arrêt* of the council, convoking the states-general in the month of May of the following year.

Brienne hoped to preside over this assembly, and direct its motions. "Are you not afraid to hold the states?" asked some one of him. "Sully held them," was the self-sufficient reply. But the archbishop was destined to proceed no farther in the emulation of Sully. The treasury was without funds; and the day was at hand for the payment of dividends to the public creditor. The minister proposed paying part in bills. The Parisian *rentiers* were in a fury to find their income thus curtailed. An insurrection was expected: several had lately taken place in the provinces,—at Rennes, at Grenoble,—and Brienne feared for the consequences. He hurried, in tears, to the royal closet, and besought the interference of the queen to induce Necker to aid and enter office. Necker agreed to supersede Brienne, but refused to take office with him. The archbishop was accordingly sacrificed. "If he did not make the fortune of the state," says Thiers, "he at least made his own:" he retired enormously rich; and even begged for a cardinal's hat in parting. In addition to the chaos and disorder to which the kingdom was reduced in his administration, his foreign policy, or rather lack of such, entailed disgrace. The popular party of the Dutch, favored by the French, had rebelled against the stadtholder. Prussia marched an army into Holland, despised the feeble menaces of Brienne, and re-established the power of the prince of Orange.

Necker was now once more enthroned in the ministeria. seat. His name was sufficient to bring money to the treasury, and to restore confidence, at least to the pensioner and the fundholder As to administrative measures, the way was marked before him. The states were already summoned; it remained to decide the important question of their organization. Should the three orders sit together, vote by orders, or by numbers? Necker was too unpresuming to decide this question; but it was necessary to regulate the respective numbers of the deputies of each class. Brienne had invited the learned to publish their sentiments on these points; of course, the opinions expressed by them were, that the commons should equal the numbers of the privileged orders united. After this rule the provincial assemblies had been arranged. The precedent told now in its favor. It was Necker's opinion also; to which the queen and court were not averse; for the idea that the crown, whose plans of amelioration were defeated by the aristocracy and by the clergy, should recur to the support of the commons, after being forced, first upon Calonne, then upon Brienne, now began to be entertained at court. Necker proposed to consult the notables on this question. The assembled chiefs of the privileged orders decided against an arrangement so fatal to them: but the bureau at which Monsieur, the king's brother, since Louis XVIII., presided, declared for the plan; in which, indeed, most of those attached to the court joined: liberality gained the ascendant. Although the majority of the notables declared against the predominance of the commons, the question was not considered as decided. A council sat to discuss it at Versailles. Necker proposed still to accede to the double return of the *tiers*, and the queen, who was present, favored the plan. Under such auspices, it was decided in the affirmative, and an order of council decreed that the number of the deputies of the *tiers état*, or commons, should equal that of the noblesse and clergy united.

CHAP. X.

1789—1791.

THE CONSTITUENT OR FIRST NATIONAL ASSEMBLY.

There is no scene, no portion of history, that can be regarded under so many different views as the revolution upon which we now enter. To some, it is all crime; to others, all glory. In England, the prevailing sentiment has been, to regard the French nation as if it were an individual actuated by one perverse will, and flinging itself, from pure love of mischief, into the agonies of suffering and the depths of crime. We have had hitherto naught but a wide anathema to bestow upon our hapless neighbor. In this, it is to be feared, we treated her with similar humanity to that with which men used to treat the leprous,—excluded them at once from society, sympathy, charity, and good-will; regarding their malady as a crime and a sin, and looking with eyes of hate on what had better merited our pity.

Revolution is one of the maladies of kingdoms, or rather the crisis of a malady. It may proceed from some latent vice in the constitution, from dissipation, from mismanagement. To avert such is often no more in the power of the nation or of the individual, than it is to be all-sound and all-wise. From early times there was something wrong in the framework of French society. These defects have been noted; above all, that marked division of classes, which refused amalgamation. Their mutual and oft-renewed struggles have been seen. The people, the great mass, not of the poor and ignorant, but often of the wealthy and enlightened, were conquered and borne down in the combat. Their defeat they could have forgiven; but the extravagant use which the upper classes had made of their victory revolted the fallen. The clergy grasped one third of the lands of the kingdom, the noblesse another; yet the remaining third was burdened with all the expense of government. This was reversing the social pyramid, and placing it upon its apex.

To reform this state of things was necessary. Flesh and blood could not bear it. Intellect, more powerful still, rebelled against it. Owing to the great exertions of the latter in print and orally, all men were agreed as to the necessity of this change. Louis XVI., however uneducated, felt and owned the need; but he was at first young, weak because ignorant, and dared not to break through the trammels of a court. The monarch, nevertheless, made every effort to bring about the desired reform peaceably. He intrusted the task first to Turgot, whose schemes were repulsed by the magistracy, Necker made no political attempt. Calonne next tried. He was defeated and overthrown by the clergy and noblesse. Brienne then was driven to repeat the attempt, and the magistracy tripped up him. What resource was left? To recur to the people. But this was revolution. True! but who rendered it indispensable? Not the people, who were all the time tranquil; not the monarch, who did his utmost; not the queen, despite the accusation that even respectable writers echo—we find her supporting Necker and approving the double representation of the commons—no. It was the resistance, the false, the blind resistance, of the privileged orders,—noblesse, clergy, magistracy,—that precipitated the revolution, and flung all power at last into the hands of the commons.

It is evident from the beginning that, in the assembly of the states, this power must soon have absorbed all others. Necker has been blamed for allowing the third estate a double number of representatives, and for not ordering from the first a chamber of peers. But Necker knew how futile any such ordonnance would have been. In times of extreme danger and convulsion, society is prone to throw off factitious distinctions, and to resolve itself into its first elements. In peace, or even in well-ordered war, the soldier obeys his officer, and looks up to him with confidence. But in the rout, in slaughter, and in the struggle for existence, each puts forth his individual exertions, and saves himself as he can. In the great English rebellion, the peerage was not destroyed: it fell. There was none of that hatred towards it which the French noblesse had excited in the people and merited from them: still it fell. From the same law, it might be augured, that in the general wreck of the social system, which was now inevitable in France, the opportunities for repairing and saving it being voluntarily lost, the members of the privileged classes could survive but as individuals, and hold influence but by their talents and character, not their rank. This is the law of every revolution in which the people are called to partake. It is here uttered as fact, not as doctrine; as warning, not as approbation.* Some argue, might not the revolution have been brought about amicably, with forbearance and mutual sacrifice? Certainly not: it was too late. The changes which even the monarch himself allowed as necessary to be effected, were too radical, too great, to be wrought by aught save force. What centuries ought to have gradually done, was here given as the work of a day. Such a task was too great, too momentous, and the time allowed too short, to permit of its accomplishment by aught short of convulsion. With never so little of fatalism in one's creed, much of that stern principle must be seen linking together and impelling the events of this dire catastrophe.

In the month of May, 1789, the deputies of the states-general thronged to Versailles. The expectation, the ferment, of the capital of the kingdom were excessive. The elections in the provinces had given rise to dissension and tumult. The noblesse and townsfolk fought in many provinces. The rumor

* The revolution of 1830 offers another exemplification of this important truth.

of a great political change had gained the very rabble, who now for the first time began to show their influence on state affairs. The distressed condition of the peasantry had swelled their disorderly ranks, in which were found those ardent tempers which war occupies and mows down, and who in long intervals of peace roam unquiet and eager for their natural element of strife. Famine, occasioned by the failure of the ast crop, rendered more severe by an inclement winter, sharpened the ferocity of this class; whilst its hordes were increased by the efforts of the benevolent, chiefly exerted in the capital, whither the indigent flocked in consequence. A few days before the meeting of the states, a tumult of a serious nature broke out, as if to offer a prognostic of the revolution. Reveillon, a rich manufacturer of the fauxbourg St. Antoine, was reported to have been severe to his workmen, and to have menaced them with a reduction of wages. A mob collected; broke into his establishment; pillaged it; grew inebriated with the contents of the cellars; and were not dislodged till after a combat, in which some hundreds perished. The dead were found to be well supplied with money; a proof that they had been hired to create sedition. Who was the suborner? Suspicion fell upon the duke of Orleans, a prince of restless temper and profligate life: hating the queen, and despised by her, for private causes, he had fomented the factious and selfish opposition of the parliament. And the obscure demagogues, that now began to agitate in the lower depths of society, made use certainly of his name and probably of his purse. The Palais Royal, where the prince dwelt, was their haunt, its precincts being sacred from the molestation of the police. Journals, too, were rare in that day; and the habit began of one person reading aloud to a body of hearers. Speech-making naturally followed reading. The *cafés* partook of the general agitation. And thus the idle and the disreputable formed in the gardens and purlieus of the Palais a kind of ever-open club, in imitation of the similar societies that now abounded throughout the kingdom. The duke of Orleans was flattered by this crowd, that assembled round his residence, and invoked his protection and his name. How far he was instrumental in pushing them to excess, is difficult to decide; but sufficient cause and pretext existed without him.

On the 4th of May, the eve of the opening of the states-general, the members of the several orders walked in solemn procession to the church of St. Louis, at Versailles. The noblesse and clergy, in magnificent costume; the third estate, or commons, in simple black: but the numbers of the latter amounting to 600, equalling those of the clergy and nobles united, formed an apter symbol of their power than all the gorgeousness of embroidery. Here were assembled the select mass of the nation, of its proud names, its intellect, and its wealth; and yet scarcely one was known to fame. Orleans was remarked, perhaps, and Mirabeau, the latter a noble rejected by his caste, and sent as deputy by the commons of Provence. A disordered life was also his chief claim to notoriety. Under the ancient *régime*, talents could only rise to fame by the aid of profligacy.

The assembly met on the following day, in a large building in the avenues of Versailles, that had been prepared for them. The monarch opened the important session with a speech characteristic at once of the benignity and irresolution of his nature. Barentin, the chancellor, followed with a kind of political homily; and Necker continued by unfolding his budget of finance, at a moment when the great question which preoccupied all minds, and shut out every other consideration, was, how the orders were to vote,—whether united, each member with a voice, or separate, each body with a *veto*. Both Necker and the king left this question undecided. The commons, supported by the popular sentiment, came prepared to insist on the union of the three orders, and for very natural reasons. Both noblesse and church had resisted in their several assemblies the ameliorations proposed by Calonne and Brienne. The states were called to effect these; and apparently this could not be done if each order remained apart, intrenched behind its veto. The monarch saw and acknowledged the force of these arguments. The previous inveteracy of the noblesse prevented him from frankly embracing their cause, and establishing their independence. The states were, therefore, left to decide the point betwixt them.

The architectural distribution of the edifice was not without influence. The large hall of assembly was allotted to the *tiers état;* two smaller ones had been prepared for the noblesse and clergy. The commons affected to expect that the two orders would join them, in order to verify their powers in common; but these, in their respective chambers, decided against the coalition. Still there was but a majority of seventy even amongst the nobles for remaining separated, and but a majority of twenty amongst the clergy. In the latter body, the number of curates, elected by the low-church, was great. The ministry in the elections had favored the popular, much more than the aristocratic or high-church, candidates. Learning this distribution of parties, the *tiers* necessarily per sisted. They were certain of succeeding in their aim. Meantime all business was deferred. The public expectation, wound up, and daily disappointed, turned to anger against the aristocrats. Irritation increased, and with it increased the influ ence of the *tiers*. The minister at length proposed a plan of accommodation as to the verification of powers, which favored the pretensions of the noblesse much more than those of the *tiers*. Nevertheless the deputies of the latter had the art and address to show no decided objection, and by this means threw on their opponents the odium of opposing all conciliation. The noblesse, indeed, at first accepted, but then demurred against, the title of *commons*, assumed by the *tiers*. This being inserted in the conferences, the peers refused to sign them, risking an open quarrel for the sake of an empty word. Their democratic opponents made decisive use of this pretext.

In the body of the *tiers état* were two parties: one, headed by Mounier and Malouet, was constitutional and moderate, anxious to secure public liberty, but to check revolution; and desirous of forming a system of government analogous to that of England. An adverse party was led by Mirabeau and Sieyes, with principles and aim yet unfixed, but bent on the establishment of one assembly, in which all rank and distinction merged. Mirabeau, smarting from a long imprisonment, was eager to retaliate on the higher classes, and on the throne itself. Ardent, conscious of the long-pent-up fire of genius, to rule by eloquence and wield the sceptre of popularity was his object. Sieyes, equally ambitious, presented a contrast with his fiery colleague: he was cold, ratiocinating, systematic; one of those temperaments which naught but the fever of political rabies could warm; and even this could but affect his head: his heart was chill as his imagination. Sieyes spoke little; his ideas were mathematically put together. This singularity won for him a character for profound and mysterious wisdom.

The parties and their chiefs now for the first time came into collision. The ultra-liberals declared, that the noblesse merely manœuvred, and raised futile objections, in order to embarrass the march of the states-general, and retain them in complete inaction. Sieyes therefore advised that, preparatory to their constituting themselves into a national assembly, a final summons should be made to the recusant orders to join the commons. This took place on the 10th of June. Its consequence was the defection of three curates from the clergy to join the *tiers*; in two days after, more of their brethren followed; amongst others, the famous Gregoire; and at length, on the 17th, took place the famous debate on the title meaning the powers which they should assume. The preamble of Sieyes stated, that they were ninety-six-hundredths of the nation; and that such a majority could no longer postpone the commencement of business, because the four-hundredths which remained, meaning the noblesse and the clergy, refused to join them. This fractional logic, which at once swept away all rights of property or birth, was adopted without dissent. And in truth the doctrine, which it discovered to be that of the overwhelming majority, might well alarm the court. Mounier, to palliate such a declaration, proposed that they should assume the title of representatives of the commons, or of the major part of the nation. But brevity in a title being justly considered dignity, Le Grand's proposal of adopting that of "national assembly" was preferred. Nevertheless, the body now self-constituted is known in French history as the *Assemblée Constituante.*

No sooner was this great and bold act accomplished, than the assembly hastened to exercise the power which it had assumed, by voting that the imposts now levied had been hitherto illegal, wanting the sanction of the representatives of the people; henceforth, however, their levy was sanctioned temporarily. These votes, this legislative power fully and exclusively assumed by the commons, startled the court and the king himself. The noblesse, thunderstruck, and conscious at once of present weakness and past imprudence, implored the monarch to support their rights. Louis had hitherto been not adverse to the union of the orders: he looked on the states as endowed with financial, merely, not political capacity. Timid himself, he had not expected such audacity; he hesitated whether he should yield or resist. His brother, his queen, the court, all struck with legitimate and prophetic terrors, entreated him to take some decisive step: Necker deprecated extremities. In the midst of this combat of principles, of prudence, and resentment, fear and hope, the clergy came to a decision on the 19th, carried by a single vote, that their order should merge in that of the commons. This came to complicate the question. Necker instantly proposed a *royal sitting*, somewhat resembling the *beds of justice* in parliament, in which the king should command the union of the orders in all subjects of general or pecuniary interest; in the consideration of others, they were to remain separate. Even this was not decided without dispute. Louis listened to all: the whole court was one distracted and noisy council, in which Necker had no predominant voice.

Orders were issued immediately for the *royal sitting*. Carpenters took possession of the house of assembly, and, by a strange oversight, the president of the assembly was made acquainted with the circumstance but on the previous evening. If, in this crisis, it must be allowed that the fears of the court were just, it must also be admitted that the commons had some reason to be alarmed: they heard of a projected *bed of justice;* they knew of the intrigues, the fears, the solicitations of the noblesse: the liberty, which it was their mandate to establish, was in peril. On the morning of the 20th, Bailly, the president, proceeded, despite the notice he had received, to the door of the hall of meeting: it was barred; the sentinels refused entrance, allowing it, however, to Bailly, upon the pretext that he wished to draw up a note of the prohibition. Some young members forced admission also: there was prospect of an altercation, when Bailly withdrew, bringing with him the angry members.

The assembly had by this time collected, and filled in a tumultuary manner the public avenue. Different proposals were made, to hold the assembly where they were, or under the windows of the royal château. There was a tennis-court at hand: it was suggested to adjourn thither, and the idea was welcomed with acclamation. Even the most moderate deputies joined in the general enthusiasm; and it was Mounier who first moved that the assembly should bind itself not to separate till they had prepared and voted a constitution. "An oath! an oath! let us swear it!" was the universal cry. Bailly, standing on a bench, now held up his hand towards the heavens that canopied the dilapidated place of meeting, and repeated the oath, whilst all the other members, one alone excepted, extended their arms and joined in the solemn adjuration. "If the privileged orders had been more formidable at the moment when they were thus attacked, or had the national party shown themselves afterwards more forbearing in their triumph, history would have consecrated this day as one of the most memorable in the annals of liberty."

This bold act of independence struck the courtiers as frowardness and sedition: it unfortunately gave fresh weight to their words, and to their influence with the king. The royal brothers were admitted to the council: the younger, then count d'Artois, since Charles X., was the leader of the anti-popular party; and he found a powerful auxiliary in Marie Antoinette, who, with the quick and single-thoughted feelings of her sex, perceived the arrogance, without being able to appreciate the motives, of the commons. In the midst of a discussion in council, a note from the queen called out Louis and interrupted the decision: the monarch was induced to modify Necker's plan of the *royal sitting*, and render it an act of severity rather than conciliation. Necker resigned.

On the 23d took place the *royal sitting*. The king made known his will. He annulled all the previous votes and acts of the assembly; commanded the orders, according to Necker's plan, to unite in the same chamber to decide on pecuniary questions, to remain separate on others. A report was then read of the reforms and concessions to be granted by the monarch, after which Louis himself resumed, "If by a fatality that I cannot bring myself to expect, you abandon me in my benevolent enterprise, I will *alone* undertake the good of my people: I will consider myself *alone* their true representative." The act here threatened might have been dangerous, but it was less dangerous than the menace. The monarch and the assembly were now at open variance: both had avowed their principles; they were incompatible and hostile; for either to recede was to succumb for ever.

The assembly felt this as it were by instinct. The last words of the king bade them instantly separate for that day; he himself retired, accompanied by the noblesse. The commons remained immovable. De Brezé, the master of the ceremonies, summoned them to depart: the president said, "that he should obey the orders of the assembly alone." Mirabeau started up, and apostrophized De Brezé,—"Tell your master we are here by the will of the people, and nothing less than the force of bayonets shall expel us." Workmen began now to remove the decorations of the hall: Bailly ordered them to cease. After much agitation, Mirabeau proposed a vote, that the persons of the members were inviolable. With this concluded the sitting.

What was the resolve of the court on learning that the commons persisted in the positions which they had taken up? In deciding on the measure and language of the royal sitting, it should have been prepared for resistance as for obedience. Now was the time to act, if ever. But no:—they had flung away the scabbard, yet feared to use the sword. The queen was the first to yield. Rumors had spread of Necker being in disgrace; the inhabitants of Versailles began to shout his name: Marie Antoinette herself summoned the popular minister, promised to support and adopt his views, and so persuaded him to resume his ministry. Thus in the morning the king was made to address the commons with the bravado of a soldier, in the evening to retract with all the weakness of a woman.

Each day of this important period forms a crisis, and comes fraught with some portentous event. The closer, indeed, that history here approaches to a journal, the more clear and perfect will be the idea conveyed of how fatuity dragged on evil and audacity brought success. On the 25th, two days after the royal sitting, forty-seven members of the noblesse imitated the clergy in coming to join the commons: they were led by the duke of Orleans. Further resistance was vain. An order of the king now requested the majority of the noblesse to unite themselves to the assembly. "I would have no blood spilt in my quarrel," said Louis to those who expostulated. On the 27th of June, the three orders sat in the same hall. "The family was united," Bailly observed; "but it gave few hopes of domestic union or tranquillity."

Whilst the assembly, or rather its popular majority, was thus completing and strengthening itself, and all its pretensions were allowed and acquiesced in by the monarch and his minister, the extreme parties of the court aristocracy, and of the seditious demagogues, were each stirring and plotting, gathering means of activity and influence. The former besieged the king through the medium of the queen, who had already recovered from momentary weakness: troops were insensibly collected and concentrated round the capital; and the château of Versailles became the head-quarters of an army, as well as the seat of a counter-revolutionary council. The populace on their part were daily getting fresh audacity and strength, or rather a knowledge of their strength. When Louis and his queen yielded on the evening of the royal sitting to the few clamors of the people of Versailles, in favor of Necker, they taught their enemies the way to conquer them. The mob of Versailles, indeed, set the example to that of Paris, bursting into the hall of the assembly on the day that the noblesse joined it, and at times drowning the debates by their clamors. Now too the municipality of Paris, self-constituted from the electors of the city, raised its head: and in common with many other clubs and assemblies, forwarded addresses of congratulation to the national assembly. The Palais Royal presented scenes of still greater disorder. Declaimers harangued in every street: the very rabble drank of the intoxicating spirit of politics. The triumph of the *tiers état* at Versailles had suspended the action of all law; journals and clubs multiplied; a pretext alone was wanted to produce open insurrection. The authority of the sovereign had quailed before that of the assembly. The populace were now determined to imitate the latter in an essay of *their* arms against the throne. When the moral power and influence of a government is defeated, it may rely on soon being driven to make trial of its physical force.

It was a short time previous to this outbursting of popular discontents, that the household troops had been disbanded; that an order had been issued forbidding the advancement of any, save nobles, to the rank of officers; and at the same time introducing the severities of Prussian discipline into the ranks of the French army. The soldiery was, in consequence, as prone to insubordination as the populace. On the last day of June, three hundred of the French guards quitted the barracks in which they had been confined, and visited the Palais Royal. They were welcomed with exultant joy. Placed in confinement on returning to their quarters, the populace broke in, and liberated them. This was the first triumph of the mob.

Foreign troops in the French service were, in the mean time, crowding to Versailles. The Orangery, the gardens, presented the appearance of a bivouac. The count d'Artois, with his friend the baron de Breteuil, took upon him to direct the attack upon the revolution.* The courage and indignation of the queen were again wound up to approve and second the intentions of this party. Whilst the theorists of the assembly were busied in preparing the constitution, the attention of Mirabeau was turned to practice. He proposed an address to the king to countermand the troops which thronged around Paris, and in the same motion recommended the formation of the citizens of Paris into a civic guard. This was no new invention; the league had had its national guard. Without deciding the question, whether this institution be compatible with monarchy, it was certainly advisable at the present moment. Had it been organized now, before the populace had tasted of plunder and of blood, the revolution might have been spared a portion of its crimes; and power, in its fall, would not have descended lower than the middle classes.

On the 11th of July, the count d'Artois's party had overcome the scruples of the king. Necker was dismissed according to his own desire, and bidden to take his departure secretly. Breteuil succeeded him. The recurrence to force, which on the 23d of June would have shown consistency, if not prudence, was now, when too late, to be employed. The

* How similar is the count d'Artois of 1789 to the Charles X. of 1830. Bezenval, after describing the prince's indignation against those who sought to overturn the throne, adds, yet, "without forces, and above all, without experience, he allowed himself to be led by a man, the most incapable of good counsel; one who was known to have failed, from his imprudence, in every thing that he undertook. This man, having a great interest to make common cause with the prince, removed from around him all the friends who could have enlightened him as to his true situation. The count d'Artois continued to consider himself chief of the party, because the noblesse came universally to pour their plaints in his ear. He always put one of them by his side at madame de Polignac's, where he dined every day. He courted and flattered them, as if men, money, or real succor could be thus obtained. Wanting these, he but opened the eyes of the demagogues, and became not so much the object of their fears as of their observation and hatred."—*Détails Historiques.*

court were anticipated in their intended blow. Necker's dismissal had taken place upon a Saturday. On Sunday, the 12th, the idle crowd of the Palais Royal learned the tidings. It was the spark upon the train, the desired pretext found. Camille Desmoulins, a low demagogue, took the lead; harangued the mob; showed himself armed; and, plucking a branch, put a leaf in his hat by way of cockade. His example was applauded and imitated. Waxen busts of Necker and Orleans were then seized in a neighboring shop, crowned with laurel, and carried in procession through the streets. Near the Place Vendôme the procession came in contact with a German regiment. Blows and shots were exchanged. A soldier of the royal guards was said to have been killed in the ranks of the people. For this cause, and from previous jealousy, some hundreds of the guards issued from their barracks near the spot, drew up, and fired upon the Germans. The prince de Lambesch, commanding them, ordered a retreat, to avoid bloodshed: whilst effecting this through the gate of the garden of the Tuilleries, an aged person was slain. Cries of vengeance followed. The populace hastened in search of arms. The Hôtel de Ville, where the electors, self-constituted as a municipality, were in the habit of daily assembling, delivered up all preserved in that establishment. They ordered the establishment of a civic guard; a vain and late attempt to separate the armed citizen from the armed ruffian.

Thus passed the 12th: the 13th saw the fermentation increase, though unmarked by events. On the morning of the 14th the Invalids were invaded by the mob; its arsenal afforded a fresh supply of muskets, and, what was more important, artillery. Thus provided, they marched to the Bastile. Some thirty Swiss and eighty invalids garrisoned this fortress. They, as well as the unfortunate governor, De Launay, were appalled by an enemy so new to the soldier,—the clamors of a ferocious multitude. The morning was spent in parleys and menaces. The municipality in vain endeavored to quiet the people, and put the fortress in the possession of their new militia. The populace was too numerous and too agitated to hearken to aught but their own passion and impatience. By a sudden assault they broke the chains of the drawbridge, and passed the outer fossé. The garrison defended the inner fortification, and the combat commenced. The French guards now took the lead; when the garrison, alarmed, compelled the governor to hoist the white flag, in token of surrender. The victors rushed in, and filled the interior of this once formidable prison. The rabble attempted to massacre the invalids: the French guards defended them. A young woman was even thrown amidst some burning mat tresses, but was rescued from the flames. De Launay was not so fortunate. Several of his officers were slain. Two French guards vainly undertook to conduct him safe through the crowd; but blows fell upon him from every side, and soon immolated the victim.

The Bastile conquered, the populace marched in triumph o the Hôtel de Ville. The assembled chiefs of the citizens were now to learn that it was not royalty alone, its officers nd its nobles, that were threatened by revolution. The municipality had chosen Hesselles, provost of the merchants, to preside. He weakly undertook to amuse the people, promising them arms and indicating where they were to be found. Exasperated by finding this information false, the provost of the merchants was massacred by the same hands as the governor of the Bastile. Thus the middle as well as the upper ranks furnished the first victims to insurrection.

In the mean time, where was the count d'Artois, the baron de Breteuil, their bold projects, and their army? They slumbered or trembled, whilst the only fortress of the capital was attacked. Louis saw their weakness and incapacity; and, abandoning their counsels, hurried to the national assembly, intending to make peace with it, to proclaim his amity and sincere cordiality with it, and to crave its support and interference to restore order to the capital. At the same time he announced, that orders were given that the troops should retire from the capital. Seeing the popular party thus victorious, the count d'Artois, the Polignacs, and inveterate courtiers, took their departure from France; as precipitate to fly as they had been tardy to act.

The national assembly, thus master of the sovereign through the influence of the Parisian mob, sent a deputation to thank the capital, and to organize anew its authorities, those of the monarchy having lost all influence. Bailly, formerly president, a man of letters and probity, headed this deputation, which was received with enthusiasm. Bailly himself was chosen to preside over the municipality, as mayor of Paris, in the place of the unfortunate Hesselles. A commander of the armed force, miscalled national guard, (for it was soon composed of disbanded soldiers, of every class save citizens,) was imperatively necessary. La Fayette, whose bust was in the Hôtel de Ville, recalling his campaigns in the cause of American liberty, was voted to this post. Lally-Tollendal, who was of the deputation, fascinated the mob by his eloquence, and, fortunately for him, was recompensed merely by their applauses. The Parisians were told, that Louis was now cordially united with the national assembly. "He has hitherto been deceived," said La Fayette and Lally; "but he now sees the merit and justness of the popular cause." The enthusiasm was general on this explication being made. Tears of joy were shed. The revolution seemed already to have closed its list of horrors and of change.

Bailly, the new mayor, entertained this opinion; but he was soon undeceived. The suspicions of the populace returned. In a few hours they recommenced clamoring and crowding, and demanded the presence of the king in his capital, to reassure them, and repeat from his own mouth his intentions. Bailly promised to do his utmost to gratify them in this; but already this simple lover of liberty perceived, that there was some mysterious agent, that excited and bribed the people to fresh sedition. It could be no other than the duke of Orleans. Already murmurs arose among the populace of the necessity of marching to Versailles, and bringing back the monarch. A deputation from the city was ordered to demand it. Louis anticipated their coming and request, by stating his readiness to visit Paris.

He accordingly proceeded thither on the 17th. Nothing is more probable, than that assassination was intended by the great mover of the base part of the rabble. They shrunk, however, from an attempt that would have been mercy to the unfortunate Louis.* Arrived at the gates of Paris, he was welcomed by the new mayor, who, with a pedantic love of antithesis little worthy of Bailly, spoke the following poignant truth:—"I present to your majesty the keys of the good city of Paris; the same which were presented to Henry IV. He reconquered his people. Here the people have reconquered their king." The procession, like funeral ones, had the appearance of a fête. The new militia was under arms. The tricolor cockade was in every hat. Green had been discarded, as being the color of the princes. Blue and red were of old the colors of the city of Paris. White was now added, out of affection to the Bourbon king. The cockade being presented to him by Bailly, at the Hôtel de Ville, he assumed it cheerfully, and bade the mayor state for him to the municipality, that he approved of their acts. This royal adhesion to the revolution being given, Louis returned to Versailles, rejoiced in heart, that he had again escaped from his capital. The queen flung herself into his arms on rebeholding him: she had been prepared for worse.

If the ruffians had been here balked of their victim, awed by his dignity, or by the general expression of regard, they

* A woman was nevertheless shot close to the royal carriage.

found means soon after to gratify their thirst of blood. Foulon, superintendent of the revenue, a peculiarly detested member of a detested profession, had been seized as one of the aristocratic conspirators. He was brought, on the 27th, to the Hôtel de Ville, then the centre of justice as of force. He was reported to have derided the sufferings of the people in famine, and to have bidden them "eat hay." He was now brought with ignominy to the Hôtel de Ville, the populace clamoring for his instant condemnation. In vain the municipality urged that they did not form a court of justice; equally in vain did they affect to go through the forms of an interrogatory to gain time. La Fayette tried his eloquence and popularity. The rabble, impatient, rushed on Foulon, tore him forth, and hanged him to a lamp-post. His son-in-law, Berthier, was soon after brought in on the same charge. The mob held up to him the streaming head of Foulon, and laughed with delight at his recoil of horror. Berthier shared a similar fate. La Fayette threw down his command in disgust, but was prevailed on to resume it.

The peasantry of many of the provinces imitated in the mean time the lower orders of the capital, in a crusade against gentility; châteaux were burned, their lords hunted forth, the possessors of birth and property menaced and proscribed. The deputies of the privileged classes now resolved to resign those rights which rendered them odious. They, too, at least a great number, however fallen, and despoiled, and calumniated, felt the patriotic excitement of the time, and were prepared to make sacrifice of every distinction and claim. The attention of the assembly being turned on the 4th of August to the excesses of the peasantry, it was observed, that their resentment was justly called forth against the upholders of *taille* and *corvée* and feudal abuses. On this the viscount de Noailles moved to abolish *corvées* and all marks of personal servitude. The duc d'Aiguillon followed; and the first nobles of the land came forward to sacrifice all seigniorial rights, jurisdiction, and exemption. The clergy followed the example. In a single hour of excitement, the proudest aristocracy, and the most unbending church, had levelled themselves with the peasant, and sacrificed those rights, rather than yield the smallest part of which, they had, during the last ten years, persisted in risking, and at length precipitating, monarchy and state.

Here closes the first act of the revolution. The privileged orders, which had so long weighed upon France, were swept away. The middle ranks succeeded to their place, and in a great measure to the difficulties and the envy of that place.

What has, throughout this history, been called the burgess-class, in which now blended the professions and smaller agriculturists, had been completely victorious in that important struggle with the court and aristocracy, which has been here minutely, perhaps tediously, described. They were now in the zenith: they formed the majority of the assembly. Bailly nd La Fayette, perfect representatives of their opinion, held the executive, as it were, of the revolutionary realm, not yet extending, it is true, far beyond the circuit of the capital. But already the working class, the artisan, the needy, began tc feel the weight of that above it, and to look even upon simple burgesses as aristocrats. The municipality was already clam ored against and bullied by the mob, which only wanted writers, orators, and demagogues to lead it on in the path of power. These did not yet exist. The dragon's teeth were sown, indeed, but the crop of mutual slaughters had not reached maturity. The shadow of royalty and of a court also existed, and attracted towards it a considerable share of popular attention and animosity. This averted for a time the struggle that was still inevitable betwixt the middle ranks of society and the lower.

An interval of two months now passed over without any flagrant scene of popular violence. The assembly employed the time in fixing the basis of the new constitution; the municipality busied in procuring bread for the Parisians; and Necker, who had returned to assume the ministry, in anguish and expedients to raise funds, at a time when neither tax could be levied nor loan raised. Although the latter was the more pressing, the constitution was the more important, question. Mounier, Lally, Necker, proposed the English model; a scheme that was neither supported by the small body of noblesse, (true to their spirit of the order, they seemed to imitate their neighbors, and now gathered hope but from the prospect of anarchy,) nor tolerated by the great majority. The very name of "noble" was so odious, that men of the most aristocratic feelings sacrificed them at once to necessity and prudence. The oracular Siéyes argued, that it was for the people to will, for the sovereign to execute. The simplicity and hardihood of this doctrine pleased. Few thought of sking, was it practicable. The existence of but one chamer was voted by an overwhelming majority. It was the uestion of the royal *veto* that excited difference. Should it exist at all? should it be absolute or suspensive? Sieyes would not allow of the word: he called it a "*lettre de cachet* against the will of the nation." The country joined in the discussion. The provincial towns sent addresses against the *veto.* The mob of the Palais Royal prepared a formidable deputation. La Fayette and Bailly stopped it at the gates of Paris. They had, for the time, recovered mastery of the popular mind. The king was advised by Necker to interfere, and state to the assembly his acceptance of the suspensive rather than the absolute *veto.* The former was accordingly decreed. Thus a single representative chamber, and a sovereign possessed merely of the power of deferring a law by his dissent, formed the outlines of the new constitution.

As yet the lower orders had no exclusive party, and scarcely an avowed partisan, in the assembly, though Robespierre and other future demagogues sat silent and unnoticed on its benches. But their voices may be discerned in the cry for a national bankruptcy, that was raised on Necker's making a statement of financial distress. The measure of spoliation would have fallen almost exclusively upon the Parisian tradesman or comfortable *rentier.* The same act was recommended, with the self-same view, by the high aristocracy under the regent, that was now demanded by the "friends of the people." Mirabeau, however, whose want or disregard of principle was often supplied by the instinct of genius, started up in behalf of the middle ranks. With ironical force he proposed to take 2000 of the wealthiest citizens and fling them into the gulf of the public debt—to immolate them in order to fill it up. Such was his hardy metaphor. The assembly recoiled. "Ay," continued he, "and what is bankruptcy but this? The other day, when mention was made of an imaginary insurrection of the Palais Royal, we heard amongst us the exclamation, 'Catiline is at the gates of Rome, and the senate does naught but deliberate.' Certes, there were round us then nor Catiline, nor perils, nor factions, nor Rome. But bankruptcy, hideous bankruptcy, is at our gates, and in the midst of us, menacing our lives, our properties, and honor—and yet we deliberate!" Struck by this apostrophe, the assembly voted by acclamation to uphold the national credit, and assent to the financial scheme of Necker.

There were plans, however, at the moment in agitation, of more serious importance than either bankruptcy or credit. Both the court and popular party had drawn breath; the one had recovered from its terrors, the latter had resumed its suspicion and impatience. Both conspired, the aristocracy as well as the rabble; whilst the middling ranks and the assembly were doomed to await, and to submit to whichever should prove conqueror. Bailly and La Fayette in vain exerted themselves to keep the capital quiet. Famine prevailed, despite the abundance of the crop. Corn is hoarded as well as coin in times of pillage and terror. The court is accused of increasing this; the duke of Orleans of having produced it. The people, always confined to one idea, and seeking in it a remedy for every woe, resumed the cry, "To Versailles! let us go to seek bread and the king at Versailles!" The courtiers were not displeased with this popular resolve, which they hoped would drive Louis to an open breach with the revolution. They saw no hope but in civil war. M. de Bouillé, a noble and a general, commanded at Metz, an important garrison of the frontier. He was beloved by his soldiery. The thoughts of the queen and her counsellors were turned towards him, as the restorer of the monarchy.

In the midst of this came the menaces, the plaints, the deputation, from Paris to the assembly. The court, recurring to its warlike ideas, brought the regiment of Flanders to Versailles. The Orangery, the gardens, were again occupied with troopers and body-guards. The municipality of Paris was alarmed. La Fayette himself spoke openly of the plot against liberty. The mob caught the suspicion. On the 2d of October a banquet was given by the body-guards to the officers of the newly-arrived regiment; those of the national guard of Versailles were also invited. It took place in the palace-theatre. Wine circulated; enthusiasm was excited. The soldiers of the regiments were admitted into the building: cups being handed to them, they drank to the health of the queen, and of the king. With drawn swords the banqueters pledged them. The queen, hearing of the fête, presented herself with the dauphin. A fresh effusion of loyalty ensued. Swords again flashed, with vows to support the royal cause, whilst the military band played the air of Cœur de Lion, "*O Richard, O mon roi, l'univers t'abandonne!*"

Accounts of the fête soon came to exasperate the Parisians, and to offer the agitators a pretext to excite tumult. Orleans, who might pretend to the regency, if the king was frightened away to Metz, had his interest in producing insurrection at this moment. A crowd of women was adroitly employed to besiege the guard, and the Hôtel de Ville. They could only be diverted from setting fire to the edifice by an invitation to proceed to Versailles. The tocsin, in the mean time, was sounded. The rabble, armed with pikes, forks, and sticks, crowded to the square, and soon marched off to Versailles, to ask bread of the assembly. La Fayette soon after arrived at the Hôtel de Ville. The assembled companies of the national guard awaited him. Though bearing this title, these troops were not citizens, but mere mercenary troops. They, too, demanded to march upon Versailles. La Fayette in vain dissuaded them; he was constrained to lead them. All Paris followed in their wake.

This movement took place on the 5th of October. On the very same day, in the assembly, the popular party first showed itself fully: Petion, Robespierre, Gregorie, started up, with denunciations, giving vent to the extreme of revolutionary language. Already they began to accuse and threaten Mirabeau, the representative of the *bourgeoise*. The only hope for the monarch, at this time, was to have rallied to the latter party; and his adhesion would have completed its sepa tion from the ultra-revolutionists, who at this time were but in the feebleness of birth. It was this day, however, that the monarch was advised to set himself at variance with the vote of the assembly, and to disapprove of their constitution.

The horde of women and rabble reached Versailles in the afternoon: they penetrated into the assembly, demanding bread, and saying that the aristocrats and the archbishop of Paris had bribed the millers not to grind corn. Mounier was dispatched to the palace; the women accompanied him thither, but the crowd was stopped at the iron railing in front of the château: twelve were, however, admitted, to lay their complaints before the king. At his aspect and that of the queen, their fury was dumb; they returned to their comrades, satisfied and charmed with their benign reception: these, amazed and angered at such a change, threatened to hang their unfortunate envoys.

The troops were drawn up in front of the château, consisting of the body-guard, the regiment of Flanders, and the national guard of Versailles. Although the two latter had joined in the famous banquet, the grenadiers of Flanders being the first to propose the health of the queen, yet now both were ill-affected, and openly avowed their opinions. Three hundred of the body-guard formed thus the entire force upon which the king had to depend. Yet causes of exasperation had been given both to the people and the assembly, and even now Louis refused to fly. Some of the people in the mean time mingled with the soldiers; M. de Savonnières, of the body-guard, came to drive them away with his drawn sabre, though striking merely with the flat of the weapon: he was wounded instantly by a shot. The national guard of Versailles took part with the populace, and fired upon the body-guards, which, too weak to contend with such a force, were compelled to retire.

Towards midnight La Fayette arrived, at the head of the Parisian guard and a fresh host of rabble; having made them take, during their march, a vain oath to be well-conducted and loyal. He made his appearance at the palace, promised tranquillity, and demanded that, as a mark of confidence, the external guard of the château should be committed to *his* troops. No doubt the general made this arrangement with the best intentions; but he was not sufficiently suspicious of the sanguinary and anarchic party that was now raising its head, supported by the money and the confidence of Orleans. That prince was seen amongst the midnight groups, and on the road: his agency must be allowed, though history cannot as yet assign the measure of his influence. All remained quiet through the night; the soldiers, the rabble, the women, round their fires. La Fayette had retired to rest, but in a lodging far from the château. A friend, an officer in whom he had confidence, should have watched. The person and guards of his sovereign were intrusted to his care, and their safety was neglected. No uprightness of character can here shelter him from censure. About half an hour after five, some of the boldest of the mob, bribed, there can be little doubt, to an act that no popular object could prompt, roamed along the vast extent of the palace, trying the possibility of entrance at one of its many gates. They found an avenue unguarded, summoned their chosen comrades, and rushed up the staircase. A *garde du corps*, perceiving the movement, had already fired from the window: and now this faithful troop, though not numbering more than a dozen, defended each door and apartment against the mob, under whose blows they fell one by one. The shouts and horrid imprecations of the ruffians indicated plainly that the queen was the object of their fury. "We will cut off her head! Tear out her heart!" Mismandre, the survivor of the *gardes du corps*, had time to gain the apartments occupied by the queen, opening and crying to her attendants, "I am alone against 2000 tigers: we are conquered; save the queen!" As the unfortunate princess fled, he who had just spoke the generous word of warning fell under the blows of his pursuers. They mangled his remains with disappointment and rage, on perceiving that their prey was flown. A more numerous troop of the body-guard occupied the doors through which Marie Antoinette had retreated: the assassins had but the satisfaction of making villanous jibes upon her yet warm couch. La Fayette at this moment arrived, and by his exertions prevented a renewal of their attempt, or of the slaughter. The rest of the *gardes du corps* were spared: the ruffians contenting themselves with decapitating the dead, and fixing their gory heads on pikes to adorn their triumph.

The mob and Parisian army outside now exulted in the

achievement of this barbarous feat. "The king to Paris!" was the universal cry: denial was vain. The monarch assented, and showed himself in the balcony in token of obsequiousness. The queen was then called for, with the same shout that the Romans were wont to hail a gladiator into their circus: Marie Antoinette appeared, the dauphin in her arms. "No child! no child!" cried the barbarians. The meaning was evident: they wanted a victim. With unshaken courage, the queen appeared alone: a musket was pointed at her; but the heart of the assassin failed through awe, not through mercy. La Fayette knelt, and kissed her hand: he, indeed, did his utmost to repair the fatal negligence of the morning. At midday took place the removal of the royal family to the Tuilleries. Historians dispute the greater or less hideousness of the procession: it was worthy of the victors. Thus the authority of the king was first destroyed, then his power, now all respect for him. The imprudence of the courtiers had served both as cause and pretext to this disaster, which the popular force effected, stirred in part by the gold of Orleans and the intrigues of agitators. La Fayette and the national assembly were mere spectators: the tide was too strong for this middle party; its leaders kept themselves indeed afloat, but the wind and tide of circumstances wafted them on a headlong course.

There was but one man at that epoch who truly understood the crisis, and saw whither things tended: this was Mirabeau, a profligate, but not altogether a politically dishonest man. He received afterwards pecuniary aid from the court, but not until his conviction had led him to unite with it. As for the constitutionalists, their ideas were excellent, and their reasoning plausible; but, struggling against the spirit of the nation, they neutralized efforts which, more wisely directed, might still have supported the middle class and the friends of order against the conspirators and ultra-revolutionists. Aristocracy, not such as conquest or feudality might found, but such as great and illustrious qualities give birth to, and time fosters into dignity—is indeed a natural element of every society. It is wise to uphold its existence: but if a feudal aristocracy, like that of France, abuse its superiority, and grind, by its oppression, deep hate of its name into the feelings and prejudices of the people, it is vain to hope for the continuance or re-establishment of that noblesse. The dire necessity of circumstances must be submitted to. This Mirabeau saw: this Mounier, Necker, Lally, did not see. They were theorists,—*doctrinaires*, to use a modern expression,—pursuing their *one idea* athwart the opposed and bristling prejudices of the nation. This is necessary to explain their ill success, as well as the irritation and hostility excited by efforts which, to Englishmen, appear at first sight honest, bold, and wise. They were all, except the last.

Twenty months now elapsed of comparative tranquillity. There is no striking event; much intrigue, indeed, fiery debating, the training, dividing, and forming of parties. The revolutionary monster slumbered, stirring at times, and showing life by starts, but not awakening fully. La Fayette possessed most power out of the assembly; and he exercised it with a firmness, a disinterestedness and courage, that did him immortal honor. His first act was to drive the duke of Orleans to exile. It is not well known whether his departure was procured by menace or inducement. His absence had certainly the effect of allowing agitation to subside.

The assembly pursued its legislative labors. They appropriated to the state all ecclesiastical property. As it was impossible to bring such a prodigious portion at once to sale, the church-lands were made over to each *commune* or parish, which was allowed time to sell and pay into the treasury the price. The want of supply and specie soon after obliged the assembly to represent this debt due to the government by the different municipalities in bonds, called *assignats*. These they passed to a prodigious amount, forming a paper money not without advantage, had not the facilities of its supply been grossly abused. The constituent assembly divided France into departments, breaking up the old distinction and frontiers betwixt provinces. It abolished parliaments, and remodelled the judicature. Tithes and feudal services had been previously done away with. Titles of honor were now abolished, Matthieu de Montmorency being foremost to make the sacrifice.

This career of legislation was, one should think, sufficiently democratic. It fully satisfied the middle classes, La Fayette, and those who rallied round him, as well as the majority of the assembly. Within its precincts, the demagogues, who designed to form and head a popular party, with difficulty found an opportunity to develop their sentiments or forward their plans. They succeeded, however, in becoming masters of a club, first established by the moderate friends of liberty. This, on the removal of the king and assembly to Paris, had installed itself in the Convent of the Jacobins. Here, as violence gained ground, the moderates, such as La Fayette, seceded and formed a separate club. Barnave, a young Protestant barrister, and the Lameths, assumed the lead in the Jacobins at their departure. This trio envied and detested equally Mirabeau and La Fayette, and seemed actuated more by the ambition of pre-eminence than by any profound conviction or principle, to separate and form a schism. They coquetted with the genuine party of the lower orders rather than embraced it. Talents alone gave them support.

Mirabeau was actuated by more independent opinions. Towards the end of 1789 he began to rein in the zeal which hitherto had borne him headlong in the path of revolution. His ardor cooled, and he could not but disapprove of that constitution which he had contributed to form. "He thought it too democratic for a monarchy; for a democracy there was a king too much." His sagacity saw the impracticability of the existing system. He, consequently, leagued secretly with the court to support the crown, and recover for it a portion of strength requisite for its existence. La Fayette, on the contrary, held firm to the constitution now established. It was not in the power of the king to unite in his behalf two such powerful men, who in fact represented the same cause,—that of the middle orders.

Louis XVI. is accused of irresolution by some writers, of insincerity by others. Never was a man more deserving of commiseration and excuse. In February, 1790, we find him embarked frankly with the nation, coming down spontaneously to the assembly, and giving an uncalled-for adhesion to its acts, that excited universal enthusiasm. In July of the same year he presided over the famous *Federation*, or union of the Parisians with deputations from the provinces, to swear to the constitution on the altar of the country. Talleyrand was the officiating bishop in this ceremony, so minutely detailed and honored by French historians, though in itself a pomp of little importance, a fête at once to celebrate the anniversary of the destruction of the Bastile, and to honor the birth of a constitution destined to be ephemeral. Many weeks of the same summer were passed by the royal family at St. Cloud; escape from thence would have been most practicable, but was not once contemplated.

Hence we may infer, that Louis had resigned himself to his humbled position, and resolved to look for no other than legislative support. The emigrant noblesse, collecting first at Turin, and afterwards at Coblentz, endeavored with their wonted imbecility and ill success to stir up rebellion in the provinces, for which the discontent of the clergy, and consequently of the devout, gave them ample facilities. They solicited Louis to sanction their plans and join their meditated armaments. He had already suffered too much by their counsels, to listen to them again. The marquis de Bouillé at that time fixed the attention and hopes of the royalists within the kingdom. He still commanded at Metz, restraining the froward spirit of the soldiers, and even mastering a sedition amongst them, by his firmness. A similar mutiny broke out at Nancy. Bouillé marched against it at the head of troops, of which he had so little reason to be confident. Nevertheless, when remonstrance failed to bring the mutineers to a sense of duty, Bouillé charged them, beat them, and sen the ringleaders captive to Paris.

This was alone sufficient to raise the monarch's hopes. Bu how could he resist the opinions and counsel of Mirabeau, when this leader of the redoubtable assembly owned as his opinion, that royalty, in order to exist, must be raised from its present prostrate condition; that this must be effected by a force foreign to the assembly; and that the only means to bring about this end was, that the king should retire to Metz, beyond the power of the Parisians, and there, at the head of an independent force, treat with the nation, if he could not with its present representatives, and conclude some more equitable adjustment between the rights of the crown and those of the people?

Such was the plan of Mirabeau, and it gained at once the monarch's approbation. But a fatal event came to retard it, and deprived Louis of what he most wanted,—a man of capacity to conduct him. Mirabeau kept his ascendency in the assembly to the last. Barnave and the Lameths in vain endeavored to shake his supremacy. On the great question, whether the power of deciding on war or peace should rest with the monarch or the nation, Mirabeau took the monarchic side. His enemies saw the opportunity, and attacked him with a virulence and truth that would have overborne any other man. The Jacobins made use of their arm, and the "great treason of count Mirabeau" was cried through the streets. "I had no need of this example," cried the orator, "to learn, that there is but one step from the capitol to the Tarpeian rock." Mirabeau's eloquence conquered in the assembly, and even partially exculpated him with the multitude. The 28th of February, 1791, was the day of his most memorable triumph.* The emigrants, collected at Coblentz, were menacing France with their own force, and with that of the

* It was that of La Fayette also, who in the morning attacked and dispersed an insurrectionary force that menaced Vincennes, and in the evening disconcerted a similar kind of movement of the royalists who frequented the Tuilleries. Thus, inside and outside the national assembly, the leaders of the middle class were triumphant over those of the lower orders. The death of Mirabeau and the unsuccessful flight to Varennes destroyed this superiority.

sovereigns of Europe. It was proposed to stop the tide of emigration, by intrusting the power of granting passports to a committee of three persons. Mirabeau exclaimed against such an inquisition. "As for me," cried he, "I should feel myself absolved from my oath of allegiance to any government, that had the infamy to propose this dictatorial commission. I swear it—" (loud cries interrupted him). "The popularity that I have so ambitioned, and that I have enjoyed like many others, is not a feeble reed. I will fix it deep in the earth. I will make it vegetate and live in the soil of justice and reason." This bold allusion, more to his purposes than to the question, was received with a blind applause, that maddened the popular leaders. They cried out against Mirabeau as a dictator. "Silence, ye thirty voices!" was his rejoinder. His last triumph was his greatest. The orator died, like a general, in his crowning victory. He returned thence to a bed of sickness, from which he never arose. That organic disease of the heart, supposed principally to affect men of strong passions and eloquence, carried him off. "After my death," said he, "the factions will soon tear the last shreds of the monarchy."

Though deranged in his plans by this loss, Louis still persevered in them, and meditated escape. The severity of the assembly towards the priesthood who refused to take the oaths wounded the king's conscience; and even the most meek, when touched in that point, become stubborn and determined. In the month of April the royal carriages were ordered to the palace; Louis and his queen descended for the purpose of visiting St. Cloud. At the sight the populace collected, surrounded the carriage, and forbade it to advance. La Fayette came in time to preserve his sovereigns from insult, but not to procure their liberty. They were obliged to return to their apartments. A more secret mode of escape was then planned. The emperor Joseph at this time promised to march an army to the relief of his unfortunate brother. The emigrants, on their side, proffered their aid and counsels. But Louis preferred depending upon Bouillé, who, under his direction, formed a camp of some faithful regiments on the frontier near Mont medy. The king hoped, by reaching it in safety, to avoid the reproach, at least, of emigration; and without foreign aid, as he afterwards asserted, to raise up liberty upon a firmer basis.

The time of flight was fixed for the night of the 19th of June. Bouillé gave orders, in consequence, for troops and detachments to meet the king at the bridge of Sommeville and at St. Menehould, to escort and protect his progress.

should he succeed in reaching those towns. Unfortunately owing to some difficulty excited by the female attendants of the royal family, the departure was put off to the following night, by which means, although word was sent to Bouillé, the detachments were no longer in waiting for the king when he arrived. A private door in her apartment had been prepared by the queen; issuing by this in three parties, the royal family gained the courts, and crossed them, the king with his children reaching the rue de l'Echelle without impediment. Here a *fiacre* awaited them. But the queen had in the mean time lost her way, the *garde du corps* who conducted her, being ignorant of Paris. She chanced to meet La Fayette, but passed unrecognized by him, and joined the rest at length after much wandering and trouble. The hackney-coach, driven by M. de Fersen in disguise, then bore them to a distant part of the city. At the gate St. Martin they quitted it for a berlin drawn by post-horses, and were soon on the road to Chalons. The king's brother, afterwards Louis XVIII., took, on the same night, the road to Flanders, and succeeded in reaching the frontier.

The carriage bearing the royal family reached Chalons in safety, and subsequently St. Menehould. The detachments of Bouillé, weary of waiting, had already taken their departure. At St. Menehould Louis was recognized by Drouet, son of the post-master; but the carriage was then setting off. Drouet set off also by a cross-road, and reached Varennes, the next place of halt, and within but two stages of Bouillé's camp, before the fugitives. There were no post-horses in Varennes, but an officer of Bouillé was appointed to have a relay in waiting. There were no symptoms of horses or guards about the hour of eleven at night when the royal family entered the town. They were obliged to alight, to question, to parley with the postilions; whilst Drouet had aroused the municipal officer, and called together the national guards of the canton. Whilst the carriage was slowly proceeding under an arch that crossed the road, Drouet, with the well-known Billaud, and one or two others, stopped it, demanding their passports. The *gardes du corps* on the box wished to resist. The king forbade them. Here the presence of a man of resolution was wanted. Bouillé had designed the marquis d'Agoult to accompany the monarch, but his place had been usurped by an obstinate old woman, governess of the prince and princess. They were now conducted before the *procureur* of the town; and, the national guards crowding in, Louis was arrested. The troops of Bouillé's army arrived also, but refused to rescue him. An aide-de-camp of general la Fayette soon after made his appearance, bearing a decree of the national assembly for the reconveyance of the fugitives to Paris.

Thus within an hour, a league, of safety, the unfortunate Louis and his family found themselves captive, and on their return to a capital, which, if it had before loaded them with contumely, would now, most likely, observe no moderation in cruelty. The assembly already showed that its opinions had taken a deeper dye of republicanism since the flight. Petion, a rude and rigid democrat, with Barnave, the rival of Mirabeau, were the commissaries who reconducted the king. Seated in the royal carriage, Barnave, with the sensibility ever attendant upon talent, felt his sympathy awakened for the sufferings of the fallen family.

During the eight days of their painful journey, he continually conversed with the monarch, and felt each moment deeper respect for a character so amiable and so just. Petion, on the contrary, a man of few ideas, held rigid in those which he professed, and piqued by being obliged to play an inferior part, merely murmured that he cared for naught save a republic. Previous to the return of the king to Paris, it was placarded, that whoever insulted him should be beaten; whoever applauded him should be hanged. He was received, then, with that silence which Mirabeau called "the lesson of kings."

The national assembly suspended the king from his functions, less as a punishment than to satisfy the popular outcry. The leaders of the mere rabble, the anarchists, now showed their heads openly under the guise of republicans. The Jacobins, whom Barnave and the Lameths deserted, started into full activity under the guidance of the most furious demagogues. In the assembly they argued, that the king's flight was abdication, and that nothing remained but to proclaim the republic. The majority were, however, still attached to their constitution, and pleaded that the monarch was irresponsible. Enraged at their want of predominance in the assembly, the Jacobins endeavored to agitate the people, and caused a petition to be prepared for dethroning Louis. This was to be laid on the *altar of the country* in the *Champ de Mars* for universal signature, an apt organization of sedition Immediately La Fayette and Bailly, by the orders of the municipality, marched at the head of troops to the scene of tumult, carrying a red flag, as a token that martial law was in force. They in vain endeavored to disperse the mob. Two invalids were torn in pieces by them, out of hatred to military uniform; and the troops were threatened with attack. La Fayette first ordered them to fire in the air to intimidate the rioters. It had no effect. And at last, beneath a serious and well-directed discharge, several hundreds fell, slain or wounded, and the rest dispersed. The leading Jacobins slunk in terror to their hiding-places. Robespierre did not show himself for many days.

This triumph, however, or the necessity of having recourse to it, served but to render the assembly unpopular. The public was weary of them, and longed for its successor, as it was wont to hail a new reign. The assembly determined to show itself disinterested. It proceeded to complete and give the last touches to the constitution, the immortality of which it fondly augured. Barnave, in the access of his late loyalty, had hoped to have modified its democratic principles: and the *right side*, or partisans of the English constitution, are accused of having marred his efforts by their hostility or neglect. But Barnave could never have executed his purpose. The time had gone by. And the fatal article, which excluded the present representatives from being elected members of the next assembly, was one which, in that day of affected disinterestedness, could certainly not be recalled. This part of the law had been decreed before the affair of Varennes, that is, before the anarchists and republicans had gathered strength. The members of the constituent assembly expected that their successors would be inheritors of their opinions and their parties. It totally lost sight of the natural progress of popular feelings, when agitated and excited. Their self-denying ordonnance was at once a reply to accusations of selfishness and tenacity for power, and at the same time an act of pride, as if the sages, who had framed the constitution, might intrust to younger and inferior hands the task of obeying and executing it. Having fulfilled its task of presenting the constitution to the king, and having received his solemn acceptance of it, the *assemblée constituante* declared itself dissolved, on the 30th of September, 1791.

CHAP. XI.

1791—1792.

THE LEGISLATIVE ASSEMBLY.

HAD the united wisdom of the first national assembly applied itself to put together a constitution of the least possible durability, on the same principles that cardinals are wont to elect an octogenarian pope, they could scarcely have fixed upon one more likely than that decreed, to attain the desired end. Even the plan of Sieyes, that the nation should will, and the monarch execute, was more practicable, if such a monarch could be found. But here the king was left with precisely that particle of legislative power, the suspensive *veto*, that loaded him with the responsibility of assent, and exposed him to the peril of dissent. The very originators of the system condemned and despaired of it; they knew, even before they launched it, that the vessel must founder. Still, in this moment did they abdicate all power, and abandon the country to a set of new and unknown rulers.

The three natural parties of a country, those of the upper, the middle, and lower classes, were all represented in the *constituent*. The first, considerable at the commencement, lost its force by splitting into the pure and unaccommodating royalists, and those who favored the English system of two houses: it disappeared towards the close, as the last gathered boldness and force. Those who leaned on the middle ranks, that widely extended but inactive mass of the population, were, by their large majority, complete masters of the country; but private jealousies and piques kept them asunder, and hence they lent themselves to elevate their future antagonists from the rank beneath them. Barnave hated Mirabeau; Mirabeau, La Fayette; both the former at least flattering the popular party,—the existence of which, indeed, they did not suspect till late—at the expense of their own. Thus in the assembly, the revolution, or, in other words, the descent of power through the successive ranks of society, advanced gradually and slowly: now, however, betwixt the *constituent* and the *legislative*, which followed, it proceeded *per saltum*, with astounding and fatal celerity.

One great cause of this was the little experience which the country had of liberty. Men with political knowledge were rare. The *notables*, in this respect, had been chosen in the first assembly, and their re-election being denied, the electors were at a loss where to look. The moderate and the timid shrunk at such a time from the public eye; and those whose zeal had distinguished them in the clubs, claimed and obtained universal preference. Elected under such influence, the *legislative* assembly soon displayed a totally new scheme of opinions and divisions. The upholders of even a mitigated aristocracy had disappeared: in their place, as the band most favorable to royalty, sat, now in minority, the majority of the late assembly. They were called constitutionalists or *Feuillans*, from the name of their club. Next in order sat the republicans—men who despised the vain shadow of royalty that the constitutionalists had preserved, and with reason;

for the post of king was untenable in the system. A conscientious and sage lover of royalty, to whom a monarch with kingly attributes was denied, would have embraced the idea of a republic as practicable at least, in preference to the vain idol of La Fayette's pedantic adoration, viz. the name of a king, and the essence of a commonwealth. The republicans were better known by the appellation of Girondins, their most celebrated leaders being members for the department of the Gironde, and originally lawyers in the court of Bourdeaux. To the left of these sat the Jacobins, the anarchists, men without principles or imaginable form of government: their support was the rabble; their aim to sweep away, as obnoxious to their envious mediocrity, the united aristocracy of birth, wealth, and talent.

The constitutionalists and Girondins both represented equally the interests of the middle class, and disputed its opinions; but the Girondins carried away the palm of popularity, and also the sceptre of power: they soon ruled the assembly, and guided the legislature. The executive at that time resided in the municipality, for Paris was in a great measure revolutionary France. The constitutionalists had held paramount influence over this body through Bailly and La Fayette; but now, when the mania of self-denial became general, these functionaries resigned, and ceded their posts of influence to their rivals. Petion, a Girondin, was chosen mayor in lieu of Bailly, and La Fayette did not recover the command of the national guard.

Such was the state of parties. The new assembly, that gave itself the name of *legislative*, by which it is distinguished in French history, met on the 1st of October. A deputation waited on the king to acquaint him. His reply was simple. The republicans did not find it sufficiently courteous; and, commencing their grave duties by a childish susceptibility about punctilio, they ordered the king's chair to be put on a level with that of their president. On the next day they repealed this important decree, Louis intimating that he would not come to open their session. Having, by pretending deference, enticed him to appear, they treated him with some marks of designed disrespect, such as sitting in his presence covered; advantages trifling to them, but wounding to the pride of the fallen monarch. Thus the assembly that ended in blood, began in puerility.

Their next steps, though more distasteful to the king, had still the excuse of necessity. Two kinds of enemies threatened the present order of things; the emigrants collected on the frontier, and the discontented priesthood scattered through out the realm. The former had the tacit support of all the European courts, and almost the avowed alliance of Austria; the latter were in communication with the emigrants, and were stirring and preparing the peasantry universally to revolt. The assembly passed a decree, declaring all emigrants, who continued in hostile meeting on the frontier beyond the month of January, civilly dead, and their properties seized, without prejudice, however, to their wives, children, or creditors. Another ordained measures of similar rigor against those priests who refused the oath, and continued to excite agitation. These laws were certainly but a just measure of retaliation. The king, from a personal feeling that may well be conceived, made the first use of his *veto* in suspending them: and then was instantly seen the absurd balance of powers provided by the constitution. The rage of the revolutionists in general knew no bounds, on finding their arms tied in their efforts to combat the enemies of the state; unable to attack the monarch directly, they turned their resentment against the constitutionalists, whose system thus obstructed them with its *veto*. They directed their scrutiny and eloquence against the existing ministers, whom Louis had chosen from that party. Delessart, the secretary for foreign affairs, was accused of feebleness, of betraying the dignity and interests of the country in his correspondence with the courts of Europe. Such being the opinion of the majority, Delessart was arrested, and sent for trial before the high court sitting at Orleans. Thus the constitutionalists, having yielded their influence in the senate and the municipality, were soon driven from the ministry, the Girondins and Jacobins uniting to complete their ruin.

It was in the debates excited by this question, and by the menaced interference of foreign countries, that Isnard, deputy of Provence, poured forth that eloquent diatribe, which soon resounded throughout the courts of Europe. "They would bring us back our noblesse!" cried he. "If all the nobles of the earth were to assail us, the French people, with their gold in one hand, their swords in the other, will combat that imperious race, and force it to endure the penalty of equality.

"Let us elevate ourselves in this conjuncture to a level with our high mission. Let us speak to ministers, to the king, and to Europe, with the dignity that becomes the representatives of France. Let ministers know our little satisfaction with their conduct, and that by the word responsibility we mean death. Tell Europe, that we will respect the constitution of other governments; but that if a league of kings be made against us, we, in turn, will raise a war of people against kings."

The French excuse the violence and crimes of their revolution, by pleading that every fresh excess was provoked by the enemies of freedom. Thus, the oath of the tennis-court, the insurrection ending in the capture of the Bastile, that of October which led the king forcibly from Versailles, were all indebted to the menacing approach of troops, and to the banquet of the garde du corps. The coalition entered into by the European sovereigns at Pilnitz, and their subsequent support of the emigrants at Coblentz, were destined to produce a still more fearful reaction. With Europe certainly France was not the aggressor. Disunited in councils, the interior swarming with secret enemies, and the army disorganized, she had every reason to avoid a war. It was deprecated by the furious Jacobins, who dreaded alike to see the enemy, or their own generals, victorious. They thought on Cromwell and trembled to see La Fayette, their enemy, acquire influence similar to his at the head of armies. The Girondists, on the contrary, clamored for open war. Though not military men, they had the instinct of the nation's force, and augured triumph, where others feared defeat. Almost all, being men of studious habits and pursuits, were deeply imbued with those classic ideas, that the vile Jacobins afterwards caught up and parodied. They believed themselves in ancient Rome, and looked not only to overthrow the Tarquin of the day, but to spread far and wide the glory and dominion of their country. In this proud spirit of emulation, the Girondists already carried their views beyond the poor boon of liberty, which the Jacobins, construing it however with licensė, would have been contented with. The Girondists it was, who first conceived that bold project of extended conquest, afterwards realized by Napoleon.

The constitutionalists, however, still clung to the ministry, and, as officers and generals, prevailed in the army. Luckner, Rochambeau, and La Fayette commanded. The last the Girondists forgave, and wished to preserve, hoping at that time mighty achievements from his military fame. They were compelled, indeed, to recruit for heroes, and choose them elsewhere than in their own body. Dumouriez promised, above all others, to answer their views. This was a bold adventurer, enterprising, ambitious, talented; but too selfish, wayward, and passionate, to have fixed principles. He affected to belong to all parties; flattered the king and the Jacobins,* as well as the Girondists. The latter, at the recommendation

* The very day in which Dumouriez accepted the ministry and charmed Louis XVI. by his plausibility and projects, he attended the Jacobins, and wore the *bonnet rouge*.

of Brissot, adopted him. Madame Roland, the priestess of the party, was the only one who saw through him with a woman's penetration, and described him as "a talented *roué*, a bold cavalier, prepared to mock and trifle with every thing, except his interests and his glory."

The Girondists themselves deserve more particular mention. Brissot was long considered to be their leader. He was, in fact, their journalist, and the chief point of connexion between them, who were provincials, and the capital. Being thus apparently the manager of their intrigues, the Jacobins called the whole party Brissotites. His memoirs, lately published, are far from presenting this personage in a respectable or amiable light. Vergniaud was their chief orator: he was a vulgar Fox; the same mildness, the same impassive appearance and equanimity of temper, contrasted with bursts of fervid eloquence when excited. Condorcet, of noble birth, was the philosopher and theorist of their ranks. He was their Sieyes, according to Mignet's expression, but with more elevation, more elegance, and more disinterestedness. Madame Roland, in fine, was to the Girondists, what De Staël was to the constitutionalists,—the priestess of their temple; for politics had displaced religion; and deliberation, prayer. There was beauty, talents, firmness, heroism, and, at the same time, tenderness of sentiment, in Madame Roland; and yet there is a tint of vulgar prejudice, even of ferocity, seen throughout her auto-biography, that chills all sympathy.

Roland, the husband of this lady, an honest, rigid personage, a philosophic puritan, born to be at most the chief clerk of a ministerial office, was fixed on by Louis as the minister of interior that he was to select from the Girondists. Dumouriez had the department of war, and made himself agreeable to the king and to his diminutive court; whilst Roland, unkempt, in round hat, and strings in his shoes, stalked into the royal presence. A ghost would have excited more welcome and less horror. "What! a man without buckles!" exclaimed the horrified master of the ceremonies. "Ah!" ejaculated Dumouriez, covering with gravity an inclination to laugh outright, "if it be come to that, all is lost."

The task of the new ministers and their party was to remove the state of suspense in which affairs, both domestic and foreign, remained, to bring matters to a crisis with the leagued sovereigns and with their own. An open manifestation of opinion was demanded of the emperor. He required, in reply, that France should recur to the state of government and parties which existed when the royal sitting took place at the commencement of the constituent assembly. This was a peremptory summons directed to the torrent or the whirlwind. The assembly replied, in April, 1792, by a declaration of war. One half of the scheme of the Girondists was thus fulfilled: the other was to force the king to resign himself freely to the current of the revolution, join with it, that is, with them, else their resolve was to force or to dethrone him. Their powers of reasoning were first employed to bend the monarch Vergniaud, Gaudet, and Gensonné drew up and sent to him a letter of exhortation to this effect; but Louis was by no means so meekly disposed as he had been when the assembly met. His queen was irritated by the revival of the popular feeling against her, produced by the demands of the emperor her nephew. The Girondist ministers made themselves odious to what still called itself a court, by their uncouthness and pretensions; and, above all, Dumouriez was false. Feeling himself in office, he broke with the Girondists, as he had done with the constitutionalists, and influenced the king to resist their counsels and insinuations. He sought to play the part of Mirabeau, without that great man's tact and powers. The effect of this conduct was unfortunate. It raised the spirits of the old royalist party, and induced Louis once more to listen to them. The first action that took place on the frontiers, was unfavorable to the revolutionary soldiers. They fled in a panic, and massacred their leader, Dillon, who expostulated and sought to rally them. This raised still higher the hopes of the small knot of young military that still thronged in the outer saloons of the Tuilleries. The populace were proportionally awakened and excited; and thus were sown afresh the seeds of insurrection.

Dumouriez endeavored to support himself in a medium between contending parties. He caused the infamous Marat to be accused for exciting to sedition, in his journal called the "Ami du Peuple." A royalist writer was at the same time summoned to answer; but the minister could not communicate even his own share of prudence to the king. Pique, rather than policy, now came to govern Louis. The assembly had voted him a constitutional guard, the greater part of it to be raised from the youth of the middle classes composing the national force of the provinces. It had been tampered with: its officers showed that spirit of hostility to the assembly which had gained the favor of the court. The assembly at length issued a decree, breaking this troop. They at the same time, indeed, ordered its place to be supplied by new levies; but the king, irritated at finding himself thus controlled, refused to have any guard whatever, and occupied his solitary palace, exposed at all times to the irruptions of the rabble.

From the moment that Dumouriez, and with him the monarch, broke with the Girondists, or rather with the majority of the assembly (for the Girondists and Jacobins were still united in their public measures), the latter directed all their batteries against the throne, determined to overturn the few bulwarks that yet remained, since it dared to contradict their wishes. Rash and guilty as was this determination, still more ash and guilty were the means employed to execute it. They were ashamed to make use of their open and legislative preponderance; they preferred employing the popular arm, and raising up insurrection, after the manner of the anarchists, or Orleans faction, in order to gain that unchecked ascendency which they sought. Their decrees and votes adroitly prepared the way for this audacious scheme. In the commencement of June, Servan, minister of war, a tool of the Girondists, proposed to the assembly, without consulting either his colleagues or the monarch, to establish a camp of federals from the different provinces, under the walls of the capital. The assembly welcomed the proposal with delight. The federals, or volunteers, being naturally the most furious revolutionists of the nation, would serve as auxiliaries to the Parisian mob to keep in awe the more moderate and constitutional partisans that remained still attached to the king, amongst the better class of citizens. The national guard, especially the unpaid battalions of the respectable quarters, were of this color. The republicans dreaded their stubbornness and interference. Here was the blunder and the crime of the Girondists, both of which they dearly expiated. Although enlightened, educated, professional men, they called in large reinforcements of the rabble to crush the middle ranks, which were their own, although they differed from them in degree.

This formed another crisis in the reign of Louis; had he seized it, the supremacy of the rabble might at least have been prevented. Many thousand national guards, of the more respectable citizens, petitioned against the federal camp. The middle class was aroused, perceived its danger, and its enemies; saw that the Girondists were betraying them, and that there was a necessity for defending the throne. It was the policy of Louis to have flung his whole influence into the scale of this party. Dumouriez pressed him to do so; but in order to this, it was necessary to satisfy that popular feeling which was common to all ranks. The Girondists, seeing the opportunity left open to the monarch, took care to obviate and close it, by sending to him a decree against the nonjuring and seditious priesthood. They knew he would resist this, and that his resistance would appear to the citizens a proof of his little cordiality towards the revolution. Their scheme succeeded. Dumouriez's advice was rejected. The monarch, exasperated, defied the Girondists and popular body, without rallying to him the national guard or the citizens. It was then that Roland and his wife, with pedantic impertinence, drew up a letter of advice to their sovereign. It was uncalled for, and could not be useful; for Louis, refusing to hearken to the moderate revolutionists, was little likely to assent to the violent.* The letter produced, what the Girondists might and did expect, the dismissal of Roland, and an open rupture between them and the monarch. Dumouriez would still have remained, could he have induced Louis to adopt even now the course that he had recommended. The king could not be made to comprehend his interests; and Dumouriez resigned, in tears at the certainty of the catastrophe that must follow.

La Fayette, as sensible as Dumouriez to the danger of the throne, now came to its assistance; and at least recorded his principles, and vented his indignation, in a letter to the assembly, accusing the Jacobins of anarchic views, declaring that the clubs swayed the assembly and the nation, and that there was no safety for the country till they were put down. This was a thrust with a foil against an enemy in armor of proof. The assembly struck it aside with derision. La Fayette was now Cromwell in the public voice, and the little brilliancy of his exploits at the head of his army sunk his reputation lower. The populace were terrified at the menaced invasion. Even their leaders expected no less at this time than soon to see the Prussians and Austrians masters of the capital. The rabble shared their fears, and reasoned, or were taught to reason thus—"Yet this is the moment that Louis Capet prevents, by his single word of dissent, the levy of the federal army that might save us; this is the time chosen to dismiss ministers of honesty and zeal; and see, he refuses to punish, that is, he encourages the priesthood; the sworn enemies to the revolution, those who are exciting the peasantry to aid the Austrians against us." Such was the plausible language of the rabble—in such did the Girondists address them.

The demagogues sought the first pretext to collect the people. They pleaded that it was necessary to excite their zeal, and to arm them in order to be in readiness for the approach of the enemy. Pikes were accordingly forged and distributed.

* The royal family were maddened by the daily insults heaped upon them especially on the unfortunate queen. Their enemies, by these atrocious means, deprived them of all coolness, judgment, or prudence, probably not without the diabolical purpose of instigating them to their own ruin.

And thus the mob had their peculiar force in the enrolled pikemen of the *fauxbourgs*, as the citizens had theirs in the national guard. The 20th of June was near. It was the anniversary of the oath of the tennis-court. It was resolved to celebrate this by the assembling of the pikemen in view of the Tuilleries. The Girondists favored the plan; they di not imagine that it would end in blood, but merely have th salutary effect of frightening Louis, and forcing him to abandon his *veto*. As Petion, one of the most violent of their party, was mayor, and thus in command of the police and the national guard, there was no opposition to be dreaded.

The rabble assembled accordingly on the morning of the 20th. Santerre, a brewer, was at their head. With the tree of liberty and the "Rights of Man" borne in triumph before them, a redoubtable body of some 40,000 pikemen, mustering the whole of the lower class of the capital, first proceeded to present an address to the assembly. The Girondists and Jacobins received their auxiliaries with welcome. The pikemen had the honor of defiling through the hall of sitting. then marched to the Tuilleries, in order to present another petition to the king, making known their approach by shouts of "*Down with the veto!*"—"*Vivent les sans-culottes!*"—and the chorus of "*Ca ira.*" On first arriving at the gate of the palace, they were denied entrance. The foremost hesitated; till the municipal officers, who kept the gate, either from treason, or alarm at the cannon which was pointed against them, abandoned their post. The populace immediately rushed up the grand staircase, carrying even the piece of cannon with them on their shoulders. Their purpose was not sanguinary, like that of the hired ruffians who broke, in October, 1789, into the palace of Versailles. But the torrent of popular violence was scarcely less alarming. Wherever they found an obstacle, it flew to pieces before their efforts. At length, whilst bursting the panels of a gilded door, it was opened from the inside, and Louis XVI. appeared: a few officers of the national guard, and one or two faithful followers, around him.

At the royal aspect the foremost pikemen hesitated and were silent, till some of them cried out they had a petition. Louis then led the way to the largest saloon of the suit; and placing himself in a window, the table with the "Rights of Man" before him, he stood, holding a plenary court of the mob. The pretended petition not being forthcoming, Legendre, a butcher, now came forward as the spokesman, and in rude language demanded the king's assent to the decrees for the federal camp and for the transportation of the priests.

"This is neither the time nor the place," replied Louis with a courage and dignity that confounded the rabble. Their only rejoinder was, "*Vive la nation!*" Louis repeated the patriotic cry. "*Let us try if he be sincere*," observed Legendre, extending towards the monarch a red night-cap on the end of a pike. The monarch took it and put it on; and shouts of approbation rent the palace. Another handed him some wine. Louis drank it off. By his side was his sister, the princess Elizabeth. "There is the Austrian," cried several, pointing to her as the queen. Some endeavored to undeceive them. "Leave them in the error," said the princess; "it may preserve the queen."

The Girondist members of the assembly at length came, on learning that their insurrection was likely to prove more serious than they intended. Vergniaud and others used their eloquence with the mob; and at length Petion himself, the chief magistrate of the city, appeared, and employed his persuasions to make them evacuate the palace. When the assembly met, the Girondists were ashamed of their triumph. They were silent; but their votes crushed all efforts to discover or punish the authors of the sedition. Petion, towards evening, recovered sufficient impudence to intrude upon Louis, with an intimation that "all was quiet and the people tranquil."—"That is not true," said Louis. "Sire?"—"Be silent."—"The magistrate of the people need not be silent when he does his duty and speaks the truth," retorted Petion. The most singular circumstance of the day was the forbearance of the mob, in departing without any promise of the *veto*. Never was courage more conspicuous than that of Louis on this occasion. To an observation of alarm, he replied by taking the hand of a national guard, and, placing it upon his heart, asked, "Does that betray fear? It never beat more regularly." With such characteristics on either side, who would not have hoped for happier results? The issue of that day, on which the populace were infuriated and left to their own uncontrolled propensities, leads one to cast the censure of the crimes which followed more on their atrocious instigators than upon the deluded people.

This fresh insult to the sovereign, and through him to the constitution, awakened the indignation of La Fayette. His army, his officers, joined in the sentiment; and, no longer confining himself to epistolary remonstrance, he instantly set out for the capital. He appeared the day after his arrival at the bar of the assembly, avowing himself charged to represent the opinions of his army, which were his own. He demanded the punishment of those concerned in the invasion of the palace, and the dispersal of the Jacobin club. The reply of the assembly was calm, but evasive; and the general instantly despaired of effecting his purposes by legal measures. He therefore resolved to imitate his enemies, by making use of force; a fatal, and, in this instance, an unsuccessful policy. His only support lay in the national guards or in the more respectable portions of it, who felt attached to their old general; but, without some countenance from the court, those dared not risk themselves under the guidance even of La Fayette, unsupported by any authority in the state. The general therefore repaired to the Tuilleries, and sought an audience of his sovereigns, in order to beseech them to put trust in him and aid him. But La Fayette had made himself odious to Louis; the monarch refused even to be saved by one whom he looked on as the origin of all his misfortunes: king and queen received him coldly; and he departed in despair at their fatuity. Still, despite of this disappointment, the general meditated an attack upon the Jacobins, at the head of some national guards, whom he had no recognized right to command. They failed at the place of rendezvous. The Jacobins, who had deserted their den in affright, remained unmolested, and were merely supplied with a just cause of accusation against their enemy.

The Prussians and Austrians in the mean time advanced, and the invasion became more menacing. The king persisted in objecting to the camp near Paris; but the Jacobins, by their correspondence, resolved to execute the plan despite *Monsieur Veto*, as they called Louis. The provinces of the south obeyed the call with alacrity, and enrolled troops of the most zealous, amongst whom were the afterwards redoubted Marseillais. The monarch proposed that the camp should be formed at Soissons. The assembly agreed, but gained the point that the new levies should at least march through Paris. They were then pressed to arrive, so as to be present to celebrate the 14th of July, the day of the capture of the Bastile and of the federation.

For all these violent measures, the revolutionists pleaded he insincerity of the king and court, and their secret understanding with the foreign foes who now advanced in arms. It was but too true: the court was insincere, and ample excuse it had for being so. Both sides had thus their banners and their pretexts; and a war of extermination, covertly carried on at first, commenced betwixt the monarch and the national representatives. The civil war betwixt the English parliament and Charles I., whom Louis shrunk from imitating, was far less sanguinary. The assembly appointed a commission to consider and prepare a dictatorial law. Whom did they propose as dictator? The mob. It was decreed, that as soon as the assembly should pass as a vote, "The country is in danger, thenceforth every municipality should sit permanently; the population of every age and rank was to arm, no uniform required, the holder of the pike by the side of him with a gun; and that all armed citizens called out of their native place on this service should receive pay." This established by law what the insurrection of June and the cunning of the Federals already had established in fact, the domination of the national guard or class of citizens by that of the people. Power here descended to the lower ranks, that is, fell into the hands of the most loud, unshrinking, and turbulent demagogues.

It was not until they were on the very verge of the precipice that the Girondists recoiled. In the debate upon the dictatorial law, Vergniaud, their chief orator, had insinuated in fervent words, and, it must be owned, with the very perfection of eloquence and address, the possible necessity of their being obliged to recur to the extreme measure of depriving the king of his crown. But when this cry was taken up and echoed, when the Federals, now arriving, not only repeated, but seemed bent on executing it, the Girondists, affrighted at the horrid allies whom they had called in, made private overtures to the monarch for mutual support. But he who, in firmness and disgust, had repulsed Dumouriez and La Fayette, was little likely to stoop to the alliance of Brissot or of Petion. Louis the Sixteenth preferred to perish.

The 10th of August was the day on which the people, stirred by the Jacobins and led by the Federals, upset the throne, and humbled royalty with the dust. Yet on the 14th of July preceding, the Girondists were still in full accordance with the mob. On that day of fête, the Federals thronged into the Champ de Mars, showing their aspect, and speaking in yells their still more hideous spirit and intentions. It was the Girondists, "whose incantations," to use the words of Scott, "had raised these devils; but who now, appalled and terror-stricken, were without the power to lay them." A more intimate acquaintance with some of the leading Jacobins and their views succeeded in awaking Brissot and his friends. These men might well imagine, that no demagogues could go farther in flattering and favoring democratic power than themselves. A mere lover of anarchy they could scarcely conceive, except in such a solitary instance as Marat, an infamous low journalist, whom all the world contemned and spat upon, and who had his contumely to avenge upon the whole human race. But it soon appeared that many members of the present assembly, and even of the constituent, shared his sanguinary views, and adopted them on calculation. Robespierre was one of those, and Danton, each with a hideous crew of followers. The Girondists admired popular insurrections; they deemed them innocent and glorious modes of bending an obstinate sovereign; they either did not suspect or little recked, that such might lead to effusion of blood. They approved of the invasion of the palace on the 14th of July, which seems, indeed, to have been conducted throughout by their spirit, in being audacious, menacing, levelling, but not without some touches of generosity and forbearance. The system of the Jacobins was altogether different. These wanted not to bend, but to crush; not to diminish, but to destroy; not to fight the court and the aristocrats to submission, but to sweep away and utterly annihilate them. The announcement of such intentions alarmed the Girondists for themselves, and with reason. But it was too late. The popular ranks had been called into activity, armed, allowed to taste of sovereignty and blood. They had been invited to a moral debauch, and could not be induced to depart contented till inebriated to the utmost—till satiated with crime, and drunk with blood.

The recoil of the Girondists to the cause of order and legality was too recent, however, too little concerted and confirmed, to allow of their resisting the insurrection now impending. They felt the storm behind them, and, at the same time, felt the inutility and danger of turning against it. They drove on, then, passively with the tempest, which the Jacobins directed and rode. Yet even the Jacobins were not the immediate planners of the insurrection. Even beneath their abyss there yawned a deeper still. The leaders of the Federals formed a club or secret committee for organizing the plot. Strange to say, this knot of ruffians, that overturned the throne of the Bourbons, and bathed France in blood, treading nobles and citizens beneath their feet, was, in great part, composed of foreigners: there was Fournier, an American; Kienlin, from the Rhine; Lazouski, a Pole. With these were Carva and Simon, wretched journalists; Vaugeois, a priest; and other names, unknown to fame, even in success.

Events favored the projects of these wretches. On the 30th of July, a quarrel took place betwixt the Marseillais and the national guard, which ended in the discomfiture of the latter. The duke of Brunswick's famous manifesto became known, and roused up exasperation. The assembly refused to order the arrest of La Fayette; consequently, the dethronement of the king could not be expected from that body. The discussion on this subject was to take place on the 9th of August. A dissatisfactory termination to it being conjectured, the insurrection was organized for the following day. The intention was scarcely concealed. The duc de la Rochefoucault, La Fayette, and others, prompted Louis to escape, and offered to secure the means. The monarch refused. He scorned to consult personal safety, and at the same time distrusted those who exposed themselves to rescue him.

The cry through Paris, where the rabble now reigned, became general for the dethronement of the king. As the vote of "the country in danger" had been pronounced, the great municipal council of the Hôtel de Ville sat permanently; and subordinate councils were formed in each of the districts or sections. These, in the moment of effervescence, came to be composed of the zealots and clubbists of the quarter. They were no sooner assembled, than they proceeded, after the fashion of the day, to legislate. Most of them voted addresses to the assembly, praying for the dethronement. One declared, of its own authority, this revolution effected. As the crisis of insurrection approached, these sections sent commissaries, -deputies in fact,—to the chief municipal assembly at the Hôtel de Ville, which, composed of citizens of some substance, and more Girondist than Jacobin, was little zealous in the cause of anarchy. The commissaries, accordingly, took upon them to expel the old municipality, and to establish themselves in its place. Such was the formation of the celebrated *commune*, that seconded the insurrection, and, afterwards, resisting the assembly itself, gave the Jacobins the victory over all antagonists. The municipal council of Paris was in fact the helm of revolution: whatever party succeeded in grasping it, guided the vessel of state.

The national assembly was warned, on the 9th of August, of the insurrection that approached. But they were powerless. They had scarcely separated in the evening, when the tocsin began to sound. It continued all night to toll the self-called patriots to arms at the different rallying points. On the morning of the 10th the several columns were complete, and ready for the attack. Santerre led the inhabitants of the fauxbourg St. Antoine. That of St. Marceau sent a body of equal force. The head-quarters of insurrection were at the club of Cordeliers, where Danton possessed the ruling voice. As for Marat and Robespierre, these wretches remained hidden in the hour of danger.

The royal inmates of the Tuilleries had thus ample warning of their peril. The few royalists, who still remained in Paris, hurried to defend their sovereign; but, for the most part old helpless courtiers, they merely excited the jealousy of the national guard, without offering material aid. Where then were the gay troops of emigrants, the gallant youth of the French noblesse? This was the hour and the field where they might have perished with honor, or more probably triumphed. In their stead, the defenders of the palace consisted of a Swiss regiment, mustering 800 men, and two of the most staunch battalions of the national guard. They were commanded by Mandat, an old soldier, who happened to be the colonel in authority for the day. The palace of the Tuilleries, which now presents towards the square of the Carousel one unbroken line of building, was then blocked and masked in front by a labyrinth of low ranges, divided by courts, somewhat resembling St. James's. These courts and approaches were intrusted to the national guard, the principal of them unfortunately to the artillery of that civic force, composed of low and democratic citizens. The interior of the château, its galleries, and many windows, were manned by the Swiss, and thronged by royalists, each offering counsel, and increasing the disorder.

At first the national guard was unwilling to act without orders from the municipality; but Petion, the Girondist mayor, who dared neither to approve nor disapprove the insurrection, had wandered to the palace, in order to have after-proofs that he had not participated in it, so strong were the fears that the people might fail in their enterprise. Petion, seized at the Tuilleries, was compelled to sign an order to repel force by force. Authorized by this, Mandat made dispositions to resist the insurgents; he proposed to anticipate their attack, and fall upon the columns of rabble as they advanced. A summons from the municipality now reached Mandat; he thought it necessary to obey, hurried to the Hôtel de Ville, and was astonished to find it altogether changed, and composed of new members. After interrogating Mandat, Huguenin, the president of the *commune*, ordered, with a side gesture of the hand, that he should be removed. He was removed effectually, by a pistol-shot; and thus the troops at the château were left without a commander. Louis himself might have supplied his place: the queen at one moment prompted him to this energy. Seizing a pistol from the belt of one of his attendants, Marie Antoinette presented it to Louis, saying, "Now is the moment to show yourself." Louis was endowed with passive, not with active courage. He obeyed mechanically the spirited suggestion, showed himself at the balcony, descended and reviewed the different troops, but all the time as silent and unanimated as at an ordinary scene. A short speech, the wielding of his sword, his mounting on horseback, any of these acts, in short, that strike and carry away the feelings of a mass, would here have told, and rallied all hearts round the monarch, who was still saluted with cries of *Vive le roi!* The fuel was there in a thousand hearts, that could have been kindled into loyalty, had the cold nature of Louis been capable of striking out a spark: but the review was a complete failure. The execrations of the mob gained upon the national guards more than the sight of their pale, spiritless, and weeping monarch. The cannoniers turned their guns against the château, in token of their opinions; the *gensdarmerie* dispersed; and the Swiss alone remained to defend the palace.

Seeing this, Rœderer, *procureur* or attorney of the *commune*, advised Louis to abandon the château, and retire with his family to the national assembly. The queen violently opposed this step. "Madame," said he, "you will have to answer for the lives of the king and of all his family, as well as of those collected here to defend you." This apostrophe decided Louis, and he resolved to follow at once the advice of Rœderer. A difficulty still remained,—to traverse the crowd, and to prevent the royalists of the château from following the royal family: the latter were induced to disperse. After suffering unnumbered insults, Louis, followed by his queen and children, the dauphin in the arms of a pioneer, entered the assembly betwixt eight and nine o'clock. "I am come," said he, "to spare the perpetration of a great crime: I cannot be more safe than amongst ye, gentlemen." The king was at first seated near the president, but was afterwards, on the pretext that his presence marred the freedom of debate, removed to the box reserved for the reporters.

In the mean time the masses of insurgents had penetrated into the courts in front of the château. The Swiss, and the few national guards that remained, made signs of amity from the windows, flinging down cartouches, and putting their caps upon their bayonets. The pikemen accordingly advanced to the great entrance under the vestibule, and demanded possession of the château, at the same time preparing to force a kind of barricade. Three or four Swiss sentries were stationed in low open windows. Some of the rabble amused themselves by pulling these soldiers down with the crooks of their pikes, and slaying them. Their comrades seeing this, fired down upon the assassins, and the combat became general. The Swiss, enraged, formed in a body, rushed down the grand staircase, sweeping the rabble before them. Issuing into the first court, they charged the Marseillais, who turned and fled, being imitated by the hordes of the fauxbourgs. In an instant every court and avenue was cleared; and had there been a single troop of cavalry to continue the rout of the fugitives, had Mandat or any officer been there to follow up the advantage, the *cause of the people* was forever lost and disgraced.

But the king himself was destined to strike the fatal blow to his own cause. Hearing the cannon and the tumult, he sent M. d'Hervilly with an order for the Swiss to retire and abandon the château. D'Hervilly found the soldiers victorious, bringing in the cannon of the people, planting one piece in battery, spiking others. He made known the unseasonable command, most absurdly, to only one battalion of the Swiss. It thought proper to obey, and repair to the assembly; where it was instantly disarmed; and thus the remaining two or three hundred were left exposed to all the fury of the mob, rendered vindictive by their own cowardice and defeat.

In the lapse of an hour the Marseillais, unpursued, had received courage; mustered once more their hordes; and began to flock back to the château. They found its approaches unguarded. They rushed in. The Swiss, with diminished numbers, seeing themselves sacrificed, defended for a short time the staircase. But surrounded on all sides, for others of the mob had attacked by the gardens, they were overpowered and massacred. The victorious rabble once more filled the halls and saloons of the palace, murdering most of those who fell in their way, yet sparing some from caprice more than mercy. Eighteen Swiss took refuge in the chapel, and offered to surrender, if their lives were spared. The promise was speedily given; and the Swiss not the less inhumanly butchered. The first attack took place about nine o'clock; by eleven the mob were masters of the Tuilleries. Their victory, or rather their previous defeat, is said to have cost them 3000 slain. Of the royalists and Swiss, about half that number perished. Amongst these fell, where more of his order should have fallen, on the steps of the throne, the marquis of Clermont-Tonnerre. The marshal de Mailly, though of the age of eighty-five, and commanding the little band of gentry on this day, escaped, to perish afterwards beneath the ax.

The assembly concluded worthily the crimes of the day by a decree, suspending the monarch from his functions, ordering the formation of a national convention and a new ministry. Shut up in the narrow *loge*, or box, which first received them, the royal family heard the ferocious demands and cries of the populace, which rendered compulsory this decree. A peach and some bread composed their nourishment during this disastrous day. The dauphin was asleep in the arms of his mother, and the future duchess d'Angoulême weeping betwixt her parents. They were obliged to remain in this situation till one in the morning; when two narrow cells, of the ancient monks of the convent, in which the assembly sat, received the monarch and his family, who but yesterday had still a palace for their prison.

The Girondists now wore cheerful faces. They affected delight at what had taken place; they claimed their share in the triumph and the spoils; and the Jacobins for the moment thought fit to respect these allies. The old ministers of the Girond, Roland, Servan, Clavière, were restored to their respective offices. Petion was allowed to keep the place of mayor. Such were the terms tacitly offered by the Jacobins, as the price of having their new municipality recognized by the assembly. Nevertheless the *commune* spoke bold and independent language. They sent a deputation, which thus addressed the assembly: "The people, which sends us to you, declares you still worthy of its confidence; but at the same time can acknowledge no power authorized to pass judgment on the late extraordinary measures, prompted by necessity, except the people itself, your sovereign and ours, convoked in its primary assemblies." In reply, the assembly had the weakness, inevitable indeed, to acknowledge the new municipality and applaud its acts. With the Girondist ministers were united Lebrun, who was intrusted with foreign affairs, and the redoubtable Danton, who was called, it must have been ironically, the minister of justice.

Themselves intrenched in the *commune*, and supported by Danton in the government, the Jacobins now pushed their violent measures with audacity. Marat was the soul of this diabolical faction. His was the system and conception, that it was necessary to the success of the revolution to sacrifice unrelentingly the lives of the aristocrats. "Behold the monarch," argued he, "how absurd to have compromised with him, or expected sincerity! From the first moment he ought to have been dethroned or rendered harmless. The aristocrats are the same. They can never forgive. In them the revolution will for ever find enemies. But where is the prison ample enough to contain the numbers of the upper classes, were the jailers faithful enough to guard them? The grave is the only prison, the executioner the only certain keeper. Slay! slay! such is the key of true policy. Your armies are of no avail. Give me 200 Neapolitans, armed with poniards: with them will I revolutionize France!"

Marat adopted this terrible creed, impelled by base envy; for, being asked what he meant by an aristocrat, he replied, not only every well-dressed person, every noble, but citizens too respectable. Shopkeepers formed an aristocracy insupportable to this ruffian. He would spare naught above filth and rags. Robespierre, a wretched attorney of Arras, utterly destitute of talent or capacity, adopted Marat's creed, from the same motives of envy, but without a shadow of conviction. Personal distinction and influence was all he sought. Mere selfishness was his creed. To these was joined Danton; a savage, in whom the popular spirit seemed concentrated, in whom the rabble might be said to be personified. He was a huge ruffian, with flattened features and stentorian voice, driven to extremes by his position, and by the rabid passions of the hour. The brutal force of his person seemed to be communicated, by excitement, to his mind. His harangues, and still more his actions, had at least the effects, if not the finer qualities of eloquence. His courage supplied the want of that quality in his colleagues, Robespierre and Marat. Such were the trio that now swayed the *commune* and the Parisian populace, and through them ruled the assembly.

It is a great stain upon the moral courage of the French, that in their representative assemblies, the audacious minority always overpowered the majority. The constitutionalists of the first assembly were crushed by their less numerous adversaries, and now the Girondists were at the mercy of the Jacobins. The municipality usurped all legislative power. Vengeance was their object, terror their support. In order to wreak the one and inspire the other, they proposed the composition of a revolutionary committee, by which alone passports were to be granted, and which was charged to arrest and pursue the suspected. Domiciliary visits enabled their emissaries to penetrate into all the houses of the capital. Moreover, the establishment of a revolutionary tribunal was required, as necessary to the safety of the state. This, to be composed of one member chosen from each section, was to issue summary and irrevocable judgments. To this atrocious demand, the assembly, despite its timidity, demurred; and the *commune* immediately dispatched one of its body to pronounce the following menace,—"As citizen, and as magistrate of the people, I come to acquaint the assembly, that this evening at midnight the tocsin will sound, and the drums beat to arms. The people are weary of being balked of vengeance. Beware that they do not do themselves justice. I demand, that instantly you vote a criminal tribunal, composed of one member from each section." This command was obeyed, and the decree passed.

Whilst the Jacobins were thus directing their efforts to private and domestic vengeance, the Girondists were taking counsel as to the defence of the kingdom. Longwy was taken. In a fortnight the enemies might be in Paris. It was then that the latter party conceived the plan of abandoning the capital, and defending the country behind the Loire. The domineering conduct of the Jacobins and of the municipality, no doubt, rendered this project less displeasing to them. Yet it came ill from men who had been the first to sound the cry for war, even when the anarchists deprecated its chances. Now, however, the parties had changed sides. The Girondists adopted the subdued tone of despair; the Jacobins the uncompromising language of audacity. Danton, above all, inspired those around him with courage, and prepared, rather than surrender the capital, to bury himself beneath its ruins. To this was joined an inveterate resolve, that if the revolution was destined to succumb, its internal enemies, the aristocrats and royalists, should not survive to enjoy their triumph. Such was the fierce motive of the massacres of September.

Throughout the month of August the revolutionary tribunal, and the sections, had crowded the prisons with the suspected. There was absolutely no room for more. And it was upon learning this, that an agent of the Jacobins was directed to examine the quarries beneath the Fauxbourg St. Germain. They were found to offer a capacious receptacle for the dead. The next care was to seek out the old agents of the duke of Orleans, those who had penetrated with bloodthirsty purpose into the palace of Versailles. Maillard, the man who had headed the female deputation of that expedition, was now chosen, and supplied with funds to collect a band of sturdy assassins like himself, together with all fit instruments of death, such as swords, knives, and mallets.

These preparations being made, the revolutionary tribunal purposely acquitted Montmorin, a noted royalist, on the 31st, in order to provoke the people, and prove the necessity of more summary modes of justice and of vengeance. The agitation and clamors of the mob were as great as had been calculated on. On the 2d of September (Sunday), a report was spread that Verdun was taken, and that the enemies were in full march upon the capital. Instantly a levy *en masse* was ordered; the citizens were summoned to the Champ de Mars, in order to march against the enemy. The tocsin was sounded: the cannon of alarm heard. The projects of the conspirators were announced, as if a convulsion of nature was at hand.

Soon after midday, as the mob gathered in the *Place* before the Hôtel de Ville, a number of priests under accusation, amounting to twenty-four, were brought forth and placed in coaches to be transferred to the prison of the Abbaye. They set forth escorted by the Marseillais and by the mob, who pursued them with execrations and menaces. They reached at length the court of the prison, where Maillard and his band awaited the first victims of the day. As each ecclesiastic descended from the carriage, he was stricken down by a hundred blows. Of the twenty-four, the abbé Sicard alone escaped, and that almost by miracle. Billaud-Varcennes, officer of the municipality, arrived just as the last victim fell, and exclaimed, "People, you do your duty! Immolate your enemies!' —"There is nothing more to do here," cried Maillard: "to the *Carmes !*" This was a convent, in which two hundred of the principal ecclesiastics of the kingdom were confined. One by one they were led forth and massacred. Some of the assassins had particular victims to dispatch, and were obliged to wipe the faces of the dead in order to ascertain whether the task was surely fulfilled.

Thence the assassins returned to the Abbaye, and proceeded in form. They prepared a table. Maillard constituted himself judge, with a dozen aids or assessors. He called for a list of the prisoners, which was delivered, the very jailer fainting with horror at the scene which must follow. Maillard then addressed his comrades with the mockery of reason and calmness; and passed a panegyric upon justice. "Do you," said he, to the band of assassins, "place yourselves outside the gate. When I pronounce that the culprit should be transferred to *La Force*, strike him down and slay him as he goes out." The artifice was applauded, as preventing struggles and difficulties; and the prisoners summoned. The first were Swiss. They met with no favor; were ordered out of the gate and massacred. Next Montmorin was brought forth, he whose mock acquittal served as pretext for these crimes; and underwent his fate. This scene was continued till late in the night; the assassins pausing at times to refresh themselves with wine. The women, however, were spared. The daughter of the singular Cazotte saved her aged parent. Mademoiselle de Sombreuil made the same efforts in behalf of her father, when a ruffian presented her with a goblet of blood, saying, "Drink, drink the blood of the aristocrats!" To have some claim to pity she actually swallowed the horrid draught, and M. de Sombreuil was spared. Others were preserved by the display of courage, and extorted pardon by exciting admiration; such is the caprice of crime. One thousand livres are registred in the books of the municipality as payment for these deeds. Each prison presented a similar scene. The number massacred is calculated at 13,000.

Amongst those confined at La Force was the unfortunate and lovely princess De Lamballe, the friend of Marie Antoinette. She met no mercy. The pen refuses to trace the ineffable horrors committed on her remains. Her head, borne on a pike, was brought in procession to the Temple, where the *commune* had confined Louis and his queen. They were startled by the unusual tumult, and demanded the cause. Rushing to look at a window, Marie Antoinette was prevented by her guards. She pressed for explanation; and it was given;—" they sought to prevent her beholding the head of the Princess Lamballe!" She fainted at the word in the arms of the no less wretched monarch.

Whilst the municipality, under the orders of the *minister of justice*, thus perpetrated the disgrace of the nation, the legislative assembly, ashamed, indignant, but powerless, sat witnessing the crimes which its conduct had induced, and which it could not prevent. Its legal authority was expiring: the elections had already commenced for returning the members of the future convention; not, however, ere it had abdicated all real power and influence in favor of the sanguinary *commune*. Thus the first national assembly expired in an act of folly, the last in blood and crime.

END OF VOL. II.

www.ingramcontent.com/pod-product-compliance
Lightning Source LLC
La Vergne TN
LVHW010238110826
845151LV00004B/1333

9781425524418